Books on Stagecraft

Dennis
Dorn
and
Mark
Shanda

DRAFTING FOR THE THEATRE

Southern Illinois University Press
Carbondale and Edwardsville

12 11 10 09   13 12 11 10

Library of Congress Cataloging-in-Publication Data
Dorn, Dennis.
    Drafting for the theatre / Dennis Dorn and Mark Shanda.
        p.   cm.
    1. Mechanical drawing.   2. Theaters—Stage setting and scenery—
Drawings.   I. Shanda, Mark.   II. Title.
T357.D67   1992
    792′.02′921—dc20   89-21915
    ISBN 0-8093-1508-4   CIP

Contents

To the User

When we set out to write *Drafting for the Theatre*, we had three goals in mind: 1) to develop a textbook for theatre design and technology students, 2) to create a resource for teachers of theatre design and technology, and 3) to provide an easily understood reference for the field of theatre graphics.

For the student, we have provided a progression starting with basic graphic techniques and working up to complex examples from the theatre. Each of chapters 3–21 ends with a series of problems that put into practice the material just discussed. Chapters 3, 6–11, 13, and 19–21 include 8½" × 11" worksheets that may either be drawn on directly or, better yet, be used as an underlay along with vellum or some other drafting media. Larger format drawings are used to accommodate exercises that require additional space.

For the teacher, we have developed correction masters for each of the worksheets provided. These correction masters, available from Southern Illinois University Press, Carbondale, greatly reduce the time necessary for the correction and evaluation of student work. Using a light table, the teacher places the master under the student's work to quickly make a direct comparison. Each problem is designed to be completed within a two-hour class period, allowing the teacher the option of observing students throughout the drafting process. In order to complete the problems in chapter 5 in a two-hour period, teachers are encouraged to provide the underlays indicated in the figures at the end of the chapter.

The final project is intended to be a major drafting assignment that requires both design and shop drawing skills. Two projects of different complexity have been included, but teachers may use their own design experience to develop different final projects utilizing the parameters given.

As a reference book, *Drafting for the Theatre* offers hundreds of theatrical examples for common drafting and geometric problems. Emphasis is on practical solutions, while even complex graphic techniques are broken down into step-by-step instructions. The complete index allows the advanced theatre practitioner rapid access to specific answers when preparing both design and technical drawings.

Through field tests at our two universities we have found this work to be an excellent practical teaching aid and well received by students. We hope that you find it the same.

Acknowledgments

As a trial textbook for the past nine years in the Design and Technology Program of the University of Wisconsin-Madison, *Drafting for the Theatre*'s value has been determined and is undisputed. And with the book's publication, the time has come to recognize those who contributed to it in so many valuable ways.

To begin, we thank each other for the pleasure of his company. The opportunity of working together and sharing thoughts and goals—that unique experience of joint authorship—will always be one of life's great gifts.

A very special thanks must go to the many students of Theatre 342, 370, and 621 Drafting for the Theatre, who over the years gave us encouragement and understanding.

Thanks of course must go to those who worked on the book with us. Jim Knapp collaborated on the "Computer-aided Drafting and Design" chapter. Linda Essig and Cindy Stillings critiqued the chapter "Lighting Design Drawings." Most of the production drafting used in the chapters on design is the work of several valued friends and colleagues: Linda Essig, Kent Goetz, Len Harman, Dana Kenn, Daniel Proctor, and Eugene Warner. Drafting assistance was provided by Jo Ellen Stauffacher, Chuck Mitchell, and Jim Nealon.

Thanks also to our colleagues and administrators at the Ohio State University and the University of Wisconsin-Madison for their generous financial and moral support.

Thanks certainly must go to Kenney Withers, our publisher, whose patience, quiet support and encouragement have been of great importance to us. And to Teresa White, whose firm hand and pointed observations directed this project through its final phases.

And to Lynda Jerit, whose guidance and unquestioning enthusiam really got the entire project to the stage of publication many years ago. Without her, the book never would have have happened.

And finally to our wives, Kathy and Ginny. Your patience, support, and love have helped us through this project.

Introduction

Drafting: The Graphic Language of Planning

This book is intended to serve both as a textbook for an intermediate or advanced level course in theatre drafting and as a reference resource for the experienced drafter. We assume that most students will not be able to cover all of the material discussed here within the scope of a one-semester course; however, this book assembles in one place the principal types of drawings, drawing techniques, and conventional wisdom requisite for the production of theatrical draftings.

It is hoped that the student using this text will achieve some mastery of the skills used in theatre graphics, specifically drafting. To begin, students must develop basics like lettering, line weight, and sheet layout (grammar). In time, however, they must be be able to go beyond mere mechanics in such a way that they can comprehend and be conversant with the conventions of all of the various stagecrafts. Throughout this process of growth, it is expected that student work will be presented in a manner that is clear, organized, and accurate (penmanship).

Theatre designers and technicians must learn the skills necessary to present their design ideas, as well as their technical solutions, in an appropriate graphic style. The ability to think in three dimensions and draw in two is one of the most important graphic skills one can develop. This ability to visualize objects in space and translate an idea to paper is what is learned from the study of graphic language. To visualize and then to graphically express these visions are outstanding traits of extraordinary creative ability and requisites to successful mastery of the specific knowledge of the field, since much of the information in texts and relevant resources is communicated through graphics.

Drafting skills have always been important to those practicing stagecraft. Today's demands of time and budgets employ these skills in an even more rigorous manner than before. The days ahead indicate that Computer-Aided Drafting and Design (CADD) systems will place increased demands on drafters. The ability to more rapidly add, delete, or otherwise modify information means that producers, directors, artists, and technicians themselves will demand increased exploration of the alternatives open to their imaginations and the scenic studio.

Surprisingly, for a profession that exhibits more the characteristics of a cottage industry than a hi-tech industry, the theatre world has responded with significant enthusiasm and effort to the challenge of improving standards of graphic communication. Concern has risen among professionals to the point that the United States Institute for Theatre Technology (USITT) has developed and accepted a series of graphic standards meant to address the needs of scenery and lighting and is currently working to establish standards for audio as well.

Today the relationship between the areas of theatre design and technology and graphic communication has never been clearer. With the rising mobility of designers and the remote location of many scenic studios, the need to effectively communicate design and technical data on paper has also significantly increased to the degree that any theatre practitioner who is ignorant of, or deficient in, the skills of graphic communication is, in essence, professionally illiterate.

Increased emphasis has been placed on good drafting skills for a variety of obvious reasons.

1. Designers and directors continue to introduce ideas and demands that require new materials and a dynamic interaction between scenery and performers, both of which require increased planning and coordination.
2. The work of theatre technicians has increased in quantity, variety, and complexity. In order to keep costs competitive and timetables compact, producers frequently split up shows into smaller bid units that then must be assembled for the first time at a location other than the shop, frequently the stage, with little time allocated to the correction of oversights and errors in planning or fabrication.
3. Theatre designers frequently can, and often need to, hold several jobs concurrently. Some are resident artists at college, university, or regional theatres, with several shows in progress simultaneously and thus in different phases of design or construction. At the same time these same designers might be working on the outside as free-lance artists. Whether full-time or part-time contractors, typically designers cannot be in residence the entire construction time because of demands from other productions.

A designer with good drafting skills can work on many projects at one time and distribute residency time in small doses for the purpose of initial discussions, quality checks, and so forth. The only way to effectively achieve this necessary freedom is to possess the skills to describe effectively and thoroughly, and in a language specific to the theatre crafts, the shape of all scenic units, their placement on stage, their finishes, and a myriad of detailed and complex information tailored to meet the needs of the organizations using the information.

The reality of this kind of experience is that drafting teaches the basics of neatness, speed, and accuracy; habits that serve any theatre worker well. Drafting also encourages the sketching of ideas, careful analysis of problems, and the detailed specification of materials and construction processes. Through drafting, problem solving is executed at the drawing table and not on the more costly studio floor.

Even though many students think they will not be drafting actively once they are working in the professional theatre, very few designers and technicians just starting out can afford the luxury of an assistant to do their drafting. More than likely they themselves will be an assistant to an already accomplished professional. This process of drawing someone else's work is an excellent opportunity for the drafter to enhance personal graphic communication skills while at the same time learning more about design, technology and the production process.

In spite of this onerous-sounding rhetoric, working in the design and technology field of the theatre is fun. The work is even more fun when the planning of what needs doing has been well thought out and adequately described by the production staff responsible for the project. Once the expectations are clearly articulated, the craftsperson is free to create, unencumbered by the need to seek direction from others.

Drafting is not an end unto itself, rather a means to achieving that end. Put simply, theatre drafting is not at all for the purpose of drawing pretty pictures, it is done for the purpose of producing beautiful, useful scenery of high quality for real actors in real performance situations. This text attempts to provide the information necessary to develop the skills required to produce quality drafting to meet this need.

PART ONE

TOOLS, STANDARDS, AND BASIC TECHNIQUES

Tools of the Craft

1

1.1 Tool Categories

Technical drawing requires the use of a variety of tools to produce clean, accurate, and reproducible drawings. As with most activities, only a few pieces of equipment are required, but additional equipment can make certain tasks easier. For the purposes of this text, drafting tools have been divided into three categories: **level 1**, those items necessary to draft and solve the problems in this text; **level 2**, additional basic tools that make drawing easier and solve specific drawing problems; and **level 3**, specialized or more costly tools not normally purchased by student theatre drafters.

Because of the tool dependency of technical drawing, investing in quality equipment is recommended. By initially spending a little extra money, drafters can purchase a fine set of tools that will last a lifetime. As the old saying goes, "A craftsman is no better than his tools." This speaks well for purchasing quality equipment from the very beginning. A recommended list of basic drafting tools is located in appendix H.

1.2 Level 1

There are nine tools that are essential to begin the practice of theatre drafting. They are:
1. A flat, smooth work surface
2. Media on which the drawing will be done
3. Tape to hold the media on the work surface
4. Pencils to draw the various required lines
5. Straight edge or combination of straight edges that permit drawing vertical, horizontal, and oblique lines
6. Drawing instruments for producing arcs and circles. (A set that includes 6" dividers and bow compass is recommended.)
7. Architect's scale ruler for determining sizes
8. Plastic eraser for removing mistakes
9. Erasing shield

1.1. Level 1 drafting tools

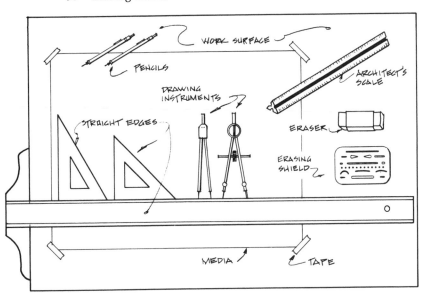

Work Surface

Any smooth, flat surface with at least one straight edge can be used as a drafting board. The kitchen table, a hollow core door across two sawhorses, drafting boards, and drafting tables all serve as work surfaces. Although the kitchen table and doors are used by many, the serious drafter should invest in a drafting board or table. These commercial products are manufactured with both a true edge and smooth surface that enhance the accuracy and quality of final drawings.

No matter how well made, commercial drafting boards are not as smooth as necessary for the creation of quality drawings. A **vinyl** or **heavy paper cover** is recommended. Vinyl board covers provide excellent work surfaces that respond well to pencil pressure and are self-healing from minor punctures and cuts.

Drawing Media

Drawings can be produced on most any paper that accepts pencil lines, but because of the need for clean, reproducible drawings, specially formulated drafting papers are preferred. **Vellum,** a 100% rag paper, is the recommended paper for use throughout the exercises in this text. A complete discussion of drawing media is located in §1.5 of this chapter.

Drafting Tape

Drafting tape is a special paper tape designed for temporary adhesion and looks like masking tape. The tape is available in rolls as well as precut dots. Drafting tape is used to secure the four corners of the drawing media to the work surface throughout the process of drafting.

Pencils

There are three different varieties of pencils that can be used in drafting. **Wood-bound pencils** are the least expensive; however, they need to be sharpened frequently, and as their length shortens through use, they become more and more awkward to handle. The **clutch holder pencil** is the traditional pencil of choice. The holder easily accepts a variety of leads, sharpened to a fine conical point using a special lead sharpener. The large diameter lead sticks are strong and not easily broken. One holder along with a combination of leads can be used to create a variety of line weights. The **mechanical pencil** produces lines of a predetermined width without sharpening. A lead is advanced through mechanical means. No sharpening is required. Mechanical pencils are identified by lead size and are available in the standard sizes of 0.3 mm, 0.5 mm, 0.7 mm, and 0.9 mm.

1.2. Leads and points common to theatre drafting

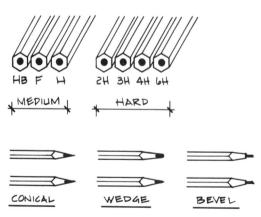

No matter what type of lead-holding device is chosen, a more important choice is the selection of the lead itself. Leads are a proportional combination of graphite and kaolin (clay), the ratio of which determines the softness of the lead. There are eighteen different grades of lead with 9H being the hardest, and 7B the softest. Most drawings on vellum are drawn with **H, 2H, and 4H** leads, with the harder leads used for construction weight lines, and the softer leads used for final lines. If mechanical pencils are used, most drafters need to choose a lead approximately one grade softer than would be used in a clutch holder because of the reduced physical strength of the mechanical pencil lead. This same rule applies to compass leads also.

Straight Edges

The **T-square** is the most common straight edge used. The head of the T-square is placed along the left hand side of the board (right hand side, if left-handed) and horizontal lines are drawn using the top edge of the blade. Vertical and angled lines are drawn using combinations of various triangles in conjunction with the T-square as a horizontal base. Two standard triangles are used for most theatre drawing: the **30°–60° triangle** and the **45°–45° triangle.**

Compass

A **bow compass** is used to draw arcs and circles and is necessary for a variety of geometric construction techniques used in the creation of drawings. Bow compasses have a pinpoint at the end of one leg and a lead holder at the end of the other. The compass lead is sharpened by rubbing the lead on a small piece of sandpaper to create a chisel point. Sandpaper pads can be purchased in most drafting supply stores.

Dividers

Dividers are similar to a compass in construction but are equipped with a hairspring to allow minute adjustments and two needle points rather than a combination of point and lead. The tool is used to divide lines into equal segments and for the rapid transfer of dimensions from one location to another.

Scale

Technical drawings are scaled representations of full-sized objects with all dimensions maintained in proportion. The scale ruler is used to measure line lengths and maintain their proper relationship to each other. Several types of scale are available, each intended for a specific task. The **architect's scale** has all of the scales common to theatre drawings. Avoid other scales such as the engineer's scale, divided into decimal units; the mechanical engineer's scale, divided into units representing inches to full size, half size, quarter size, or eighth size; and scales that are a combination of all three types.

Erasers

Four different types of erasers are recommended for the removal of errors from drawings. The most universal is the **vinyl compound** eraser that easily removes pencil lines. Vinyl compound erasers are sturdy and when used break down into very fine strands that can easily be brushed off your drawing. The **hard beveled rubber** eraser is also handy to have. Beveled rubber erasers are more abrasive than the vinyl compound but are less expensive and work well when large areas must be erased to revise

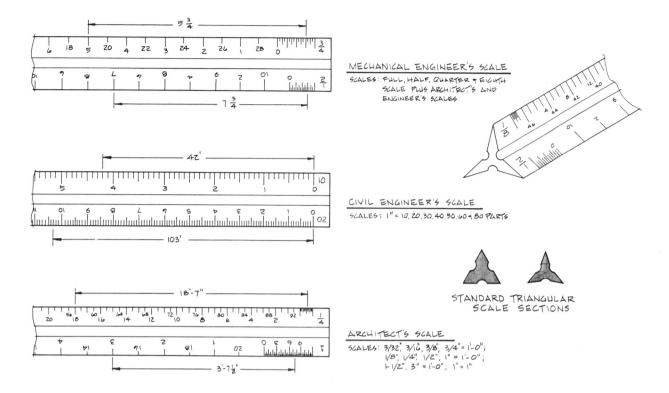

MECHANICAL ENGINEER'S SCALE
SCALES: FULL, HALF, QUARTER & EIGHTH
SCALE PLUS ARCHITECT'S AND
ENGINEER'S SCALES

CIVIL ENGINEER'S SCALE
SCALES: 1" = 10, 20, 30, 40, 50, 60 & 80 PARTS

STANDARD TRIANGULAR
SCALE SECTIONS

ARCHITECT'S SCALE
SCALES: 3/32", 3/16", 3/8", 3/4" = 1'-0";
1/8", 1/4", 1/2", 1" = 1'-0";
1-1/2", 3" = 1'-0"; 1" = 1"

1.3. Scale ruler types

work done long ago. The **art gum** eraser is very soft and used for cleaning smears and removing pencil lines from inked drawings. Useful for picking up excess graphite from heavy lines is the **kneaded rubber** eraser.

Erasing Shield

An **erasing shield** is a thin metal shield that protects lines near those being erased. Shields are available with a wide variety of hole sizes punched in them, and the drafter may wish to have several different types. One corner of the shield may be bent up to facilitate picking it up from the drawing surface.

1.3 Level 2

The second level of drafting tools are those that can make drawing easier and solve specific drafting problems. They are:

1. Parallel bar
2. Ames Lettering Guide
3. Adjustable triangle
4. Protractor
5. Cleaning pad
6. Dusting brush
7. Beam compass
8. Irregular curves
9. Adjustable curves
10. Templates
11. Colored leads
12. Ink pens and supplies

Parallel Bar

While long horizontal lines can easily be drawn with a T-square, the farther out on the blade the line is drawn the greater the chance for an error. The **parallel bar** eliminates this danger. Parallel rules are securely mounted to drafting boards, and their ends are controlled by a system of cables and pulleys. The control system allows the parallel to be moved up and down the board while remaining in a horizontal position. Provision is also made to allow the bar to be aligned with the drawing after a sheet has been taped to the board.

6

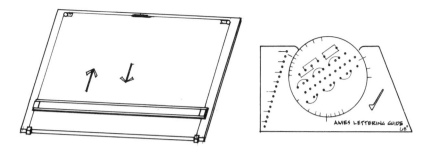

Ames Lettering Guide

The **Ames Lettering Guide** facilitates drawing guidelines for a variety of letter heights and is easily adjusted to permit rapid drawing of both vertical and horizontal guidelines. Use of the lettering guide is explained in detail in §3.4.

Adjustable Triangles and Protractors

Adjustable triangles have an adjustable hypotenuse attached to a locking sweep that is ruled with degree designations, allowing lines of most any angle to be drawn. A **protractor** permits the exact measurement of angles.

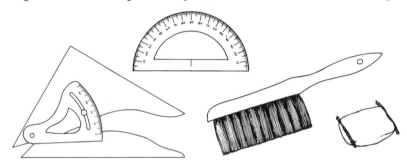

Cleaning Pad and Dusting Brush

To maintain the cleanliness of drawings a **cleaning pad** and **dusting brush** are helpful. A cleaning pad picks up excess graphite and coats the surface of the drawing with eraser dust. A dusting brush is used to remove eraser dust without smearing the drawing.

BEAM COMPASS

Beam Compass

Large arcs are impossible to draw using a bow compass because of tool-size limitations, therefore a **beam compass** may be required. The long arm of the beam with adjustable pinpoint and lead holder allows for great accuracy and is more easily manipulated than a bow compass.

Irregular and Adjustable Curves

Curved lines that are not arcs and circles can be drawn with the aid of **irregular curves** (commonly called French curves) or **adjustable curves.** Both are used to provide an edge along which various line segments are drawn after the irregular points of the curve are plotted and connected.

IRREGULAR OR
"FRENCH" CURVES

ADJUSTABLE CURVE

7

Templates

Repetitive shapes like lighting instruments, identification symbols, and hardware symbols utilize **templates.** Templates are available to help draw any geometric shape desired, as well as providing a shorthand to a host of proprietary and standard symbols used by professionals such as engineers, architects, and computer programmers.

1.9. Templates

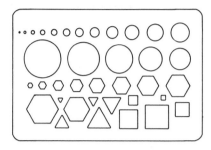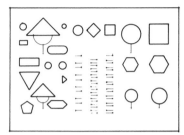

Colored Leads

Colored leads are useful to help differentiate between details and levels of overlays. In addition, a nonreproducible blue lead, one of the many colors available, is invaluable for planning layout and roughing in ideas, as this shade of blue line will not appear during the printing process.

Ink Pens and Associated Supplies

Supplies for inking drawings are included in level 2 although they are seldom used. Inked drawings in the theatre are normally restricted to permanent theatre plans, sections, and circuit plots. The equipment most commonly used includes **technical pens** with fixed diameter tips to draw constant width lines, lettering devices such as the **Leroy® system,** and a range of drawing inks available in varying opacities and colors.

1.4 Level 3

The items in level 3 are specialized or costly tools not normally purchased by student theatre drafters. The convenience and efficiency they afford the drafter may, however, make their purchase worth the investment.

1. Light tables
2. Drafting machines
3. Electric erasers
4. Flat scales
5. Multiple instruments and templates
6. Preprinted media

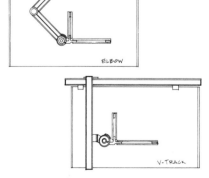

1.10. Light table

Light Tables

A **light table** can greatly ease the ability to draw tracings and utilize overlays. Light tables may be purchased in a variety of sizes from small portable units to full table-size models.

Drafting Machines

A **drafting machine** is a set of scaled drawing arms set at 90° to each other and secured to a movable head. Drafting machines effectively replace T-squares, triangles, protractors, and scales. Two types are available: arm machines, commonly referred to as "elbow machines," and track machines, which require a horizontal track attached to the top of the drawing board. The head of either style may be set at any angle and the interchangeable arms are available in a variety of scales. Although expensive, drafting machines are very easy to use and are great time savers.

1.11. Elbow and tracking machines

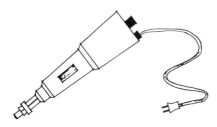

1.12. Electric eraser

1.13. Flat scales

Electric Erasers
An **electric eraser** removes mistakes much faster. Changeable cores allow the use of both vinyl compound and hard rubber erasers in these motorized units. Both cordless and corded models are available.

Flat Scales
Triangular scales combine many scales on one ruler, but a drafter can waste much time searching for the required scale. **Flat scales** are essentially ⅓ of a triangular scale, therefore several flat scales are required to replace one triangular scale.

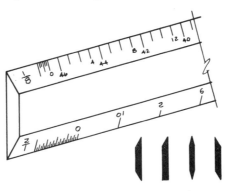

STANDARD FLAT SCALE SECTIONS

Multiples
Multiple copies of triangles, compasses, dividers, templates, and pencils in a variety of styles and sizes are often helpful to the experienced drafter. Tools can be selected to match the specific needs of an individual drawing. Although one size will do, time can be saved and frustrations reduced if the right tool is available.

Preprinted Media
Any of the available drawing media may be preprinted with borders, title blocks, logos; virtually anything desired. Large architectural and engineering firms utilize preprinted media in all of their work, however, the costs do not warrant its use in theatre applications.

1.5 Drawing Media

An ideal drafting paper has great physical strength to withstand erasing and use; is highly stable, resisting temperature and humidity changes; is transparent to ease drawing reproduction; and has "good tooth," the coarseness of the drawing surface affecting line quality and ease of erasure. Drawing media are available in a variety of types meeting the specific needs of the drafter.

Drawing Paper
Drawing paper is useful for pencil drawings that are not intended for reproduction. This fairly heavyweight paper is usually buff, light cream, or green in color. The nonreproducible quality of drawing paper makes it inappropriate for theatre drafting.

Tracing Paper
Intermediate drawings or sketches may be drawn on tracing paper, a low density, naturally transparent media. Tracing paper does not have the strength or stability of other papers and as a result is much less expensive. Its low cost makes tracing paper an excellent choice for temporary

overlays, layout work, "roughs," and sketching. Available in standard-sized pads and rolls, pads are usually white, while rolls come in two colors: white and canary (yellow).

Vellum

Vellum, a 100% rag paper, meets the qualities outlined and is the most popular paper choice for theatre drafting. Vellum easily accepts both pencil and ink and can be tinted to relieve eye strain. A variety printed with a nonreproducible grid is available that makes layout and sketching much easier.

Tracing Cloth

Tracing cloth is linen that has been sized with a starch or plastic compound to provide a good drawing surface that resists smearing. With a natural fiber as a base, tracing cloth is subject to humidity and deteriorates over time. While once considered stable and useful for permanent drawings, its use has largely been replaced by drafting film.

Drafting Film

Drafting film has excellent stability for use with both pencil and ink. Film has replaced cloth as the media of choice of archival quality drawings. Plastic leads are required when working on drafting film to obtain the needed opacity. These leads are available for both clutch holders and mechanical pencils. Drafting film is the most expensive of the media discussed, and because most theatre drawings are not of archival quality, drafting film is seldom used for production drawings.

1.6 Reproduction

To be of any value all technical drawings must be easily reproduced. Originals take far too long to create to allow them to be used in the field, where they will almost certainly be damaged. A variety of reproduction techniques are used to create the necessary copies of a technical drawing.

Blueprinting

The blueprint process is the oldest method of drawing reproduction and is seldom used today. Blueprinting is a photographic process that utilizes original drawings as the negative. The original is placed over chemically treated white paper and exposed to light. The paper turns blue wherever the light passes through the original. The exposed print is then placed in a stop bath of clear water, removed, and allowed to dry.

Diazo and Ozalid

Similar to the blueprint process are the diazo and ozalid processes. Diazo and ozalid also utilize the original as a negative and burn off chemically treated paper through exposure to light. Ammonia vapors are used to develop the final print. Nonammonia machines are available for use in nonventilated areas. These techniques are much less costly than blueprinting and result in a whiteprint; a drawing with a white background and blue lines. Other line colors, principally black and sepia, can be achieved through the use of special print papers using the same process.

Intermediates

Polyester film duplicates (slicks) and paper sepia prints are known as intermediates in the graphic reproduction industry. Both can be created using special chemically coated materials run through standard diazo-style machines. Intermediates are of lesser quality than other forms of prints but are especially helpful for overlays and composite drawing work. Many theatre drafters use "reverse" paper sepias when drawing ground plans and center-line sections (see chap. 16).

Photography
A variety of photographic processes may be used to duplicate drawings. Large format cameras create film negatives for efficient storage and high-quality reproduction of technical drawings. Photographic techniques are costly but invaluable to operations where extreme accuracy of reduction or reproduction is needed.

Photo Duplication
Large format photo copying machines (xerography) are available that are capable of producing continuous prints up to 36" × 16'-0". Full-sized copies as well as reductions and enlargements can be made on bond, vellum, and film media with this equipment.

1.7 Storage of Drawings

1.14. Sample cover sheet

Drawings are ideally stored flat in large drawers or hung vertically in specially designed racks or cabinets. Large drawings may be loosely rolled and stored in tubes. When a project is complete, all drawings should be bound together in a single package with an appropriate cover sheet. The drawing package is bound along the left-hand margin with a strip of excess print paper. The strip of paper is folded several times and then joined to the rest of the drawing using staples.

1.8 Checkpoints

√ A number of basic tools are required for mechanical drafting.

√ Additional tools aid the drafter and speed the creating of drawings.

√ All technical drawings must be reproducible to be of value.

2 Graphic Standards

2.1 Communication Is the Key

The primary purpose of drafting is to convey technical information in a graphic manner. In the specific field of theatre, drafting must be viewed as a means to an end. Theatre graphics are used to communicate design and construction ideas to members of the production team and shop craftspersons. Although drafting should be seen as a tool rather than a product in itself, in order for the information on the drafted plate to be effectively communicated, drawings must be of a high quality and follow established graphic standards. Factors such as drawing arrangement, line weight quality, and presentational style play a significant role in graphic communication.

Recently the theatre industry followed the practice of other professionals who make extensive use of graphics in their work by establishing a standard graphic language in scene design and technical production. According to the United States Institute for Theatre Technology (USITT) Graphic Standards Board, this action was taken for several reasons.

The primary reason cited for standardization is the ever-increasing mobility of theatre designers and technicians. It is not uncommon for a designer in New York to be working on a production in San Diego that is being built in Phoenix and directed by someone from Minneapolis. Expenses for personal, on-site conferences can be exorbitant in relationship to overall production budgets. Consequently, much information is exchanged through the mails and other information delivery systems. As mobility increases, so does the need for a standardized graphic language that is equipped with symbols and notation unique to the needs of theatre practitioners.

The second reason for standardization is enhanced education. For educators to successfully prepare students to enter fields of theatre design and technology, industry standards must be defined. Assumed information, which in fact could be incorrect, may well have a harmful effect on a student's professional growth.

A significant benefit of standardization is increased efficiency. Theatre drafting is frequently done under severe time constraints. The use of standardized schematic symbols reduces drafting time while maintaining high quality.

2.2 Drawing-Sheet Standards and Handling

Standard Sheet Sizes

Two systems of sheet sizes are approved by ANSI (American National Standards Institute) and are normally stocked by all graphics supply stores. System 1 is based on the universal 8½″ × 11″ sheet size and its multiples. This system allows the filing of small tracings and folded prints in standard manila files along with related correspondence. The al-

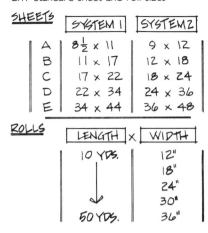

SHEETS	SYSTEM 1	SYSTEM 2
A	8½ × 11	9 × 12
B	11 × 17	12 × 18
C	17 × 22	18 × 24
D	22 × 34	24 × 36
E	34 × 44	36 × 48

ROLLS	LENGTH ×	WIDTH
	10 YDS.	12"
		18"
	↓	24"
	↓	30"
	50 YDS.	36"

ternative, system 2, is based on 9″ × 12″; it has the advantage of a larger surface area. Both systems permit all sizes to be cut, with little or no waste, from a standard 36″ roll of paper or film.

Borders

Once the paper is secured, use T-square and triangles to draw a border around the page. Though the use of borders is not mandatory, it is highly desirable, since they prevent the placement of valuable information too close to the edge of the sheet, where it is easily lost during drawing reproduction.

Initially the border is drawn, using light construction lines; later, it will be darkened as one of the last steps in the drawing process. Standards for the border are ½″ along the bottom, top, and right sides, with a 1″ border along the left-hand side. The 1″ dimension is used to facilitate the space lost when binding the complete set of production drawings.

Title Blocks

All drawings require a title block to provide proper identification. The title block should be placed in the same position for all drawings of a single project. USITT recommends that the title block be located in the lower right-hand corner of the drawing or drawn as a strip across the bottom of the drawing. Often the right and bottom edges of the border coincide with the same edges of the title block.

2.2. Title block examples

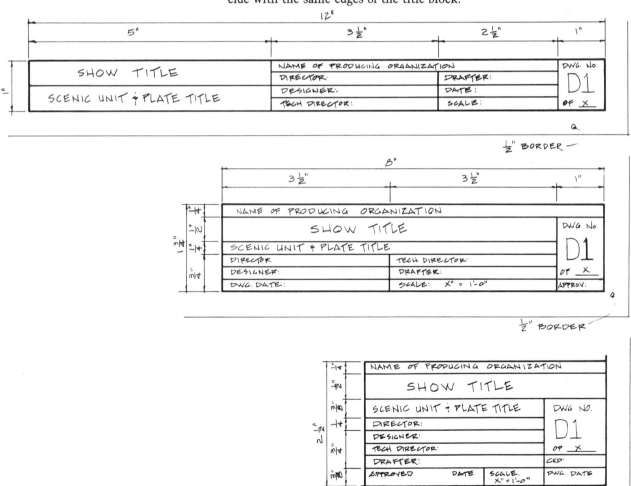

Figure 2.2 shows a variety of title block examples. Each is acceptable and may be adopted for use by the individual drafter. Title block formats vary considerably, but all should include the following information:

1. Name of producing organization and/or theatre
2. Name of production, act and scene if appropriate
3. Drawing title
4. Drawing number
5. Predominant scale of the drawing
6. Date the drawing was drafted
7. Director of the production*
8. Designer of the production
9. Technical director of the production*
10. Drafter of the drawing
11. Approval of drawing, if applicable

*All items other than those asterisked are USITT mandated.

2.3. Standard title block for this text

The title block format shown full size in figure 2.3 is the standard title block recommended for use with this text.

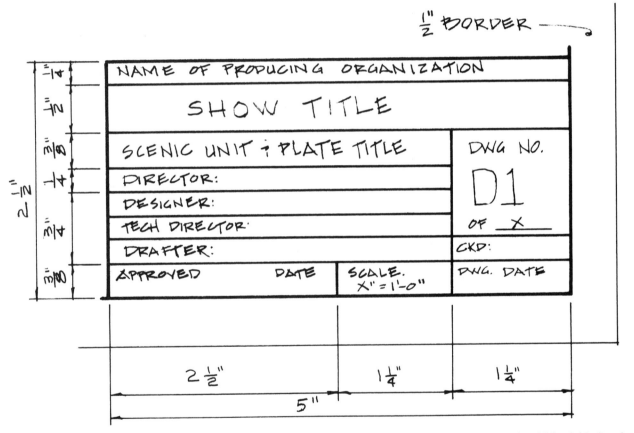

2.3 Folding and Rolling of Prints To facilitate handling, mailing, and filing, prints should be folded to letter size in such a way that the title block will always appear on the front face, and the last fold will always be at the top. In filing, this prevents other drawings from being pushed into the folds of filed prints. Recommended methods of folding standard-sized prints are illustrated in figure 2.4.

Because marks caused by folding can often result in loss of clarity, drawings are frequently rolled and handled directly or stored in tube. Always

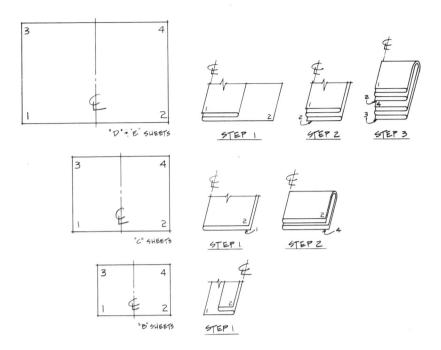

roll drawings loosely, with the face out, and with the title block exposed. If this orientation is used, when unrolled, the drawings will flatten out themselves and be much easier to read and handle. If drawings are received rolled face inward, reroll them tightly in the opposite direction. This will help, but probably not entirely correct the situation.

2.4 Line Weight

No other single factor has a greater impact on the graphic quality of drafting than does line weight. The term **line weight** references a combination of thickness and opacity that when properly used allows both reproduction and line differentiation in your work. In 1983 the USITT adopted a two-thickness line weight system for both pen and pencil. A modified ANSI standard, the USITT standard for theatre drafting is shown in figure 2.5. In fact, the USITT standard permits the use of three thicknesses, although the "extra thick" line weight is specified for infrequent and very specific uses.

2.5. USITT-approved line weights. Reprinted by permission of USITT

EXAMPLE	PENCIL	PEN
THIN	.3 MM	#3Ø - 2Ø .25 - .30 MM
THICK	.5 MM	#1 - 2 .45 - .5 MM
EXTRA THICK*	.9 MM	#3 - 3½ .8 - 1.0 MM

*SPECIAL APPLICATIONS ONLY

While no one in the theatre has the time nor the need to measure the width of lines on a given drawing, the drafter has the responsibility to have thick lines that are thicker than thin lines and, conversely, thin lines that are thinner than thick. The sizes listed in figure 2.5 serve primarily as a guide.

2.5 Alphabet of Lines

To further aid the reader of a drawing in making distinctions between various lines and their respective meanings, a set of standard line symbols has been adopted. This "alphabet of lines" is to be observed on all plates assigned in this text and is included here as a ready reference. Should a drawing require use of a line(s) not listed in the alphabet of lines, e.g., multiple set-piece locations on a composite ground plan, the new line(s) should be defined in a legend placed on the drawing near the title block.

2.6. USITT standard alphabet of lines. Reprinted by permission of USITT

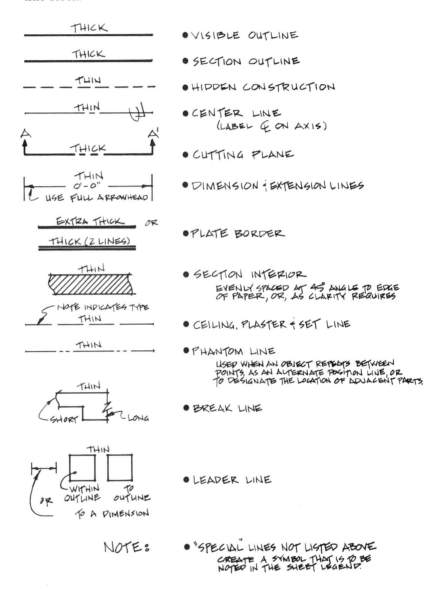

2.6 General USITT Symbols

Many of the objects that appear on drawings are hardware or construction techniques that are used throughout the theatre industry. To facilitate drawing ease and promote standardization, USITT has also established a set of standard symbols. These symbols serve to effectively communicate complex information with minimal drawing effort. More will be discussed on the use of symbols later.

16

2.7a. USITT dimensioning and lettering standards. Reprinted by permission of USITT

USITT DIMENSIONING & LETTERING STANDARDS

- WRITING DIMENSIONS:

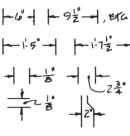

a) LESS THAN 1'-0"

b) 1'-0", OR GREATER

c) SMALL SPACES
PLACE THE DIMENSION IN PROXIMITY TO THE AREA MEASURED, PARALLEL WITH THE BOTTOM EDGE OF THE SHEET & DIRECTED TO THE POINT OF REFERENCE BY MEANS OF A LEADER LINE.

- PLATFORM & STAIR TREAD HEIGHTS
GIVE IN INCHES (ABOVE THE STAGE FLOOR) PLACE IN CIRCLES AT OR NEAR THE CENTER OF THE PLATFORM OR TREAD.

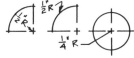

- RADII

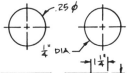

- DIAMETERS

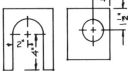

- LOCATING CENTERS

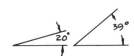

- ANGLES

ABCDEFGHIJKLM
NOPQRSTUVWXYZ   - ALPHABET

1234567890   - NUMERALS

- NOTE: ALL "FIGURES" MUST BE CLEAR, CONSISTENT & EASILY UNDERSTOOD. ORIENT THEM TO BE READ FROM EITHER BOTTOM OR RIGHT SIDE OF THE SHEET.

2.7b. USITT shop drawing standard symbols. Reprinted by permission of USITT

USITT SHOP DRAWING STANDARD SYMBOLS

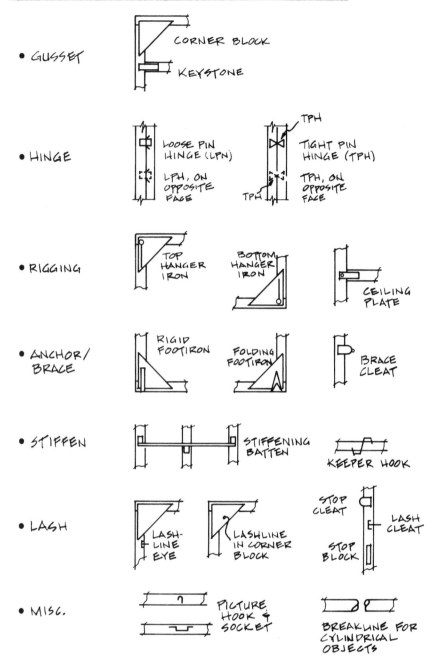

- GUSSET — CORNER BLOCK, KEYSTONE

- HINGE — LOOSE PIN HINGE (LPN), LPH, ON OPPOSITE FACE, TPH, TIGHT PIN HINGE (TPH), TPH, ON OPPOSITE FACE

- RIGGING — TOP HANGER IRON, BOTTOM HANGER IRON, CEILING PLATE

- ANCHOR/BRACE — RIGID FOOTIRON, FOLDING FOOTIRON, BRACE CLEAT

- STIFFEN — STIFFENING BATTEN, KEEPER HOOK

- LASH — LASHLINE EYE, LASHLINE IN CORNER BLOCK, STOP CLEAT, STOP BLOCK, LASH CLEAT

- MISC. — PICTURE HOOK & SOCKET, BREAKLINE FOR CYLINDRICAL OBJECTS

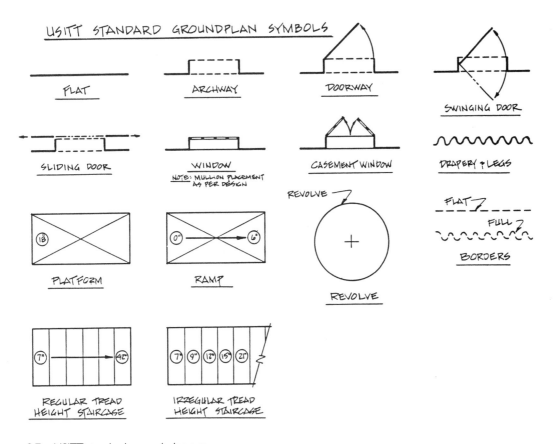

USITT STANDARD GROUNDPLAN SYMBOLS

FLAT

ARCHWAY

DOORWAY

SWINGING DOOR

SLIDING DOOR

WINDOW
NOTE: MULLION PLACEMENT AS PER DESIGN

CASEMENT WINDOW

DRAPERY & LEGS

PLATFORM

RAMP

REVOLVE

FLAT

FULL

BORDERS

REVOLVE

REGULAR TREAD HEIGHT STAIRCASE

IRREGULAR TREAD HEIGHT STAIRCASE

2.7c. USITT standard ground plan symbols. Reprinted by permission of USITT

2.7 Checkpoints

√ Theatre drafting is clear in presentation, consistent in style, and efficient in method.

√ Line weights and symbols serve to help the reader identify exactly what is being seen.

√ Symbols provide an efficient means of conveying complex information.

3 Lettering

3.1 In Defense of a Lettering Style

In drafting, lettering is like the frosting on a cake. The cake itself may be perfectly shaped and possess excellent flavor and texture, but if the frosting is not uniformly and attractively applied, the observer is unlikely to judge the cake first-rate. Likewise with lettering: a clean, accurate, and organized drawing can often be rendered unattractive by ill-formed and randomly positioned lettering. Even a cursory examination of theatre graphics will reveal many instances in which detailed notation is necessary to fully explain a drawing. Since lettering should enhance, not detract from, the overall quality of the drawing, from the very beginning, emphasis is placed on the importance of competent and attractive lettering . In this chapter a variety of lettering options are shown: lettering devices as well as freehand lettering techniques.

3.1. Lettering examples

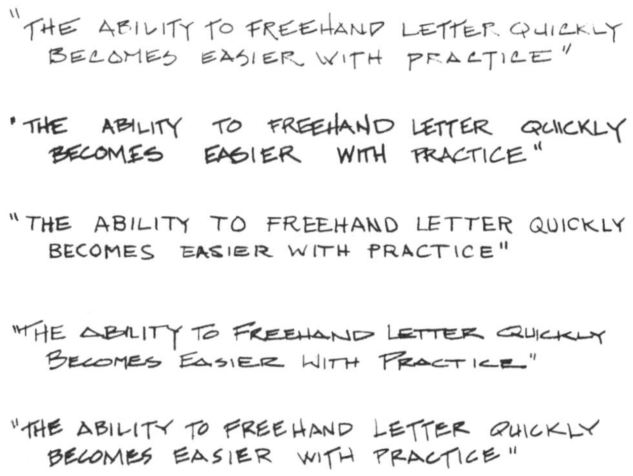

3.2 Freehand Lettering

The most common and inexpensive method of lettering theatrical drawings is by hand. Because this system requires only pencil, paper, and guidelines, and is a skill that can be learned by all, it is the recommended lettering technique.

Anyone can learn to letter if persistent and intelligent. Interestingly enough the ability to letter has little relationship to writing ability; excellent letterers often have poor penmanship.

3.3 Freehand Lettering Techniques

The Vertical American Standard Alphabet is a single-stroke Gothic lettering style commonly used in architectural as well as theatre drafting and is the USITT standard alphabet. As seen in figure 3.3, the American Standard can easily be expanded and condensed to fit visual and space needs. Note that this alphabet does not use serifs in forming the I, J, Z, and 7.

No one expects all theatre drafters to learn to letter in the same manner.

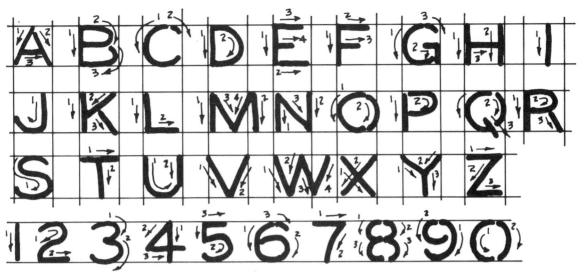

3.2. The Vertical American Standard Alphabet

Each drafter should work to establish a "style" within the guidelines of the recommended standards and to conform to that style throughout all the drawings for a particular project. To do this the drafter must have a thorough knowledge of the proportions and forms of the letters and the order of the strokes, along with a complete knowledge of composition—the spacing of letters and words. A consistent freehand lettering style can be achieved only with much persistence and faithful adherence to industry standards. However, in the most blunt terms possible, there is only one way to develop an acceptable lettering style: PRACTICE! PRACTICE! PRACTICE!

3.3. Expanded and condensed lettering styles

LETTERING IS EASIER
WITH PRACTICE

EXPANDED

LETTERING IS EASIER
WITH PRACTICE

CONDENSED

3.4 Lettering Guidelines

Guidelines for vertical capital letters are shown in figure 3.4. Theatre drawings commonly use letters and numerals ⅛" high, with the space between lines of lettering ranging from ⅗ to the full height of the letters. Letter heights vary, however, dependent upon the relative importance of the information to be lettered. The maximum size for single stroke lettering is ¼". Letters larger than ¼" appear weak owing to the narrow line weight. For those drafters who are hesitant to freehand large-sized letters, a common alternative is to underline ⅛" letters, leaving a ¹⁄₁₆" space between the letters and the underline.

3.4. Lettering guidelines

1) LETTERING IS EASY
WITH PRACTICE

SPACING IS
3/5 HEIGHT

2) LETTERING IS EASY
WITH PRACTICE

(EVEN
SPACING

Two methods are commonly used to lay out guidelines. The first involves drawing a vertical construction line near where the lettering is to be done. Using a scale ruler, divide the line into appropriate segments for

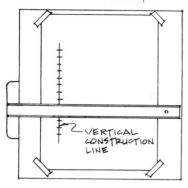

letter-height and line spacing. Horizontal guidelines are then projected using T-square and pencil.

The second method involves the use of a commercially available lettering guide and is much faster. The Ames Lettering Guide is a convenient tool for drawing guidelines for lettering and dimensions, as well as drawing section lines. The guide is a plastic frame having an interior rotating disc perforated with three columns of holes. The vertical distances between the holes may be adjusted by rotating the disc. Along one edge of the disc are numbers that indicate letter size in 1/32". For example, for 1/8" high letters, use the no. 4 setting. On the opposite side of the disc is another gauge, this one being for lettering in the metric system.

3.6. Ames Lettering Guide

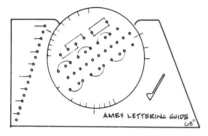

The holes in the center column are spaced equidistant; this column is intended to be used to draw guidelines for numerals and fractions, but many drafters use it to draw equally spaced guidelines of whatever size needed. The two outer columns are intended to draw guidelines for lowercase letters. The column marked 3/5 is used where it is desired to make the lower portions of letters three-fifths the total height of the letters. The column marked 2/3 is used for the same purpose, but the proportions are set at two-thirds this time. The fraction designation also indicates the space between lines. The middle hole of each of these columns is not used when lettering capitals. The vertical side of the frame contains another column of equidistant holes; these are nonvariable and spaced 1/8" apart.

3.5 Spacing Letters and Words

Equally as important as proper letter formation is the proper spacing between letters and words. Uniformity in spacing of letters is a matter of equalizing spaces by eye. The background areas between letters, not the distances between them, should be approximately equal. Space words well apart, but space letters closely within words. Letters should not touch; for the sake of clarity each must be a distinct entity. Make each word a distinct unit separated from adjacent words with a space large enough for a capital *M*.

Centering words in a note is often desirable. To space letters symmetrically about a center line, number the letters as shown; consider the space between words as one letter. Place the middle letter on center, visually making allowance for narrow letters (*L*'s) or wide letters (*W*'s) on either side.

3.7. Lettering on center

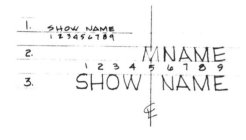

A second method is to letter a trial line along the bottom edge of a scrap of paper. The scrap can then be placed as shown or, if using tracing paper, may be placed directly underneath the final position. These same techniques may be used when lettering to a fixed margin.

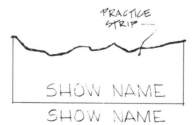

3.8. Lettering, using a trial strip

3.6 Basic Rules of Lettering

1. Choose one style of lettering and practice the formation of the letters. The Vertical American Standard Alphabet is the recommended style.
2. Use only the capital alphabet. Lowercase letters are rarely used.
3. Use a soft lead, preferably an H or HB, which will glide and is more easily controlled than a hard lead.
4. Make letters bold and distinctive. Letters must be uniform in thickness of stroke and opacity. Keep the lead point sharp. This can be assisted by routinely twirling the pencil while lettering. The twirling will help keep the pencil point conical.
5. Form the habit of lettering whenever possible: letter notes, envelopes, your name. Practice lettering both words and sentences to enhance spacing skills.
6. Do not try to develop speed at first. Make individual strokes quickly but take time between letters and strokes to assure letters are being correctly formed.

3.9. Lettering inconsistencies

EXAMPLE	CONCERN
Theatre TEChNoLoGY	• STYLE
THEATRE TECHNOLOGY	• HEIGHT
THEATRE TECHNOLOGY	• VERTICALITY
THEATRE TECHNOLOGY	• LINE WEIGHT
T HEATRE TEC HN O LoGY	• DIST. BETWEEN LETTERS
	• DIST. BETWEEN WORDS

THEATRE TECHNOLOGY IS HARD WORK, BUT CAN ALSO BE FUN!

7. Always use guidelines.
8. Space letters closely without touching. Separate words with enough space for a capital *M*.
9. Practice with larger letters (about ¼″) and gradually reduce the size until you can letter effectively at ⅛″. Never letter smaller than ⅛″ on any drawings for the stage.
10. Letter drawings last to avoid smudges and overlapping with other areas of the drawing.
11. Fractions are 1⅔ times the height of the whole number. Numerator over denominator is preferred practice.
12. The size of the lettering should be related to the importance of the labeling. (See chap. 8.)

ALL NUMERALS SAME HEIGHT

$1\frac{1}{2}$ $2\frac{5}{8}$ $6\frac{7}{8}$

3.10. Lettering fractions

SIZES	USES
1/8"	ALL NOTES AND DIMENSIONS
3/16"	SCENIC UNIT & PLATE TITLES
1/4"	SHOW TITLES

3.7 Lettering Devices

Lettering Templates

As mentioned in chapter 1, several styles of lettering templates are readily available in most graphic supplies stores. Templates produce a rigid uniform look, common to engineering plates for which templates are commonly used because these drawings often are the work of several drafters. This need for uniformity is not so pronounced in the theatre, where drawings and lettering are produced quickly and usually by one person. Lettering templates are certainly useful when lettering titles and labels that might require lettering 1/4" high or larger, since even experienced drafters find it difficult to neatly letter in such a large size. For the most part, however, templates are ultimately too slow and cumbersome to be useful in producing the amount of lettering required on theatrical drawings.

Dry Transfer Letters

Dry transfer letters are another alternative to freehand lettering. Transfer letters are actually typeset style alphabets, commonly sold in sheets. The letters are transferred from the full sheet to the drawing surface by rubbing the surface of the sheet with a blunt object and burnishing the letter to assure uniform adhesion. Dry transfer letters readily attach to both vellum and film. They print nicely, using the diazo process, because of their opacity. While they can be ideal for bold lettering needs, the use of transfer letters is very time-consuming and can be expensive.

Typewriter Copy

A recent innovation in lettering needs is the use of a photocopy machine and adhesive backed repro film, commonly known as "sticky-back" film. Normally information is typed or drawn on a standard 8½" × 11" sheet of paper. Next, the information is photo duplicated onto the sticky-back media. To mount on the drawing, remove the waxed backing and position the adhesive-backed film at the correct location. Once aligned, cover the top surface of the film with a waxed surface and burnish out all wrinkles and air bubbles. Sticky-back is most useful for large blocks of information, such as general notes, schedules, and legends; it is rather cumbersome for small blocks, such as local notes.

The LeRoy® Lettering System

The Leroy® system, a lettering device widely used by engineering firms, produces a uniform ink letter. The device uses a guide pin that traces letters grooved in a template, while an ink cartridge pen moves on the paper or film. By adjusting the arm, the letters can be made vertical or inclined. A large number of templates and pen sizes are available.

Other Systems
There are many other commercial lettering aids available at a wide range of prices. Most of these devices, however, are too slow, costly, or cumbersome to be of great use in the production of theatre drawings.

3.8 Problems

The following three exercises give practice forming letters. Be patient and take time to study the American Standard Alphabet style sheet. Much practice is required to learn to letter rapidly in a uniform style. By starting slowly, paying careful attention to correctly shaping letters, and following the rules of uniformity, drafters will provide themselves with the best possible foundation.

3.12. The Vertical American Standard Alphabet

Worksheet 3.1
Copy the American Standard Alphabet shown below three times on the sheet provided. Use the order of strokes given as a guide.

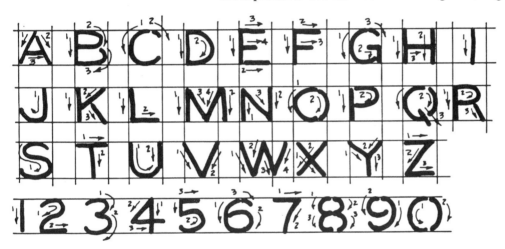

Worksheet 3.2
Copy the lettering example given. Do your best to fit the entire line in the space given; wrap around if necessary.

3.13. Lettering examples

ABCDEFGHIJKLMNOPQRSTUVWXYZ — 1234567890 $\left(\frac{1}{8}"\right)$

WHEN LETTERING NOTES, LEAVE A SPACE THE SIZE OF THE $\left(\frac{1}{8}"\right)$
LETTER 'M' BETEEN WORDS. CONSISTENT SPACING WILL HELP
CONVEY DIRECTIONS THAT ARE BOTH LEGIBLE AND UNDERSTANDABLE.

FRONT ELEVATIONS — UNITS 'A' THRU 'H'; $\left(\frac{3}{16}"\right)$
SECTION A-A; "AS YOU LIKE IT"

Worksheet 3.3

This exercise concerns itself with spacing, one of the most difficult aspects of good lettering. Copy this speech on the guidelines provided. Center the title and use a left margin line. Use capital letters only.

JACQUES' SPEECH: "AS YOU LIKE IT," II.7

ALL THE WORLD'S A STAGE,
AND ALL THE MEN AND WOMEN MERELY PLAYERS.
THEY HAVE THEIR EXITS AND THEIR ENTRANCES,
AND ONE MAN IN HIS TIME PLAYS MANY PARTS,
HIS ACTS BEING SEVEN AGES. AT FIRST THE INFANT,
MEWLING AND PUKING IN THE NURSE'S ARMS.
THEN THE WHINING SCHOOLBOY, WITH HIS SATCHEL
AND SHINING MORNING FACE, CREEPING LIKE SNAIL
UNWILLINGLY TO SCHOOL. AND THEN THE LOVER,
SIGHING LIKE FURNACE, WITH A WOEFUL BALLAD
MADE TO HIS MISTRESS' EYEBROW. THEN A SOLDIER,
FULL OF STRANGE OATHS AND BEARDED LIKE THE PARD,
JEALOUS IN HONOR, SUDDEN AND QUICK IN QUARREL,
SEEKING THE BUBBLE REPUTATION
EVEN IN THE CANNON'S MOUTH. AND THEN THE JUSTICE,
IN FAIR ROUND BELLY WITH GOOD CAPON LINED,
WITH EYES SEVERE AND BEARD OF FORMAL CUT,
FULL OF WISE SAWS AND MODERN INSTANCES,
AND SO HE PLAYS HIS PART. THE SIXTH AGE SHIFTS
INTO THE LEAN AND SLIPPERED PANTALOON
WITH SPECTACLES ON NOSE AND POUCH ON SIDE,
HIS YOUTHFUL HOSE, WELL SAVED, A WORLD TOO WIDE
FOR HIS SHRUNK SHANK, AND HIS BIG MANLY VOICE,
TURNING AGAIN TOWARD CHILDISH TREBLE, PIPES
AND WHISTLES IN HIS SOUND. LAST SCENE OF ALL,
THAT ENDS THIS STRANGE EVENTFUL HISTORY,
IS SECOND CHILDISHNESS AND MERE OBLIVION,
SANS TEETH, SANS EYES, SANS TASTE, SANS EVERYTHING.

WM. SHAKESPEARE, 1599

3.9 Checkpoints

√ Lettering should enhance, not detract from, drawings.

√ Always use guidelines when lettering.

√ To master lettering, practice it daily.

√ Personal style is developed from the firm foundation of basic lettering skills.

3.1

3.2

Name:	LETTERING	Worksheet 3.3
Date:		

4 Tool Use

4.1 Using the Right Tools Properly

There is a flip side to "a craftsman is no better than his tools," which is "tools alone do not a craftsman make." To get the best possible results from their equipment, drafters need to possess a detailed knowledge of the needs and capabilities of their tools and how each contributes to producing a successful final product: the technical drawing.

An ongoing focus of this book is the need to create reproducible drawings. Because of the high cost of time (labor) involved in drawing preparation, original draftings are rarely used in the field. Typically, originals are stored in a safe location and prints are made, using one of the reproduction processes discussed earlier. However, in order to create good prints, drawings must be drawn with excellent line quality. This is achievable only when drawing technique is appropriate and consistent. This chapter addresses many of the techniques and areas of which the drafter must be concerned.

4.2 Line Quality

Drawing is the language of lines. Therefore, it is appropriate that this discussion begins by examining the topic of line quality. Line quality refers to:

> Sharpness (results from a sharp lead)
> Blackness (opacity)
> Appropriate line weight (width or thickness of line)

This book is devoted to pencil drafting and does not discuss ink drawing, except by mention. Nevertheless, ink remains the benchmark by which the quality of pencil drawings are measured. The finish lines of any completed drawing should be very dark. Dark crisp lines give punch or snap to a drawing. The rules given below provide guidelines for satisfying line quality needs.

1. Construction lines should be made with a sharp, hard lead (4H or harder) and drawn so light that they need not be erased when the drawing is complete.
2. All finish lines of a completed drawing, regardless of line weight, should be very dark.
3. Contrast in line weight is created by use of distinct line widths, with little or no difference in the degree of darkness. Line opacity can be checked by holding a drawing up to light. Lines that are not opaque will not print well.
4. Opacity is controlled by the density of the lead used, as well as the pressure placed on the lead as lines are drawn.
5. Rotate the pencil as lines are drawn to maintain line thickness and even lead wear.
6. Ends of lines should be accented by a little extra pressure on the pencil; lines that fade out become arbitrary.
7. All lines should touch or intersect crisply at corners.

4.1. Creating a crisp line

4.2. Creating a crisp corner

4.3 Positioning the Drawing Sheet

The first step in the development of any drawing is to place the sheet of paper on the drawing board. Right-handed persons generally locate their drawing near the lower left-hand corner of the board; left-handed persons use the lower right-hand corner. In either case, the paper should be positioned at a location that is comfortable and that the T-square can easily reach.

To secure the paper, place the T-square on the paper, near the top. By inspection, adjust the paper until the top edge is parallel with the T-square blade. Lowering the T-square a few inches, place a piece of drafting tape over the upper corners to secure the sheet. Next, carefully slide the T-square down the page, smoothing out all wrinkles and air bubbles until the square is just above the bottom edge. Secure this edge with tape as well.

4.3. Placing the paper on the board

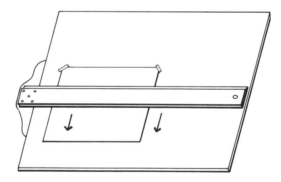

Once the paper is secured, it is time to arrange the sheet, see §4.6. In this introduction of tools, however, the discussion of drawing arrangement must come later. Before being concerned about the organization of a drawing, give attention first to the use of the following various basic tools. Use is demonstrated by function rather than tool name.

4.4 Drawing Straight Lines and Curves

All lines on a drafted plate are drawn with the aid of a specific tool or combination of tools. Lettering is the only time when freehand drawing is recommended, but even then tool-drawn guidelines must be used.

Horizontal Lines

Horizontal lines are drawn using a T-square. With the head of the T-square tight against one side of the drawing board, the top edge of the square is placed at the location of the desired line. Holding the T-square head firmly, pull the pencil point along the top edge, moving from the head in the direction of the drawing hand. For right-handers, this action is from left to right. Twirl the pencil slowly as the line is drawn to maintain a sharp conical point; do this for all lines.

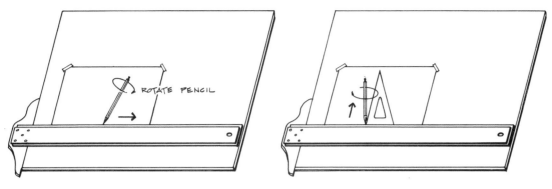

4.4. Drawing a horizontal line

4.5. Drawing a vertical line

Vertical Lines

Vertical lines are drawn in a similar manner. This time the T-square functions as a base to support a triangle. The vertical leg of the triangle is used as the guide for the pencil and is placed so that the triangle is under the drawing hand. This will prevent possible smudging caused by the hand moving across previously drawn lines. The pencil should be pulled, not pushed, up the edge. Pulling gives greater control of the pencil, producing better line quality and reducing the chance of cutting the paper.

Lines at an Angle

Triangles are also used to draw angled lines. Using a combination of 30°–60° and 45°–45° triangles, any angled lines in 15° increments can be drawn. Finer degree designations are drawn with the aid of an adjustable triangle or a protractor and straight edge.

4.6. Drawing angles, using combined triangles

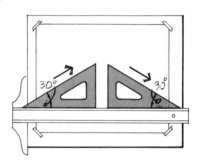

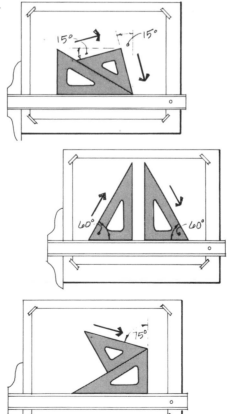

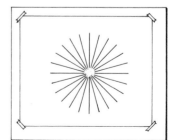

Arcs and Circles

Anytime a regular curved line is needed, the tool of choice is a compass. As illustrated in the chapter on tools, the most commonly used type is the bow compass. When drawing arcs and circles, be sure to firmly position the center point. To ensure a smooth line, draw arcs in a continuous motion.

4.7. Drawing an arc, using a bow compass

4.8. Setting a compass to a given distance

To set a compass for a given radius X, draw a construction line slightly longer than X. Using a scale, make two marks X length apart. Set the point end of the compass at one of the marks and adjust the bow until the lead end touches the other mark exactly. The compass is now set for use to draw a circle of given radius X.

4.5 Measuring in Scale

Technical drawings are scaled reductions in which all dimensions retain the same ratio as the full scale. For example, if a 4'-0" × 12'-0" flat is drawn using the scale 1" = 1'-0", then the scaled representation would be 4" × 12" and easily fit on a standard 18" × 24" sheet of vellum.

4.9. The triangular ruler

A variety of scale rulers are available, with each appropriate to a given task. For the preparation of theatrical drawings the architect's scale rule is used. The most common scales for theatre drawings are: ¼" = 1'-0"; ½" = 1'-0"; 1" = 1'-0"; 1½" = 1'-0"; and 3" = 1'-0". Note: In drafting, numerals expressing dimensions in feet and inches are separated by a hyphen.

Each edge of the scale rule is marked for use by the two different scales represented. To properly read a scale, follow the steps provided in figure 4.10.

4.10. Measuring a line, using a scale ruler

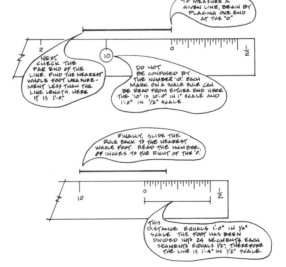

4.6 Drawing Arrangement

With only this basic introduction to drafting tools, it is now possible to begin drawing. Several problem plates are provided to incorporate the concepts discussed in this chapter.

Most problem plates are provided with a predetermined sheet arrangement, therefore these remarks on drawing arrangement may not seem immediately pertinent. Keep in mind, however, that all technical drawing needs to be organized on the sheet. The composition of a finished drawing has an impact on any assessment of its graphic quality. From the viewpoint of appearance, objects should be spaced evenly on a sheet and as much of the entire sheet used as possible.

As discussed in §2.2, each drawing begins with a sheet of paper being fastened to the drawing board and space allocated for the border and title block. Before further putting pencil to paper, however, devote a few minutes to planning the placement of the views (objects) that need to be drawn.

A good way to determine a satisfactory arrangement is to rapidly rough in the object outlines, using a soft lead pencil and a piece of tracing paper laid over a ¼" square grid. If the initial arrangement is not to the satisfaction of the drafter, a second tracing paper overlay can be made, copying only what is wanted from the first rough. Perhaps a third overlay may be needed. Avoid erasing; it takes too much time. These quick sketches double as planning tools to determine how objects are actually going to be drawn. The use of "roughs" is a significant element in most graphic problem solving and will be discussed in more detail later in this text.

Once the overall arrangement of the drawing has been determined, use the "rough" layout as an underlay for the actual drawing sheet. Begin the final layout by using construction lines to block out the major horizontal and vertical lines. Use them to establish the perimeters of each object to be drawn. Next, fill in the needed details. Once all the views of all objects are complete, and the necessary dimensions and notation added, all construction lines are "heavied up." Be sure to use lines of the appropriate symbol and weight (thickness).

4.7 Keeping the Drawing Clean

One of the real challenges of achieving high-quality graphics is keeping the paper clean of smudges and graphite buildup. Lead choice, paper choice, humidity, and technique all impact on how clearly lines will be drawn and how difficult smearing will be to overcome. One way to help prevent excess graphite from smearing is through the use of eraser dust. Eraser dust can be purchased in a shaker can or in a cleaning pad sometimes known as a "dead rat." The dust is sprinkled on the drawing and serves to pick up stray graphite and keep white space white. Proper use of eraser dust is an acquired skill, and much practice is required to determine how much dust to use and how often to brush it off. Care should be given, however, to not use so much dust that it becomes impossible to successfully draw a line.

The drafter may wish to concentrate and fully develop only one portion of a drawing page, and then move onto another. To protect the work already completed, two techniques are used. The first is to place a protective cover of tracing paper over the area already drawn. This cover allows drawing tools to pass over the completed area without smearing. Work may also be protected through the use of a spray fixative. There are a variety of fixatives on the market that essentially apply a sealing coat to the drawing. Fixatives work well but are difficult to control. All areas that are not to be sealed should be masked prior to application. "Workable fixatives" allow for erasures to be made even after a drawing has been sealed.

4.8 Problems

The following problems practice the use of various combinations of tools including T-square, 30°–60° triangle, 45°–45° triangle, and bow compass. Each section of the two drawings focuses on the use of one or more of these tools. Concentrate on line type and weight, as well as accuracy, in the development of each drawing. Check carefully the scale used in the dimensioning of each exercise.

Problem 4.1

On an A-size sheet, draw the figures shown in figure 4.11 full size. Use proper line symbols as detailed in the USITT Alphabet of Lines. When necessary, locate the centers (C) by use of the intersection of the diagonal lines that connect each corner of the given rectangle. All constructions are developed from that point. Omit dimensions and instructional notes. Complete the title strip.

Part A.   Draw horizontal lines, using a T-square and the appropriate symbol from the USITT alphabet of lines.

Part B.   Draw vertical lines, using a T-square, triangle, and the appropriate symbol from the USITT alphabet of lines.

Part C.   Draw the pattern shown, using T-square and triangle. Work lightly when drawing construction lines. Heavy up all final lines when complete.

Part D.   Draw the pattern shown, using the appropriate tool combinations. Work lightly when drawing construction lines. Heavy up all final lines when complete.

Part E.   Draw the pattern shown, using a 30°–60° triangle. Work lightly when drawing construction lines. Heavy up all final lines when complete.

Part F.   Draw the pattern shown, using a 45° triangle. Work lightly when drawing construction lines. Heavy up all final lines when complete.

Problem 4.2

Draw the figures shown in figure 4.12 full size.

Circle A.   Use T-square and triangle to locate all centers and points of tangency. Use a bow compass to draw the circle and arcs. Omit dimensions and instructional notes. Complete the title strip.

Circle B.   Use a T-square and triangle to locate all centers and points of tangency. Use a bow compass or circle template to draw the circles.

  Scroll: Use the same tools as above to complete this figure.

4.9 Checkpoints

√ Good line quality requires sharpness, blackness, and proper line weight.
√ Scaled drawings are reductions in which all dimensions remain proportional.
√ All lines drawn on a drafted plate are done with the aid of drafting tools. Use no freehand lines.
√ Draw object outlines first lightly, then "heavy" them up to conform to proper line weight.
√ Careful arrangement and cleanliness of drawings improve graphic quality.

4.11. Layout dimensions, problem 4.1

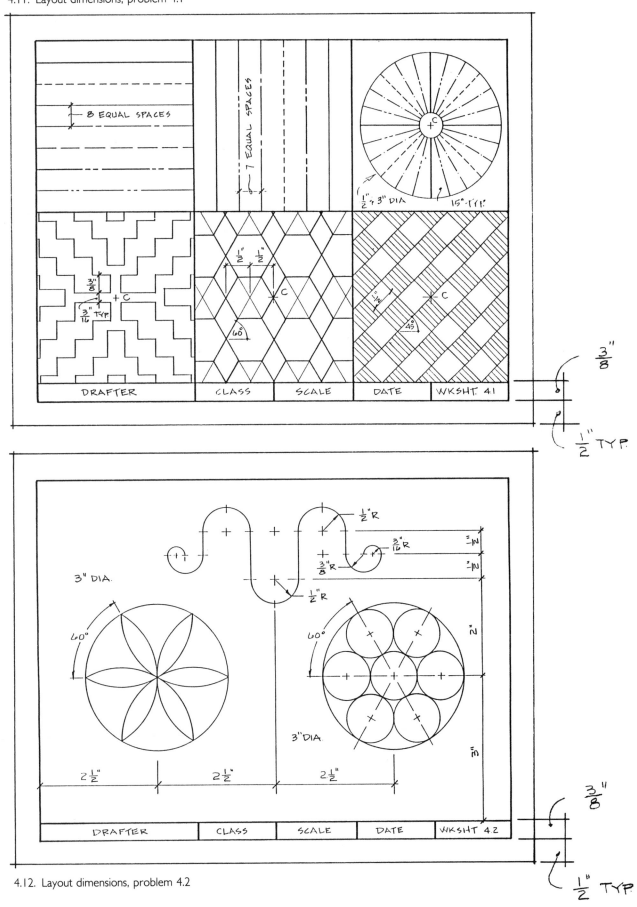

4.12. Layout dimensions, problem 4.2

5   Geometric Construction

Technical drawing involves a great deal of geometry, although this fact is often not acknowledged. In many instances, solving a design or a construction problem means drafting something out in scale to determine dimensions, joinery, or some other aspect of the object that was not at first apparent. Geometric constructions can result in easier and more accurate drawings than those developed through mathematical or transferring techniques. Furthermore, ont only do the techniques investigated in this chapter apply to scaled representations for the preparation of design and construction drawings, but most can be used in studio work in the development of full-scale patterns.

This chapter is designed to investigate selected geometric constructions considered to be of importance in the creation of technical drawings for the theatre. Beyond the informational value afforded beginning drafters, this study of geometric construction is intended to provide the opportunity to become more familiar with drawing tools and their use before beginning the study of more complex drawings.

STRAIGHT-LINE CONSTRUCTIONS
5.1 Bisect a Line, Using a Triangle and T-Square

Given line AB to be bisected:
1. From end A and B, draw construction lines at 30°, 45°, or 60° to form an intersection at point C.
2. Through intersection C, draw a line perpendicular to the given line AB.
3. Label the intersection of the perpendicular and AB as point D, the bisector of line AB.

5.1a. Bisecting a line, using a triangle and T-square

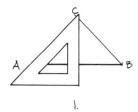 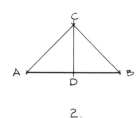

1.   2.

5.1b Bisect a Line or an Arc, Using a Compass

Given line or arc AB to be bisected:
1. From A and B draw equal arcs with a radius greater than half of AB, forming points of intersection D and E.
2. Join intersections D and E with a straight line to locate center point C, the bisector of AB.

5.1b. Bisecting a line or an arc, using a compass

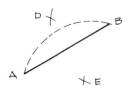 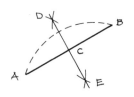

1   2.

5.2 Bisecting an Angle, Using a Compass

Given angle BAC to be bisected:

1. With A as the center point, strike arc R of any convenient radius less than AC, forming points of intersection E and F along AC and AB.
2. From points E and F, strike equal arcs S of any convenient radius greater than ½ of BC to form intersection D.
3. Draw line AD, which bisects the angle.

5.2. Bisecting an angle, using a compass

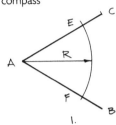

5.3 Transfer a Given Angle

Given angle BAC, transfer that angle to new location A'B':

1. With A as the center point, strike arc R of any convenient radius to create points of intersection E and F along AC and AB.
2. With A' as the center point, strike arc R' (R' = R) to create an arc that intersects A'B' forming point E'.
3. With E as the center, set the compass to a radius length of EF.
4. With E' as the center, strike an arc with radius length E'F' (E'F' = EF) that intersects the arc constructed in step 2, forming point F'.
5. With a straight edge, draw side A'C', using points A' and F'.

5.3. Transferring a given angle

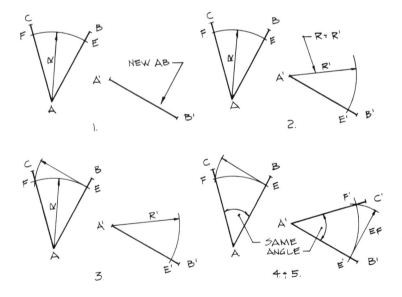

5.4 Draw a Line Parallel to a Given Line at a Given Distance

Given line AB and R as the distance:
1. With any point E of the line AB as center and R as the radius, strike an arc.
2. Place one leg of a triangle along AB and another triangle or T-square along another leg.
3. Hold the T-square firmly and slide the triangle until its edge is tangent to the arc.
4. Draw the required line CD.

5.4. Drawing a parallel line at a given distance

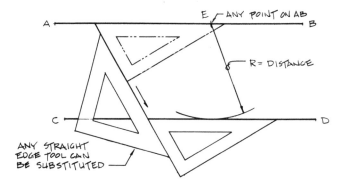

5.5 Draw a Perpendicular to a Parallel Line

Given line AB and CD as the perpendiuclar:
1. Choose any point C along AB. Place one leg of a triangle along AB and another triangle or T-square along the hypotenuse of the first.
2. Hold the lower triangle firmly and slide the top triangle until its other leg intersects with point C. Draw the required perpendicular CD.

5.5. Drawing a perpendicular to a parallel line

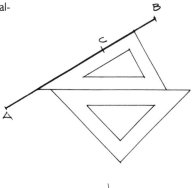 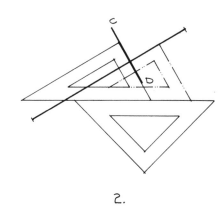

5.6a Divide a Line into Eleven Equal Parts

Given line AB:
1. Draw a vertical construction line at one end of line AB.
2. Set the zero of any convenient scale at the other end of line AB.
3. Swing the scale until a scaled unit divisible by eleven intersects with the construction line.
4. Make tiny dots or prick points along the scale where the individual units lie.
5. From these points draw vertical construction lines that intersect line AB dividing it into eleven equal parts.

5.6a. Dividing a line into equal parts

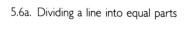

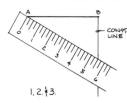 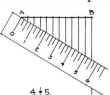

5.6b Divide a Line into Proportional Parts

5.6b. Dividing a line into proportional parts

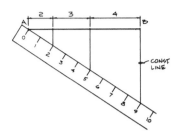

Given line AB:
1. Draw a vertical construction line at one end of line AB.
2. Set the zero of any convenient scale at the other end of line AB.
3. Total the number of proportional parts and swing the scale until a unit divisible by the total of the parts intersects the construction line.
4. Make tiny dots or prick points along the scale where the proportional units lie.
5. From these points draw vertical construction lines that intersect line AB, dividing it into proportional parts.

5.7 Draw a Triangle with the Sides Given (Triangulation)

Given the sides A, B, and C:
1. Draw one side, C, in the desired location of triangle ABC.
2. With an end point of C as center, strike an arc with a radius of length A.
3. With the other end point of C as center, strike an arc with a radius of length B, forming an intersection with the first arc.
4. Connect the end points of C and the intersection point.

5.7. Triangulation

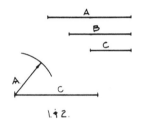

1. ² 2.

3.

4.

5.8a Draw a Square (Using Triangles)

Given one side AB:
1. Draw vertical construction lines at points A and B.
2. From points A and B, draw 45° construction lines that intersect the vertical lines of step 1, forming points C and D.
3. Connect A, B, C, and D.

5.8a. Drawing a square, using triangles

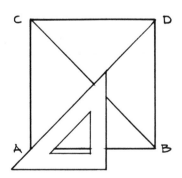

5.8b Draw a Square (Inscribed in a Circle)

Given a circle E:

1. Draw two diameters at right angle to each other forming lines AC and BD.
2. Connect A, B, C, and D to form the sides of an inscribed square.

5.8b. Drawing a square, inscribed in a circle

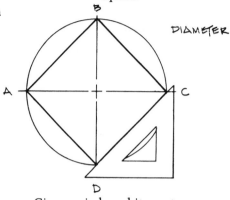

5.9a Draw a Regular Hexagon (Inscribed)

Given a circle and its center:

1. Draw vertical and horizontal center lines.
2. Draw diagonals through the center point, using either 30° or 60° angles.
3. With a straight edge, connect the points of intersection of the four center lines created and the outside of the circle.

5.9a. Drawing a regular hexagon, inscribed

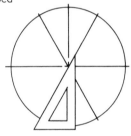

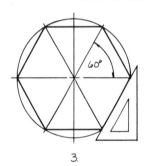

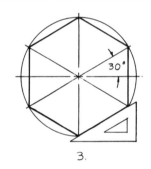

5.9b Draw a Regular Hexagon (Circumscribed)

Given a circle and its center:

1. Draw vertical and horizontal center lines.
2. With a 30°–60° triangle and T-square, draw the six sides tangent to the circle
3. To check accuracy, diagonals may be added.

5.9b. Drawing a regular hexagon, circumscribed

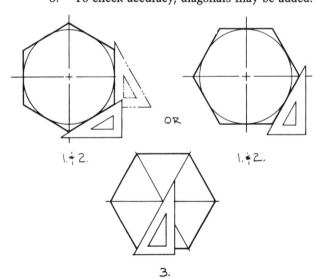

40

5.9c Draw a Regular Hexagon (Using T-square and 30°–60° Triangle)

Given points A and B that are corners of the hexagon:
1. From points A and B, draw vertical and 60° construction lines, forming points C and D.
2. Draw two horizontal lines, one that passes through point O, the other connecting points C and D.
3. Form the remainder of the hexagon by drawing 60° lines from points A, B, C, and D.

5.9c. Drawing a regular hexagon, using T-square and 30°–60° triangle

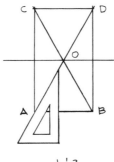 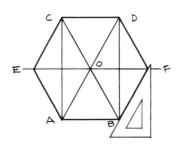

ARCS AND CIRCLES
5.10 Find the Center of a Circle

Given a circle:
1. Draw any chord AB, preferably horizontal.
2. Draw perpendiculars from A and B, creating points D and E.
3. Draw diagonals DB and EA.
4. The intersection of DB and EA will be the center of the circle.

5.10. Finding the center of a circle

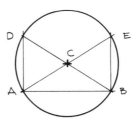

5.11 Draw a Tangent to a Circle through a Point

Given a circle, its center, and point P on the circle:
1. Move the T-square and triangle as a unit until one side of the triangle passes through both point P and the center of the circle.
2. Slide the triangle until the other side passes through point P and draw the required tangent.

5.11. Drawing a tangent to a circle through a point

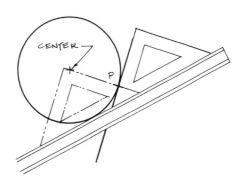

5.12 Draw a Tangent to Two Circles

Given two circles with centers A and B:
1. Move the triangle and T-square as a unit until one side of the triangle is tangent, by inspection, to the two circles.
2. Slide the triangle until the other side passes through the center of one circle and mark the point of tangency where the leg of the triangle intersects with the outside of the circle.
3. Slide the triangle until the side passes through the center of the other circle and mark the point of tangency.
4. Connect the points of tangency.

5.12. Drawing a tangent to two circles

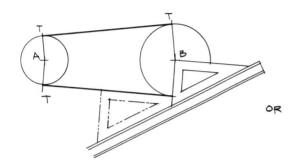
OR
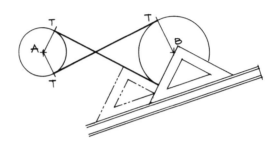

5.13 Draw an Arc Tangent to a Line through a Point

Given line AB, with tangent point T on AB, and point P:
1. Draw line PT.
2. Draw the perpendicular bisector of PT, forming line DE.
3. Draw a perpendicular at point T that intersects with DE, forming point C. The intersection point C forms the center of the requried arc.
4. With C as center and CT as radius, draw arc PT.

5.13. Drawing an arc tangent to a line through a point

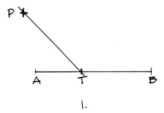
1.

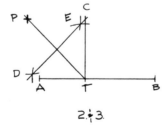
2.÷3.

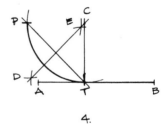
4.

5.14 Draw an Arc Tangent to an Arc through a Given Point

Given an arc with center O and radius X, and point P:
1. With P as center, draw an arc with radius R. R is any convenient radius greater than ½ the distance and less than the whole distance from P to the given arc.
2. With O as center, draw an arc with radius X + R that intersects with the arc from step 1.

5.14. Drawing an arc tangent to an arc through a point

3. The point of intersection, C, is the center of an arc with radius R that is tangent to the given arc through point P. Point T is the point of tangency of the two arcs.

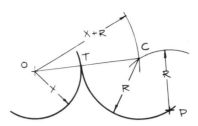

5.15 Draw an Arc Tangent to Two Lines at Right Angles

Given two lines at right angles:

1. With the intersection of the lines as center, draw an arc with any convenient radius R that intersects the lines, forming points A and B.
2. With A as center and B as center, draw two arcs of radius R that intersect, forming point C.
3. With C as center, draw the required arc of radius R with points of tangency A and B.

5.15. Drawing an arc tangent to two lines at right angles

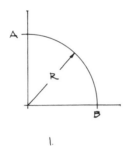

1.

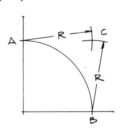

2.

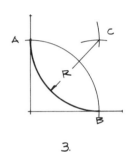

3.

5.16 Draw an Arc Tangent to Two Lines at Acute Angles

Given two lines forming an acute angle and any radius R:

1. Draw lines parallel to the given lines at distance R from them. The intersection of these parallel lines forms point C, the required center.
2. From C, draw perpendiculars to the given lines. The intersection of these perpendiculars and the given lines forms the point of tangency A and B.
3. With C as center and R as radius, draw the required arc with points of tangency A and B.

5.16. Drawing an arc tangent to two lines at acute angles

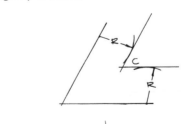

1.

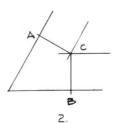

2.

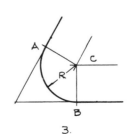

3.

5.17 Draw an Arc Tangent to Two Arcs (Side by Side)

Given side-by-side arcs with radii A and B and any radius R:

1. Draw arcs parallel to the given arcs at a distance R from them. The intersection of these two arcs, C, is the center of the required tangent arc.
2. From the centers draw lines to point C to locate the points of tangency T on the given arcs.
3. With C as center, R as radius, and T as points of tangency, draw the required arc.

5.17. Drawing an arc tangent to two arcs, side by side

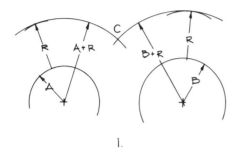

1.

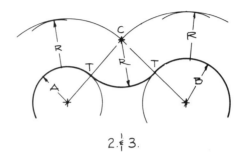

2. & 3.

5.18 Draw an Arc Tangent to Two Arcs (One Enclosing the Other)

Given arc A with radius X, arc B with radius Y and any radius R:

1. With A as center, draw an arc parallel to the given arc at distance X + R.
2. With B as center, draw an arc parallel to the given arc at distance Y − R.
3. The intersection of these two arcs, C, is the center of the required tangent arc.
4. Draw lines AC and BC to locate points of tangency T on the given arcs.
5. With C as center, R as radius, and T as points of tangency, draw the required arc.

5.18. Drawing an arc tangent to two arcs, concentric

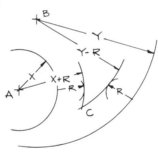

1, 2. & 3.

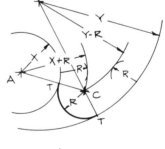

4. & 5.

5.19 Draw an Arc Tangent to Two Arcs (Enclosing Both)

5.19. Drawing an arc tangent to two arcs, enclosing them both

Given arc A with radius X, arc B with radius Y and radius R (R≥AB):

1. With A as center, draw an arc with radius R − X.
2. With B as center, draw an arc with radius R − Y.
3. The intersection of these two arcs, C, is the center of the required tangent arc.
4. Extend lines CA and CB to intersect with the given arcs to determine the points of tangency, T.
5. With C as center, R as radius, and T as points of tangency, draw the required arc.

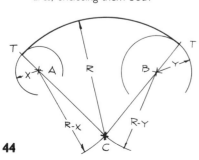

5.20 Draw an Ogee Curve Connecting Two Parallel Lines

5.20. Drawing an ogee curve connecting two parallel lines

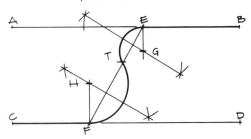

Given parallel lines AB and CD:

1. Connect AB and CD with any line EF and establish point T on EF. (If T is the midpoint of EF, the ogee curve will have equal arcs.)
2. At points E and F, draw perpendiculars.
3. Draw the perpendicular bisectors of lines ET and FT.
4. The intersection of the bisectors and the perpendiuclar create points G and H (center points of the required tangent arcs).
5. With G as center and GT as radius, draw one of the tangent arcs.
6. With H as center and HT as radius, draw the other tangent arc.

INSCRIBED FIGURES AND LESS COMMON CONSTRUCTIONS
5.21 Draw a Pentagon inside a Circle

Given a circle with center O and points A, B, C, and D:

1. Bisect radius OA to find point E.
2. With ED as the radius and E as the center, strike an arc to find point F.
3. With DF as the radius and D as the center, strike an arc to find point G.
4. Chord DG forms one side of the pentagon; using this measurement, draw the remaining sides.

5.21. Drawing a pentagon inside a circle

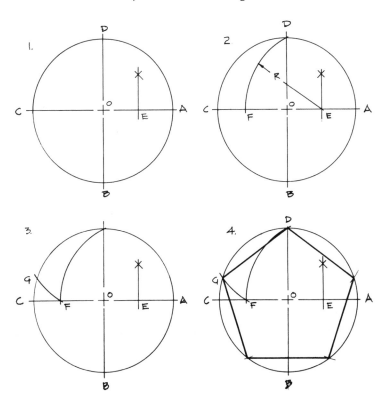

5.22 Draw an Octagon, Using a Square

Given a square:

1. Connect the corners of the square, forming lines AC and BD and point E.
2. With AE as the radius, strike an arc from each point A through D that intersects the side of the square.
3. Connect these points of intersection to form the eight sides of the octagon.

5.22. Drawing an octagon, using a square

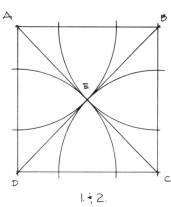 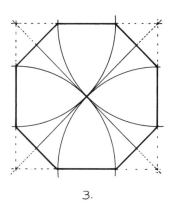

1. ÷ 2. 3.

5.23 Draw a Seven-Sided Polygon in a Circle

Given a circle with diameter AB:

1. Divide the diameter into seven equal units. (This number corresponds to the number of sides the resulting polygon will have.)
2. From points A and B, strike arcs with radius AB to form the point of intersection C.
3. Draw a line from point C through point 2 along the interval line that intersects with the circle to form point D.
4. Chord AD will be the length of one side of the desired polygon; using this measurement, draw the remaining sides.

5.23. Drawing a seven-sided polygon in a circle

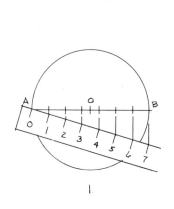 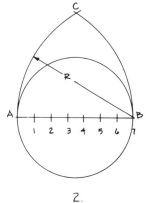 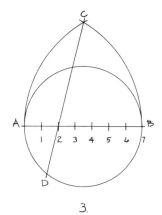 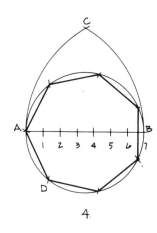

1. 2. 3. 4.

5.24a Draw an Ellipse (Trammel Method)

Given the minor axis AB, the major axis CD, and the intersection O:

1. With a scrap piece of paper, mark a line the distance AO.
2. With O as one end point, mark a corresponding line CO.
3. Place point A of the line drawn on CD and at the same time, place point C on the line AB, and mark point P that is a point on the ellipse.
4. Reposition the paper, keeping A on CD and C on AB to mark other points of the ellipse.

5.24a. Drawing an ellipse, trammel method

5. Connect the points, using an irregular curve or a flexible curve.

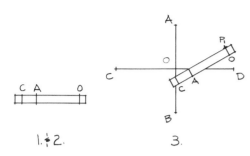

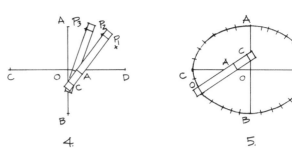

1.÷2.   3.   4.   5.

5.24b Draw an Ellipse (Two-Circle Method)

5.24b. Drawing an ellipse, two-circle method

Given the minor axis AB, the major axis CD, and the intersection O:
1. Draw two concentric circles with radii AO and CO.
2. Divide the circles into a convenient number of equal parts (twelve).
3. From the intersection of the radial lines and the outer circle, draw lines parallel to AB.
4. From the intersection of the radial lines and the inner circle, draw lines parallel to CD.
5. The intersection of the parallel lines drawn from the same radial lines form the points of the ellipse.
6. Connect the points, using an irregular curve or a flexible curve.

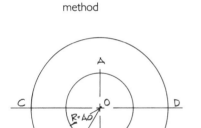

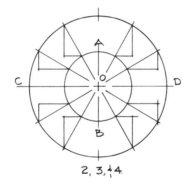

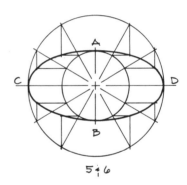

1.   2, 3,÷4.   5÷6

5.25 Draw a Parabola

5.25. Drawing a parabola

Given the focus, point F, and the directrix, line AB:
1. Draw a line perpendicular to AB through point F; this forms the axis. Label the intersection of this line and AB as point O.
2. Draw a line parallel to AB that intersects the axis at any point X.
3. With F as center and OX as the radius, strike an arc that intersects the parallel line drawn above and below the axis. These points of intersection are points on the parabola.
4. Repeat this process to develop as many points as necessary, then connect the points using an irregular curve or a flexible curve. Note: The point H where the parabola intersects with the axis is the bisector of line OF.

47

5.26 Draw a Spiral of Archimedes

5.26. Drawing a spiral of Archimedes

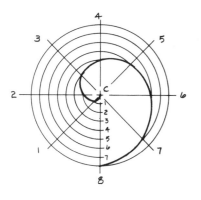

Given a circle with center C:

1. Divide a radius into equal parts and number them.
2. Divide the circle into the same number of equal parts.
3. With C as center and C–1 as radius, draw the arc that intersects with line 1.
4. Repeat this procedure for all other points.
5. Starting at C, draw a smooth curve through the intersection of the arcs and lines with corresponding numbers.

5.27 Rectify an Arc (Finding True Length of an Arc When Straightened)

Given an arc with center O:

1. Draw chord AB that connects the ends of the arc to be rectified.
2. Bisect AB and label the point of intersection C.
3. Extend the bisector to the center point O.
4. Draw AO and BO.
5. With A as center and AC as length, draw arc CD that intersects with an extension of AB.
6. With D as center and DB as length, draw arc DE that intersects with a tangent to A that is perpendicular to AO.
7. Line AE is the true length of arc AB when straightened.

5.27. Rectifying an arc

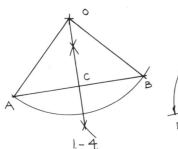

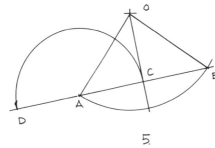

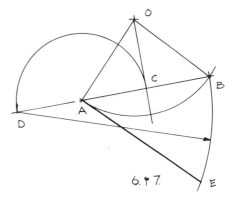

5.28 Problems

The problems of this chapter are to be drawn on three C-size (18″ × 24″) sheets. Each problem studies a particular classification of geometric constructions. Problem 5.1 examines straight-line constructions; problem 5.2 examines arcs and circles; and problem 5.3 examines inscribed figures and less common constructions. Each sheet is divided into a series of boxes as shown in figure 5.28. Within each box, starting lines and points need to be established for the various constructions. This information is given in the figures provided with the instructions for each problem, in addition a reduced copy of the finished sheet is provided for reference.

Instructors may use all three sheets or perhaps create a new combination of constructions. Regardless, this chapter will provide the opportunity to lay out a full-sized drawing for the first time, complete with border and title block.

In drawing geometric constructions, accuracy is of the utmost importance. Use a sharp hard lead, i.e., 4H to 6H, in both pencil and compass. Draw construction lines extremely light: so light they can barely be seen at arm's length. When the entire sheet has been completed, heavy up all finish lines with a **dark thin line.**

5.28. Typical sheet layout

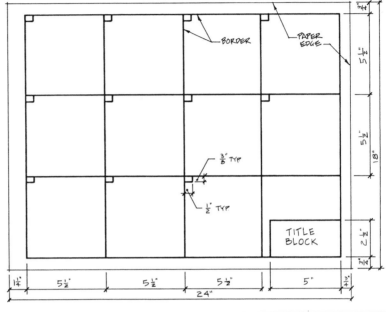

5.29a. Problem 5.1 layout

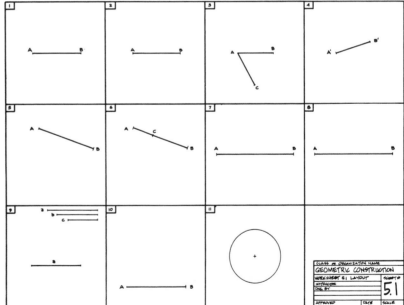

Problem 5.1

Draw the listed geometric constructions on a sheet of vellum formatted as shown in figures 5.28 and 5.29a. Follow the step-by-step instructions for each construction in the section identified. All work is in ½" = 1'-0" scale.

	Construction	Section Reference	Line Dimensions
1.	Bisect a line, using a triangle and T-square	§5.1a	AB = 5'-3"
2.	Bisect a line or an arc, using a compass	§5.1b	AB = 5'-3"
3.	Bisect an angle, using a compass	§5.2	AB, AC = 4'-0"
4.	Transfer a given angle	§5.3	AB, AC = 4'-0"
5.	Draw a line parallel to a given line at a given distance R	§5.4	AB = 6'-5" R = 2'-3"
6.	Draw a perpendicular to a parallel line	§5.5	AB = 6'-5" CD = 2'-9"
7.	Divide a line into eleven equal parts	§5.6a	AB = 8'-8"
8.	Divide a line into proportional parts (2, 3, 5, 3, 2)	§5.6b	AB = 8'-8"
9.	Draw a triangle with the sides given (triangulation)	§5.7	a = 5'-6" b = 4'-6" c = 3'-3"
10.	Draw a square, using triangles	§5.8a	AB = 6'-7"
11.	Draw a regular hexagon (inscribed)	§5.9a	R = 2'-10"

5.29b. Problem 5.1 complete

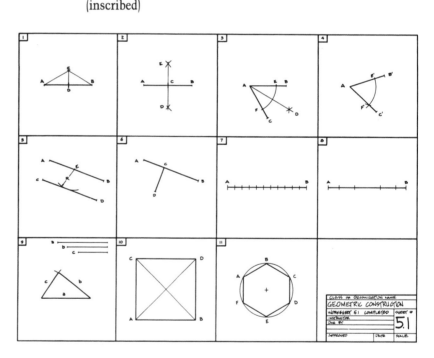

50

Problem 5.2

Draw the listed geometric constructions on a sheet of vellum formatted as shown in figures 5.28 and 5.30a. Follow the step-by-step instructions for each construction in the section identified. All work is in ½" = 1'-0" scale.

	Construction	Section Reference	Line Dimensions
1.	Find the center of a circle	§5.10	DIA = 5'-6"
2.	Draw a tangent to a circle through a point	§5.11	DIA = 5'-6"
3.	Draw tangents to two circles	§5.12	DIA A = 2'-0", DIA B = 3'-6", AB = 5'-0"
4.	Draw an arc tangent to a line and through a point	§5.13	R = 3'-9"
5.	Draw an arc tangent to an arc through a point	§5.14	R = 2'-6", X = 3'-10"
6.	Draw an arc tangent to two lines at right angles	§5.15	R = 5'-4"
7.	Draw an arc tangent to two lines at acute angles	§5.16	Angle = 55°. R = 3'-6"
8.	Draw an arc tangent to two circles (side by side)	§5.17	DIA A = 2'-0" DIA B = 3'-6" R = 1'-9" AB = 4'-0"
9.	Draw an arc tangent to two arcs (concentric)	§5.18	X = 3'-7" Y = 8'-8" R = 2'-0"
10.	Draw an arc tangent to two arcs and enclosing both	§5.19	DIA A = 1'-3" DIA B = 2'-0" R = 5'-1", AB = 6'-4"
11.	Draw an ogee curve by connecting two parallel lines	§5.20	AB = 10'-0" CD = 10'-0" BD = 4'-7" EFB = 50° DT = 2'-4"

5.30a. Problem 5.2 layout

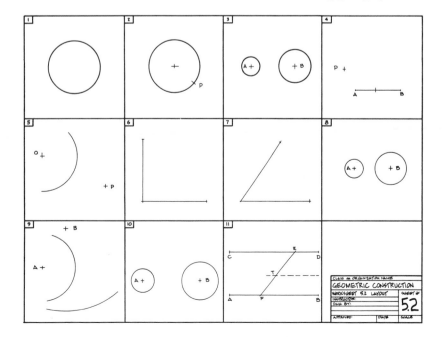

5.30b. Problem 5.2 complete

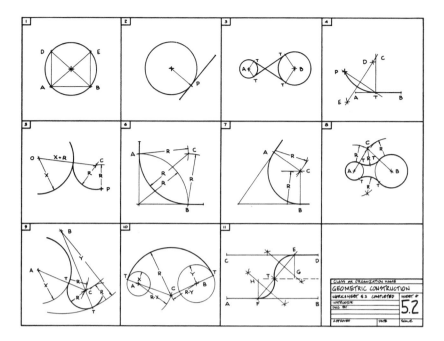

5.31a. Problem 5.3 layout

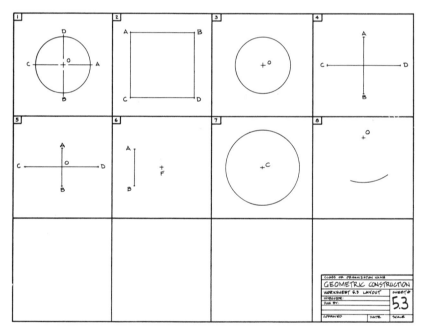

Problem 5.3
Draw the listed geometric constructions on a sheet of vellum formatted as shown in figures 5.28 and 5.31a. Follow the step-by-step instructions for each construction in the section identified. All work is in ½" = 1'-0" scale.

	Construction	Section Reference	Line Dimensions
1.	Draw a pentagon inside a circle	§5.21	Radius = 3'-0"
2.	Draw an octagon, using a square	§5.22	AB = 7'-0"
3.	Draw a polygon, using a circle	§5.23	Radius = 3'-0"

4.	Draw an ellipse (trammel method)	§5.24a	AB = 6'-0", CD = 8'-0"
5.	Draw an ellipse (two-circle method)	§5.24b	AB = 4'-0", CD = 8'-0"
6.	Drawing a parabola	§5.25	OF = 3'-0", OX_1 = 2'-3"
7.	Draw a spiral of Archimedes	§5.26	Radius = 4'-0"
8.	Rectify an arc	§5.37	R = 4'-10", AB = 4'-0"

5.31b. Problem 5.3 complete

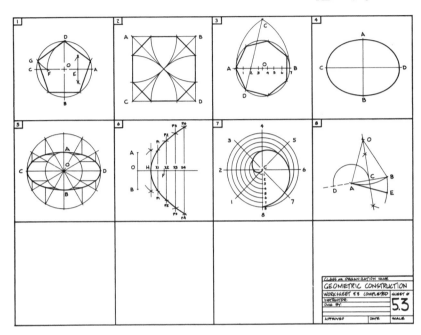

5.32 Checkpoints

√ Geometric construction techniques can be used both at the drafting board for scaled drawings and in the scenic studio for solving full-scale construction problems.

√ Geometric constructions often produce more accurate results than mathematical or transfer methods.

√ Always use a sharp, hard lead for construction lines in a geometric constructions.

PART TWO

MULTIVIEW DRAWINGS

6 Orthographic Projections

6.1 Technical Drafting

At the very root of technical drafting is the challenge of describing three-dimensional shapes, using a two-dimensional medium. To be useful, technical drafting must be accurately drawn and provide all the information necessary to successfully construct the needed object. Drawings that relate the true size and shape of the object are required for accurate construction. Once drawn, understanding is further enhanced by the addition of dimensions and notes describing materials, finishes, and assembly techniques. Ideally, the drawing process works to the benefit of both the user and the drafter. Whenever possible the drafter should use the drawing as a problem-solving opportunity to clarify on paper the many decisions that might otherwise wait for answers until the more costly construction phase.

All the drawing techniques discussed in this text rely on the conventions of orthographic (right-angle) projection. Figure 6.1 illustrates the classification of projections available to the drafter. Two major headings are used: 1) central projection and 2) parallel projection.

6.1. Types of projection drawings

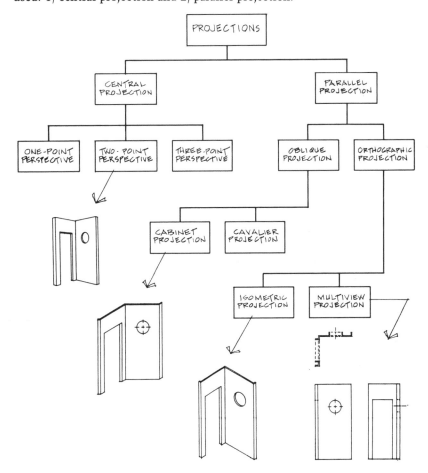

6.2 The Glass Box

To develop a set of drawings using multiview projection, an object is placed within an imaginary glass box. The object images are then projected to the surface planes of the glass box (fig. 6.2). Once all views of the object have been projected to the respective planes of the box, the box is unfolded revealing six views that accurately describe the three-dimensional object in two-dimensional terms.

6.2. The glass box

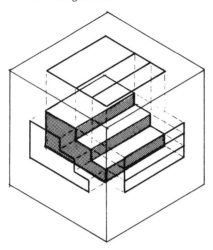

6.3. Unfolding the glass box

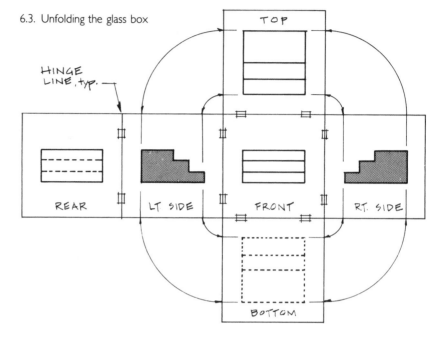

6.4. Standard dimension relationships

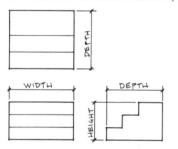

In most cases, not all six views are necessary for complete object description; in fact most objects can be described with only three views—front, top, and right side. Using these views, height, width, and depth dimensions can be shown (fig. 6.4). The term **elevation** is often used in place of "view" when referring to either front, rear, or side views, i.e., those views in which height is shown.

6.3 Arrangement of Views

The specific arrangement of orthographic views is very important. Proper orientation allows for the straightforward transfer of dimensions from one view to another, as seen in the American National Standard arrangement in figures 6.3 and 6.4. When views are placed in these relative positions, it is rarely necessary to identify them. When they are positioned out of order, the "removed view" must be clearly identified.

6.4 Meaning of Lines

Any line within a single orthographic view has three possible meanings. The line can be:

1. The intersection of two surfaces
2. The edge view of a surface
3. The contour view of a curved surface

Contemporary drafting practice discourages the use of shading on working drawings, since the technique, although attractive, is very time-consuming. Consequently, it is necessary that blueprint readers carefully examine all the views of an object to determine the meaning of the lines, since a surface can be interpreted in several different ways (fig. 6.5). Line AB at the top of the front view might be regarded as the edge view of a flat surface, if we look at only the front and top views and do not observe the curved surface seen in the right-side view. Similarly, the vertical line CD in the front view might be regarded as the edge view of a parallel surface, if we look at only the front and side views. The top view shows that the line is the intersection of an inclined surface.

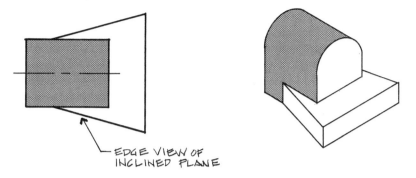

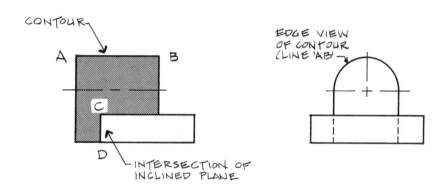

Figure 6.6 further explores the subject of line interpretation. The top view is shown divided into four distinct areas—A, B, C, and D. Each represents a surface at a different level. The one top view accurately describes all five of the objects shown, but by itself does not provide enough information to select one object over another. The only information that is certain is that no two adjacent areas lie in the same plane.

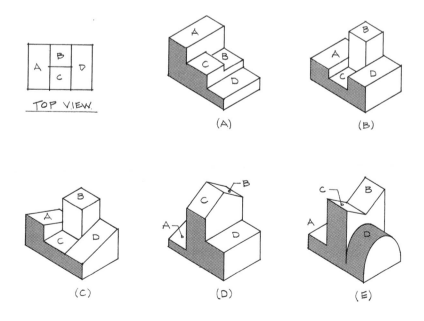

6.5 Transferring Dimensions

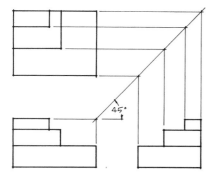

6.7. Miter line transfer

Width, height, and depth dimensions are shared between the various views in an orthographic projection. Therefore, given any two views, the third may be developed. By projecting vertical lines up from the front view, the width of the object is transferred to the top view. By projecting horizontal lines from the front view, the height of the object is transferred to the side view. Both of these transfers can be reversed as well. The dimension that is most challenging to transfer between views is the depth. There are four common methods for making this transfer:

The miter transfer method: The most commonly used method for transferring depth dimensions between the top and side views is through the use of a 45° miter line. First, inscribe the front view of the object in a rectangular box (fig. 6.7). Next, draw a 45° construction line extending from the upper right-hand corner of the rectangle. The depth dimension is then projected, using horizontal lines from the top view to this miter line. From the points of intersection of the projected lines and the miter line, vertical construction lines are drawn, completing the transfer of the depth to the side view.

Alternative transfer methods: Other methods of transfer involve the use of **dividers,** a **tick strip,** or a **scale ruler.** These methods frequently afford a higher degree of accuracy than the miter line technique but are more cumbersome in regard to tool handling and are therefore commonly used when only a small number of very accurate measurements are to be transferred. The least accurate among these systems is probably the scale ruler. When using a scale to transfer dimensions on views not drawn to scale, the drafter may be required to use interpolation, leading to the possibility of error.

All four of these processes may be used to transfer any dimension, interior or overall, and are completely reversible, i.e., transfer the depth dimension from a side view to the top view.

6.8. Alternative transfer methods

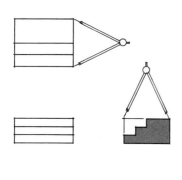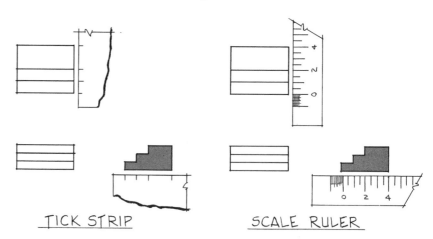

6.6 Precedence of Lines

Visible lines, hidden lines, and center lines often coincide on a drawing. In these situations it is necessary to know which line to show. Fortunately there is a simple rule of thumb to follow: **A visible line always takes precedence** over (covers up) a center line or a hidden line, while **a hidden line always takes precedence over a center line** (fig. 6.9).

6.9. Precedence of lines

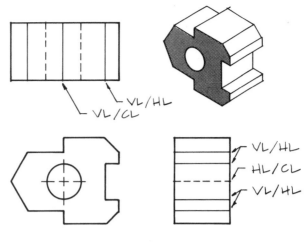

VL/HL
VL/CL

VL/HL
HL/CL
VL/HL

KEY:
VL —VISIBLE LINE
HL —HIDDEN LINE
CL —CENTER LINE

6.7 Hidden Line Practices

6.10. Hidden line practices

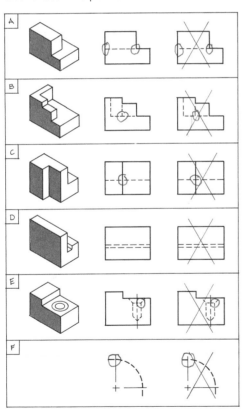

Since the use of hidden lines can frequently confuse the reader, even when drawn properly, correct drawing practice must always be followed. To assist the drafter, conventions have been established governing the use of hidden lines in a drawing. Samples of both correct and incorrect drawing techniques are illustrated in figure 6.10.

a. Leave a gap whenever a hidden line dash forms a continuation of a visible line; observe this convention for both straight and curvilinear lines.
b. Intersect both visible and hidden lines at L and T corners.
c. "Jump" the visible line whenever a hidden line crosses a visible line.
d. Stagger the dashes when drawing parallel hidden lines.
e. Intersect the dashes when two or three dashes meet at a point, regardless of the angle formed by the intersection.
f. Draw hidden line arcs so that these arcs touch the center line but do not extend beyond.

Poorly drawn hidden lines can easily spoil the appearance of a drawing as well as lead to confusing interpretations. Conventional practice is to draw each dash by eye about ⅛" long and spaced about ¹⁄₃₂" apart. Accentuate the beginning and end of each dash by pressing down on the pencil. This will produce sharp crisp dashes and aid drawing clarity.

61

6.8 A Brief Overview of Standard Orthographic Conventions and Views

View Selection

Views should be chosen that will best describe the object to be drawn. Use only the minimum number of views that will completely portray the size and shape of the unit; except for complex objects, more than three views are seldom necessary. For describing simple units, drawing only one or two views will often be adequate. Theatre flats and platforms typically fit this situation.

6.11. Draw only necessary views

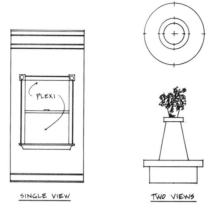

SINGLE VIEW   TWO VIEWS

Avoid Hidden Lines

Select the view to be drawn so that hidden features are avoided whenever possible. As a rule of thumb, do not incorporate any hidden lines that are not really necessary for clarity.

6.12. Avoid views with hidden lines

6.13. Half view

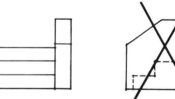

Partial Views

The term **partial view** is used to describe several types of drawings. Symmetrical objects may often be drawn using **half views**. The half view is a timesaving convention, used either alone, as shown in figure 6.13, or as a combination view showing both elevation and section (interior) features in one drawing. If the latter, the two halves are separated by a center line and clearly labeled.

On objects where drawing both side views would aid clarity (usually this means avoiding hidden lines), each partial view need not be complete if together they depict the shape. The only hidden lines shown in this type of drawing are those immediately behind the view. A partial view drawing is considered a type of removed view and must be clearly labeled in the manner "RIGHT SIDE PARTIAL VIEW."

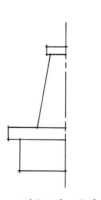

HALF VIEW

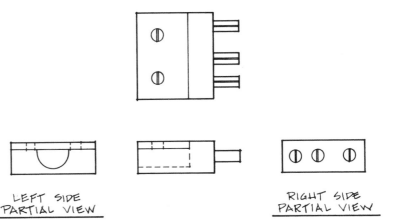

LEFT SIDE
PARTIAL VIEW

RIGHT SIDE
PARTIAL VIEW

Removed Views

Detail views are examples of drawings that may be **removed views.** Enlarged views are used when it is desirable to show a feature in greater detail or to eliminate the crowding of details or dimensions. Ordinarily the enlarged view should be oriented in the same direction as the main view. In those circumstances when the drafter determines it is helpful to rotate the drawing, both the direction and amount of rotation must be clearly indicated, as should the scales of both the initial and the detail views. Two alternative systems of identification are shown in figure 6.15.

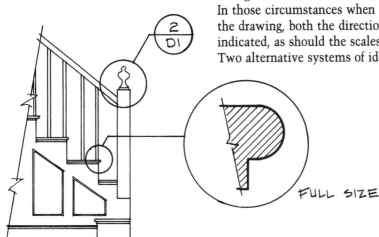

FULL SIZE

Rear Views

At times it is necessary to draw the **rear view** of an object. The rear view is typically drawn to the left of the left-side view; the extreme right of the right-side view is also acceptable. When either placement is not practical, possibly owing to the length of the unit, the rear view may be relocated, but the orientation (top, bottom, side) must remain the same. Locate the drawing where most appropriate and clearly label it as a "REAR VIEW REMOVED."

Key Drawings

A **key drawing** is a technique emerging from "simplified drawing" practice. This convention is particularly well suited to the description of repetitive patterns that might be found in a deck framing or the repeat pattern of a decorative wall application.

There are no rules governing the drawing of a key plan, but in most situations it is advisable to include a partial view of the actual object. The partial view will clarify for the reader the actual object being discussed. The remainder of the drawing is single line and schematic, reducing drafting time.

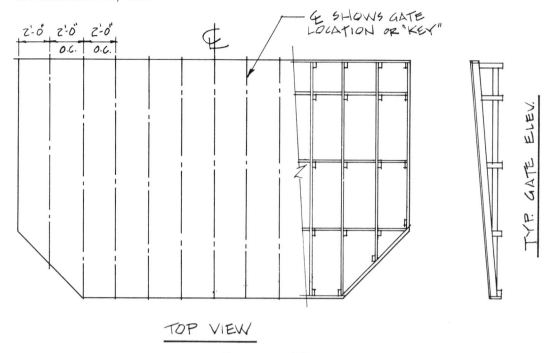

¢ SHOWS GATE
LOCATION OR "KEY"

2'-0" 2'-0" 2'-0"

O.C. O.C.

TYP. GATE ELEV.

TOP VIEW

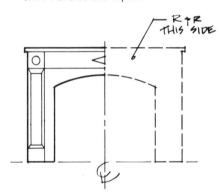

6.17. Reverse and repeat

R+R THIS SIDE

Reverse and Repeat

The convention of **reverse and repeat (R&R)** is frequently used when drawing detailed symmetrical objects. Also known as "opposite hand" and "mirror view" drawings, the practice of R&R is used as a form of drafting shorthand. Typically, the drawing is oriented on the object's center line, one side of which is drawn in full detail, while the opposite side is outlined with a long dashed line and notated "R&R THIS SIDE."

6.9 Problems

Worksheet 6.1
An isometric drawing of each object is provided along with an incomplete set of orthographic views. Two of the three views are complete, but the remaining view is missing some lines. Locate the missing lines, showing all construction lines. Darken up the finish lines; include all visible and hidden lines.

Worksheet 6.2
Given two views of each object, construct the missing views. Include all visible and hidden lines. Transfer dimensions using one of the techniques discussed (the drawings are already set up for the miter line method). Darken up the finish lines; include all visible and hidden lines. Do not erase construction lines; show all work.

Name:	ORTHOGRAPHIC PROJECTIONS	Worksheet 6.1
Date:		

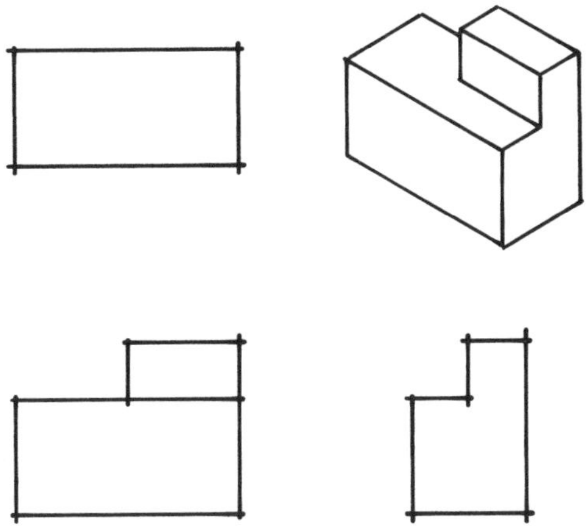

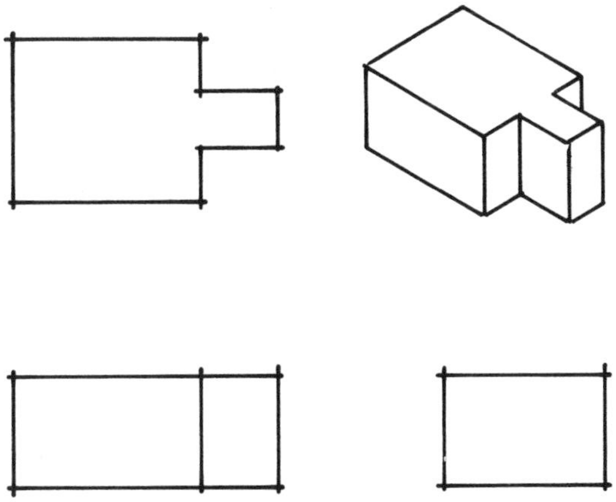

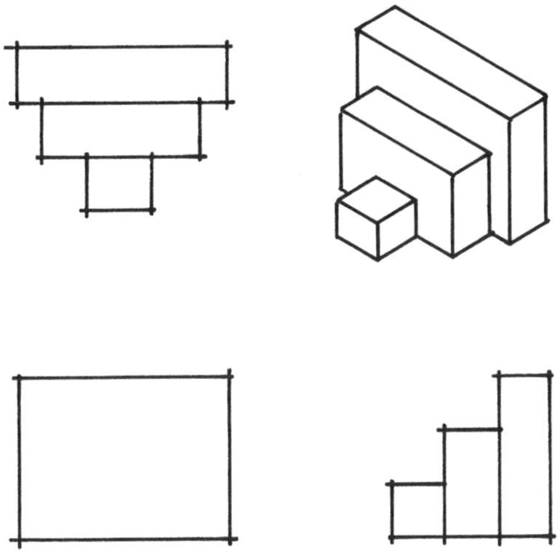

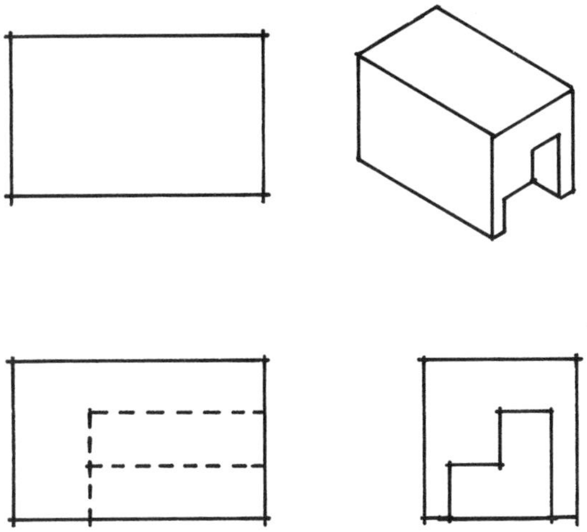

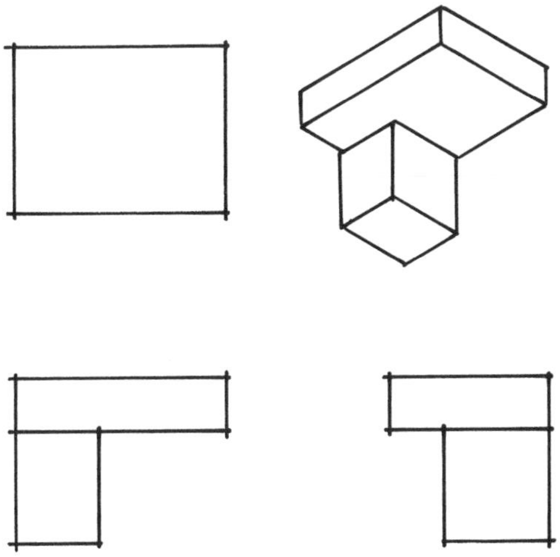

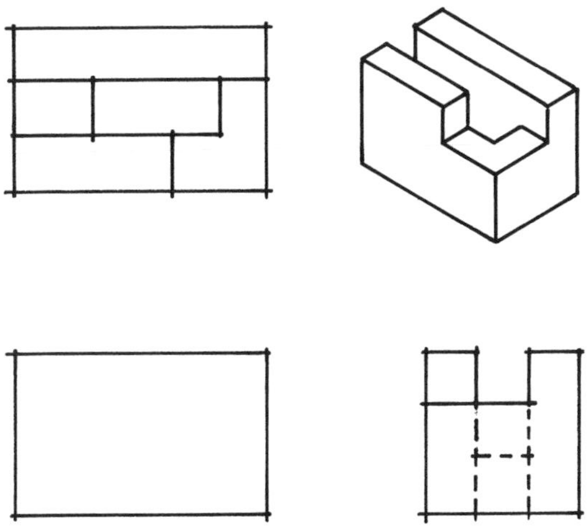

Name:	ORTHOGRAPHIC PROJECTIONS	Worksheet 6.2
Date:		

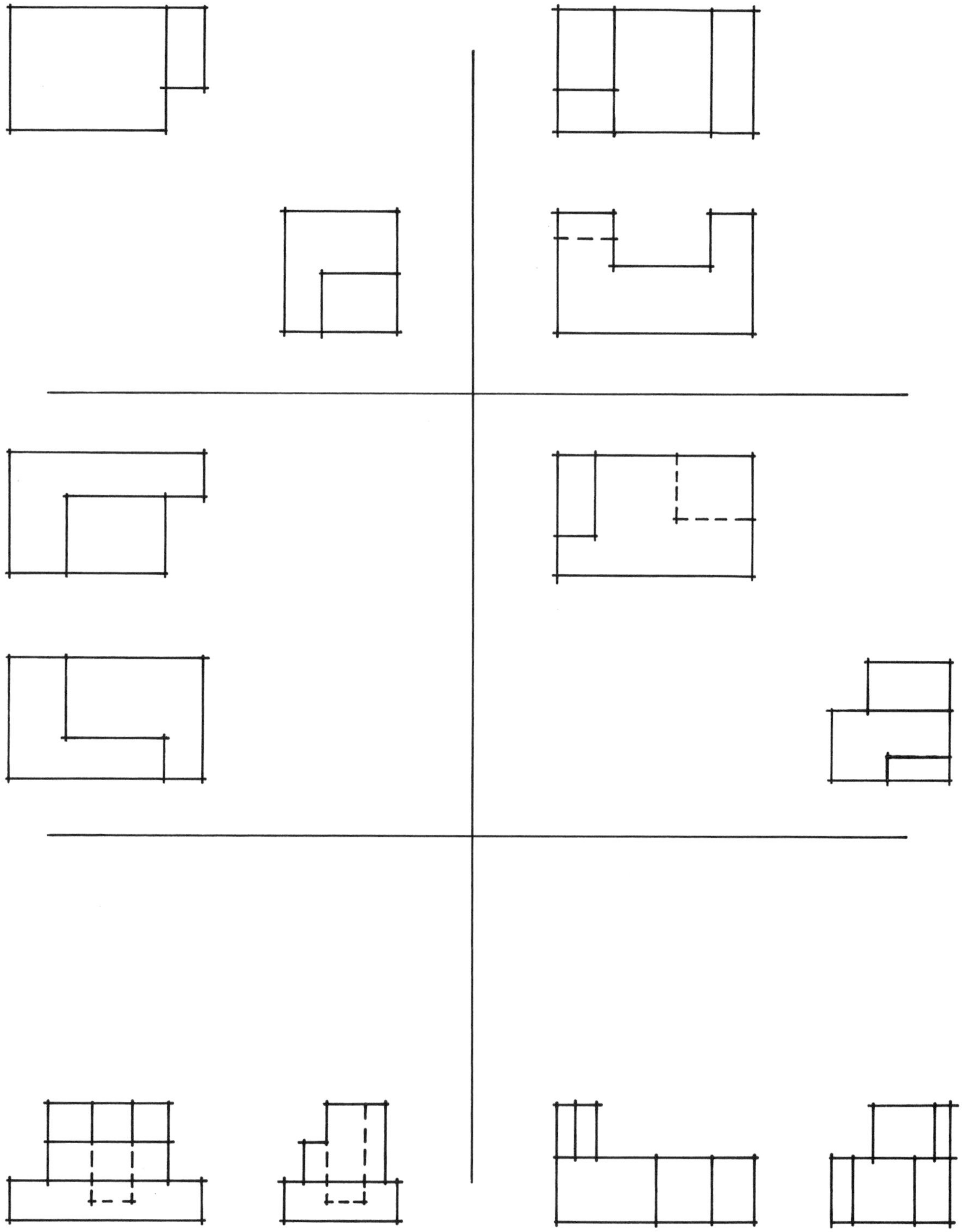

6.10 Checkpoints

√ Orthographic drawings allow three-dimensional objects to be described in a two-dimensional format.

√ Orthographic drawings solve problems at the drawing board rather than in the scenic studio.

√ The standard arrangement for a multiview drawing includes three views: front, top, and one side.

√ Dimensions may be transferred between the various views of a multiview drawing, using a variety of methods.

√ There are various types of projections. The choice of which type to use depends on the information needed to satisfactorily describe an object.

7 Dimensioning

7.1 The Need for Dimensions

Although the importance of accurately drawn graphics cannot be over-stressed, a drawing is of little use to a craftsperson if it does not contain dimensions and notation (written instructions). Although this logic seems obvious enough, the need to include dimensioning and notation creates real difficulties for many drafters. Too often, the schedule "forces" the drafter to take shortcuts, leaving many dimensions and assembly choices to the craftsperson. When drawings reach the shop in this condition, the resulting situation is time-consuming for the craftsperson and problematic for the design because now there is no check in the system.

Thorough dimensioning and notation require many skills, among them, computation, lettering, layout and a knowledge of construction processes. To assure each subject sufficient discussion, this chapter focuses only on the rules of dimensioning; notation conventions are covered in the next chapter. In actual practice, of course, the two cannot be separated.

What follows are the major themes regarding dimensioning practice. Keep in mind though that despite the volume of material covered, some situations remain unspecified. Where no established convention applies, focus on the basic question of dimensioning and notation: **Can the specifications provided be interpreted in only one way and are they complete enough to build and finish the project without additional information?** As a check, mentally walk through the layout or construction process. Almost certainly the answer can be "discovered" from within this framework.

The dimensioning guidelines that are addressed in this chapter are presented under several headings to provide a focus to what is a lengthy and sometimes bewildering list of rules. These rules, however, are all part of the dimensioning conventions and should be observed, not simply because they are rules, but because they assure that information is presented in a form that is both thorough and familiar to drafters and readers alike. Just as none of us would question observing the "rules of the road," a similar observance of dimensioning practices is beneficial to everyone working on a project.

7.2 Orientation of Dimensions

Two orientations for the reading of dimension figures are approved by American National Standards Institute (ANSI). Either is acceptable, but drafters are encouraged to adopt either one system or the other. Regardless of the choice made, use one system exclusively on any one drawing.

In the **unidirectional system** both notes and dimension figures are lettered horizontally on the sheet and are read from the bottom of the drawing. The unidirectional system has been adopted in many industries because it is easy to use and read, especially on large drawings.

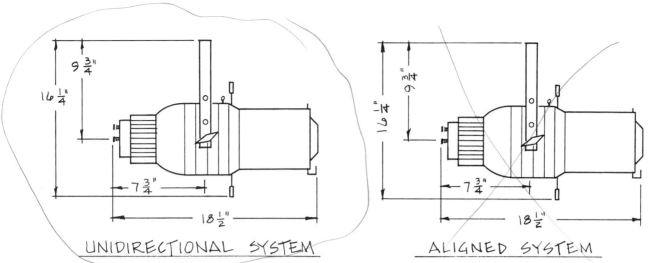

UNIDIRECTIONAL SYSTEM

ALIGNED SYSTEM

7.1. Unidirectional and aligned dimensioning

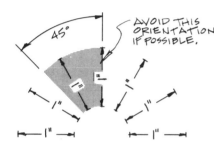

7.2. Direction of dimensions

AVOID THIS ORIENTATION, IF POSSIBLE.

In the **aligned system** notes are still lettered horizontally on the sheet, but all dimension figures are aligned with the dimension lines so that they are read from the bottom or from the right side of the sheet. An effort should be made, however, to avoid locating dimensions in the shaded area of the fourth quadrant shown in figure 7.2, since this position is awkward to read.

7.3. Extension line conventions

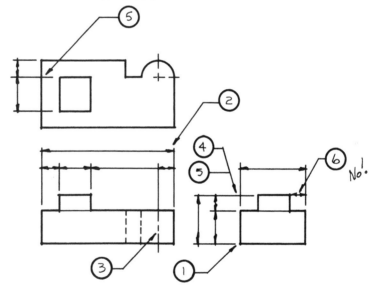

7.3 Lines and Arrowheads

Extension Lines

1. Run extension lines perpendicular to visible profile lines. Allow a ¹⁄₁₆" gap between them. *do ⅛" gap for this class*
2. Attach dimensions to one view only; do not connect two views with extension lines.
3. A center line may be extended and used as an extension line, in which case it is still drawn as a center line.
4. Do not cross dimension lines and extension lines if avoidable. Extension lines, however, may cross each other.
5. When extension lines must cross extension lines or visible lines, do not break either line.
6. Do not use a profile line of the object as an extension line.

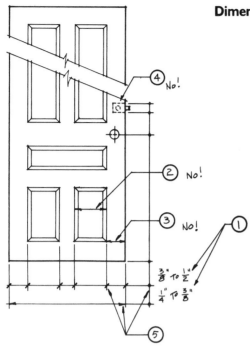

Dimension Lines

1. Dimension lines run between extension lines and should be spaced uniformly. Allow ⅜" to ½" between the object outline and the closest dimension line; allow ¼" to ⅜" between dimension lines. (Using increments of ⅛" makes the layout easy.)
2. Do not use any line of a drawing as a dimension line.
3. Do not join a dimension line end to end (chain fashion) with any line of the drawing.
4. Avoid dimensioning to hidden lines wherever possible.
5. Punctuate the ends of all dimension lines with either an arrowhead, 45° slash, ~~or dot~~, but use only one method in any one drawing. Arrowheads should be solid and proportioned so that their length (⅛"–³⁄₁₆" long) is approximately three times the width.

7.4. Dimension line conventions

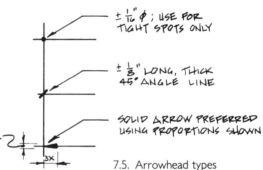

7.5. Arrowhead types

Leader Lines

1. Draw leader lines with a horizontal component originating from either the first or last word of a note or dimension, at mid-height of the lettering. Then draw an oblique line (usually 60°) ending in either an arrow (if pointing to an edge) or a dot (if pointing to a surface). Do not choose an angle that is parallel to dimension, extension, or section lines.
2. Letter the note or dimension first, then place the leader.
3. Leader lines drawn with a straight edge are preferred over leaders drawn freehand.
4. Avoid long leader lines.
5. Do not cross leader lines.
6. Avoid the use of leader lines for dimensions unless the dimension absolutely cannot be written within the space between extension lines.
7. Locate leaders on the view that shows the profile of the surface to which the requirement applies.

7.6. Leader line conventions

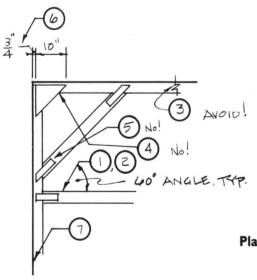

Placement of Dimensions

1. "Line up" intermediate dimensions in chain fashion; place longer dimensions outside all intermediate dimensions.
2. Center dimension figures approximately between the arrowheads, except those in a "stack" of dimensions, then figures should be "staggered."

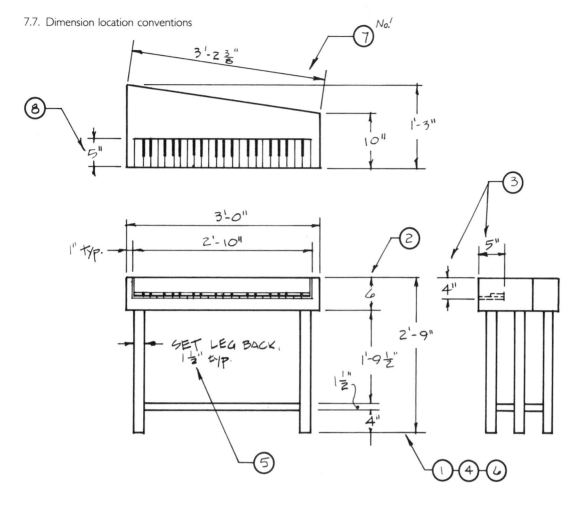

3. Attach dimensions to the view where the shape is most characteristic and is shown true size and shape.
4. Place dimensions applying to two adjacent views between views unless clarity is promoted by placing them outside.
5. Do not place dimensions directly upon a view unless clarity is promoted and long extension lines are avoided.
6. Provide sufficient dimensions so that it will not be necessary to calculate, scale, or assume any dimension.
7. No dimensions should be given except those needed to fabricate the item.
8. Dimensions should not be duplicated or the same information be given in two different ways.

Lettering Dimensions
1. Position dimensions either above the dimension line (allow a ¹⁄₁₆″ gap) or set in the center of a broken dimension line. Use only one system on any one drawing.
2. Express all dimensions of one foot or larger in feet and inches. Separate the numerals with a hyphen, e.g., 4′-1³⁄₄″. Do not omit foot and inch symbols.
3. Letter dimension figures about ⅛″ high for whole numbers and approximately ¼″ high for fractions. Figures lettered smaller than this are difficult to read under shop conditions.

7.8. Conventions used in lettering dimensions

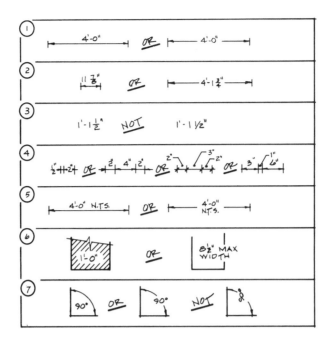

4. Do not draw fraction bars at an incline except in confined areas, such as tables.
5. Do not touch the fraction bar with either the numerator or denominator figures.
6. Do not squeeze dimension figures into spaces too small or reduce them in size in order to fit. Rather use leaders or the techniques shown.
7. Mark a dimension "NTS" or "NOT TO SCALE," if it does not match the scale of the drawing.
8. Do not letter dimensions over profile lines or sectioned areas; if unavoidable, leave a halo of white space behind and around the dimension figures.
9. Letter dimension figures for angles horizontally, in the manner of a note.

7.9. Dimensioning arcs and circles

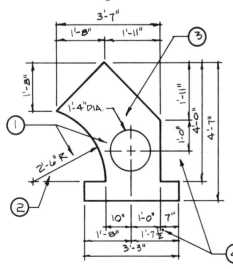

Circles and Arcs
1. Dimension a circle by its diameter, an arc by its radius.
2. Follow or precede a radius dimension figure with the letter R. The radius dimension line should have only one arrowhead, and it should touch the arc.
3. Circles are dimensioned by a note that points toward a circular view of the hole. Follow or precede a diameter dimension figure with "DIA."
4. Locate holes or arcs using dimensions from profile edge to center line.

7.4 Problems

In solving the accompanying worksheets, take the time to incorporate all the guidelines contained in this chapter. Observe the recommended spacing, line-weight conventions, locations, and sizes. As with lettering, practice with the goal of building good habits. Time spent now in developing a good foundation will pay off in the future.

These worksheets begin a new benchmark. All worksheets that follow will require dimensions and notation. Proper dimensioning will be considered as one of the "musts" to go along with accuracy, scale, line-weight, and reproduction.

Worksheets 7.1, 7.2, 7.3

Given the orthographic projections on the worksheets provided, completely dimension all figures incorporating the guidelines covered in this chapter. All figures are $\frac{1}{2}'' = 1'\text{-}0''$ scale unless otherwise noted.

7.5 Checkpoints

√ Use only one system of dimensioning, either the unidirectional or the aligned, on any one drawing.

√ Place dimensions between the views, attached to the view that best shows the characteristic profile of the object.

√ Do not duplicate dimensions in drawings or force the reader to calculate, scale, or assume any dimension; provide all dimensions necessary for fabrication but do not provide redundant information.

√ Align intermediate dimensions and place longer dimensions outside all intermediate dimensions so that dimension lines will not cross extension lines.

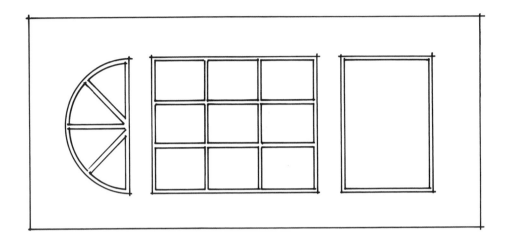

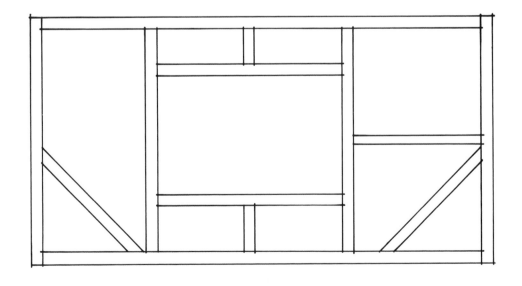

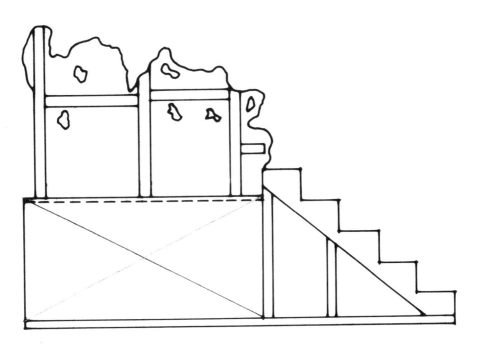

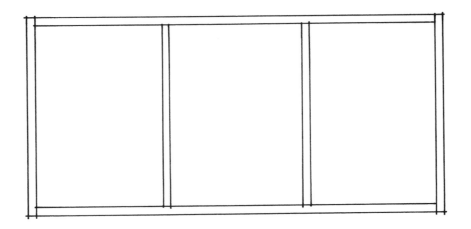

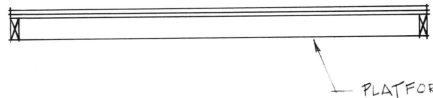

PLATFORM $\frac{3}{4}" = 1'-0"$

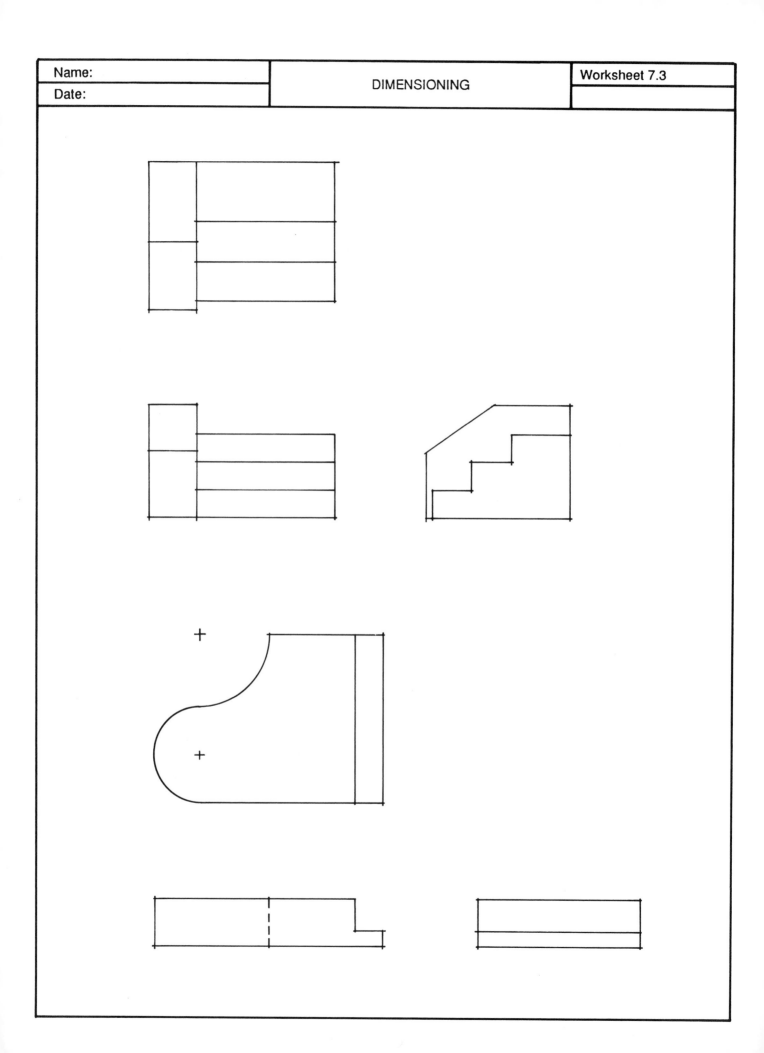

8 Notation

8.1 The Importance of Notes

Few elements of theatre drafting are as neglected as notation. Perhaps it is due to the ever-present urgency to get drawings off the drafting table and into the studio, or perhaps it is simply a lack of appreciation of the great importance that notes hold to the end users: scenic carpenters, welders, prop builders, and painters.

Information such as material choices, assembly procedures, fastening techniques, and desired finishes must be effectively communicated from the planning level to the implementation level. A complete set of notes will take much of the burden of decision making off the work crew and place it in the hands of designers and technical directors where it belongs. All too frequently these managers have thought out the construction process and arrived at a solution when developing drawings but have failed to take the time to add appropriate notes to communicate their ideas.

8.1. Cradle from *The History of American Film.* Courtesy Leonard Harman, scene designer

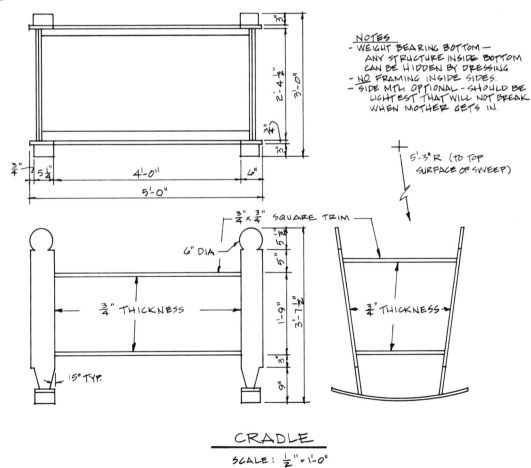

NOTES
- WEIGHT BEARING BOTTOM — ANY STRUCTURE INSIDE BOTTOM CAN BE HIDDEN BY DRESSING.
- NO FRAMING INSIDE SIDES.
- SIDE MTL. OPTIONAL - SHOULD BE LIGHTEST THAT WILL NOT BREAK WHEN MOTHER GETS IN.

5'-3" R (TO TOP SURFACE OF SWEEP)

¾" × ¾" SQUARE TRIM

6" DIA.

¾" THICKNESS

15° TYP.

¾" THICKNESS

CRADLE
SCALE: ½" = 1'-0"

Like dimensioning, the study of notation involves learning conventions that guide technique. The content of any note, however, is controlled by one simple rule of thumb: **provide only that information you would need to construct the unit you are drawing—but provide it all.**

8.2 Notation Guidelines

1. Notes are used to complement or simplify dimensioning by indicating information on a drawing in a condensed and systematic manner. Notes should be brief, written in present or future tense, and carefully worded so as to be capable of having only one interpretation.

2. Notes should always be lettered horizontally on the sheet, using guidelines, and arranged in a systematic manner. Use standard upper-case Gothic lettering. Vertical, ⅛" high lettering is preferred. Notes and other lettering should not be underlined.

3. Notes should not be lettered in crowded places. Avoid placing notes between views, if possible. Do not letter them so close together as to confuse the reader, or so close to another view or detail as to suggest application to the wrong view.

4. Notes (and leaders) should not be placed on the drawing until the dimensioning is substantially completed. If notes are lettered first, almost invariably they are in the way of necessary dimensions and will have to be moved.

5. There are two principal types of notes: general notes and local notes.

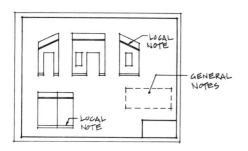

8.2. Note locations

General notes refer to units or drawings as a whole. They are lettered in the lower right-hand corner of the drawing, above or to the left of the title block, or in a central position below the unit to which they apply. Typical examples of this type of note are:

    a. ALL UNITS MUSLIN COVERED, EXCEPT AS NOTED
    b. CASTERS ARE 3" TIRE, SWIVEL, DARNELL SERIES 70

Local notes apply to local requirements only and are connected by a leader to the exact point to which the note applies. Typical examples are:

    a. 45° BEVEL
    b. LINE OF PLATFORM "P3"

6. Abbreviations and symbols are used on drawings to conserve space and time, but only when their meanings are quite clear. When in doubt, spell it out! Only commonly accepted abbreviations such as the examples shown in figure 8.3 are to be used. A complete list of accepted abbreviations is found in appendix G.

8.3. List of abbreviations

ALTERNATE	ALT	OUTSIDE DIAMETER	OD
CENTER LINE	CL	PLASTER LINE	PL
DIAMETER	DIA	PLYWOOD	PLY
DO NOT COVER	DNC	REVERSE & REPEAT	R&R
EACH	EA	SHEET	SHT
HARDWARE	HDW	STAGE LEFT	SL
INSIDE DIAMETER	ID	STAGE RIGHT	SR
LOOSE PIN HINGE	LPH	TIGHT PIN HINGE	TPH
MUSLIN	MUS	TONGUE & GROOVE	T&G
NOT TO SCALE	NTS	TYPICAL	TYP
ON CENTER	OC	WHITE PINE	WP

COMMON ABBREVIATIONS FOR THEATRE USE

8.3 Labeling Scenic Units

Every stage set comprises many pieces. To keep track of all the components, it is incumbent upon the production team of designer and technical director to establish a uniform labeling system. Inconvenient as it is, the unique nature of scenery typically demands a tailor-made system for each production. Such systems are not always easy to organize, since scenic units are often unconnected and may lie in a helter-skelter series of planes.

A consistent format of labeling enhances clarity. Users become "trained" to look for uniform information regarding **unit designation, view identification, scale, and number of pieces required.** Such a system also provides a ready means of cross referencing units between design drawings, shop drawings, and constructed units. Since labeling systems are typically developed at the drafting table, guidelines are provided to assist the drafter in the creation of an efficient system.

Figure 8.4 shows a suggested labeling system based on those found in architectural graphics that identifies specific units on a sheet of drawings. Figure 8.5 is a modification that allows for identification of the unit drawing on a specific sheet as well as providing a shorthand for referencing views shown on other sheets. Objects are numbered from the top left-side corner of the sheet, left to right moving toward the bottom right-hand corner where the title block is located.

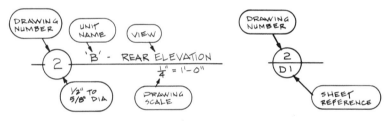

8.4. Labeling sample   8.5. Referencing another sheet

8.4 Labeling Guidelines

1. For a box set or similar arrangement, label principal continuous wall units beginning with the DSR return (if used) and progressing in sequence toward DSL. Use uppercase letters, moving from A toward Z (fig. 8.6).
2. Masking or backing units can follow one of two sequences:
   a. A continuation of the sequence begun in 1, above
   b. A double letter symbol such as A-A, D-D, indicating that the unit is a masking unit and is located offstage of flat A or flat D
3. Non-box sets (fig. 8.7) are not so readily labeled. In such cases try to establish a system that facilitates unit identification. For example, label masking units with a M-#; steps with a S-#; platforms with a P-#. Again the units should be labeled numerically, beginning DSR, e.g., M-1, M-2; S-1, and so on. Symmetrical sets can use nomenclature such as M-1R, M-2R, M-2L, which directly indicates the side of the stage on which the unit is located.
4. Ideally, unit labels are established in the design-drawing phase. Once into the shop-drawing phase, the component pieces of each unit should bear the initial label plus an add on. As before, the logic must be straightforward and unwavering (fig. 8.8).

8.8. Component-labeled shop drawing

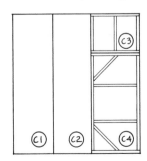

8.6. Box set ground plan

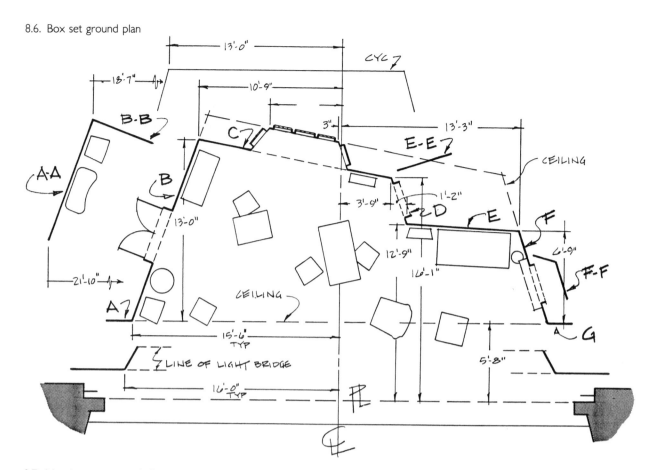

8.7. Non-box set ground plan

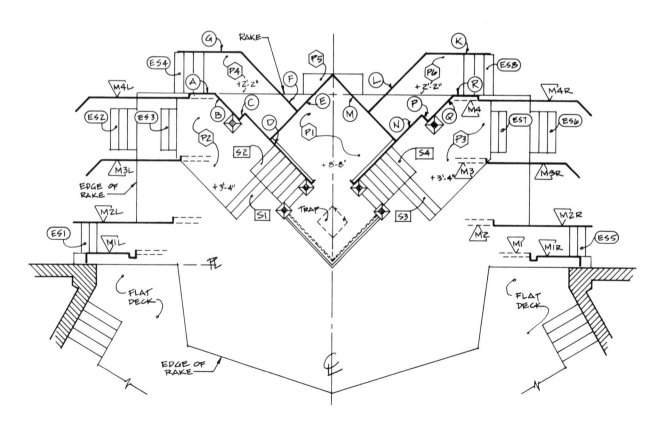

8.5 Problem

Given the design elevation of a street lamp used in a production of *Spokesong*, dimension, label, and notate each drawing. Notes should include suggested materials, fabrication techniques, or other pertinent information. Provide a minimum of eight such notes.

8.6 Checkpoints

√ Notes are used to provide detailed information about material choices, assembly procedures, fastening techniques, and desired finishes.

√ Place notes on drawings only after the drawing has been dimensioned.

√ All objects on a drawing should be labeled as to unit designation, view identification, scale, and number of pieces required to promote clarity.

√ Shop drawing labels are a further breakdown of the labels established on the design drawings

POTTINGERS
ENTRY

LAMP POST
SCALE: $\frac{3}{4}$"=1'-0"

9   Section Drawings

9.1 Looking at the Inside

Standard multiview drawings provide information about the six surface planes of an object, but any information about the interior must be shown through the use of hidden lines. Since hidden lines are often confusing, section drawings are used to provide the needed clarity.

9.1. Section drawings

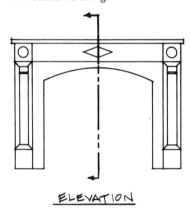

ELEVATION

9.2 The Cutting Plane

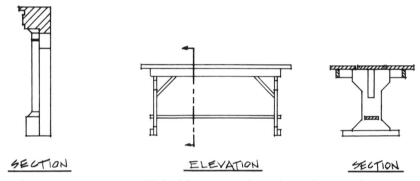

SECTION   ELEVATION   SECTION

The section view is established by cutting through an object with an imaginary knife, creating an interior "cutting" plane that is then viewed in a manner identical to other multiview drawings. The location of the cutting plane is chosen by the drafter to provide the most complete information possible. Although there are some conventions intended to reduce the number of drawings needed, often several section drawings are necessary if an object is to be adequately described for construction purposes.

The exact location of the cutting plane is shown in another view as a cutting plane line. The cutting plane line is a thick line, terminating at each end with arrows that indicate the viewing direction (fig. 9.2). In the event two or more section views are drawn, identify the arrowheads of the cutting plane lines, using an alphabet label such as A-A, B-B, etc.

Typically, the cutting plane line will pass through the entire length or width of a drawing. The resulting section is a full section and may be referenced as either a **longitudinal section** (cuts through the object parallel with the longest dimension) or a **transverse section** (parallel to the shorter dimension). Alternatively, the cutting plane line may be staggered, front to back or side to side, to provide additional details not possible to show if the cutting plane line was a straight line. This type of drawing is known as an **offset section** (fig. 9.6). The bends in the staggered cutting plane line are always at 90° and are never shown in the corresponding section view.

Ground plans of stage settings are actually section drawings with a horizontal cutting plane located approximately 4'-0" above the stage deck, permitting all openings such as doors, windows, fireplace openings, etc.,

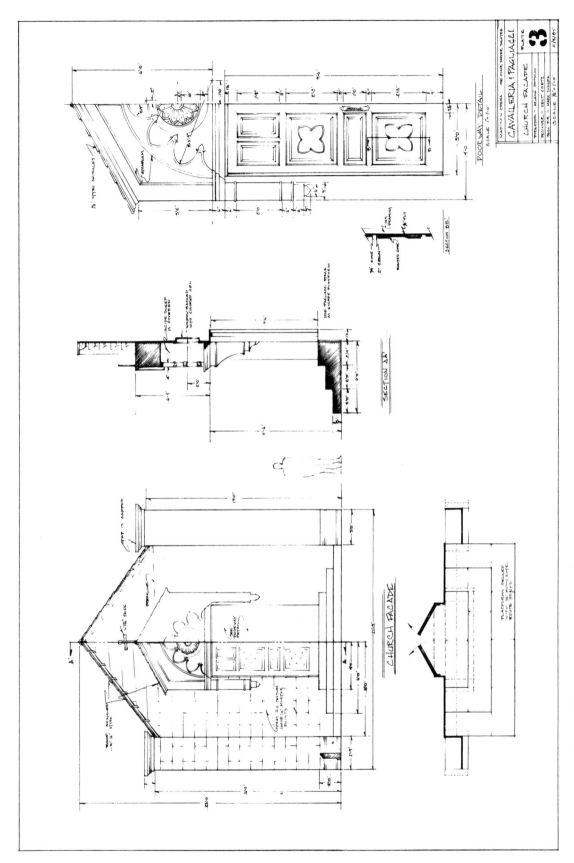

9.2. Doorway from *Cavaleria Rusticana.*
Courtesy Kent Goetz, scene designer

to be clearly shown. Unlike all other section drawings, the location of the ground plan's cutting plane line is not referenced on another view.

9.3 Line Symbol Conventions

What enhances the reading of a section drawing is the use of some special line symbols. All shapes that have been cut are highlighted by the use of conventions: the section outline and section lines. The section outline is a solid thick profile line, identical in appearance and use to the visible outline. The surface of the plane being exposed is indicated by **crosshatching,** the term commonly applied to section lines. Section lines are thin lines, usually drawn at 45° to the horizontal and uniformly spaced $\frac{1}{16}''$ to $\frac{1}{8}''$ apart depending on the size of the drawing being done. (The average $\frac{1}{2}''$ scale drawing utilizes a spacing of $\frac{3}{32}''$.) An angle other than 45° (usually 30° or 60°) is used in the event 45° section lines would be parallel or perpendicular to a prominent visible outline.

Unless the drawing is a shop drawing indicating component materials, the object is treated as a solid, with all section lines running parallel. In the case that the drawing is done for the purpose of identifying of individual materials, the section lines of the various parts are drawn in opposite directions to distinguish one component from another. Surfaces too narrow to permit the practical use of crosshatching are often screened, either lightly shaded or completely opaqued. A series of thin lines parallel with the section outline are frequently used to crosshatch panel or sheet materials.

Surfaces that are not cut through are treated as elevations in a manner identical to that of standard multiview drawings, although the use of hidden lines should be kept minimal. In areas that are crosshatched, hidden lines are never used, since one of the principal purposes of section drawings is the elimination of hidden lines.

9.3. Section line standards

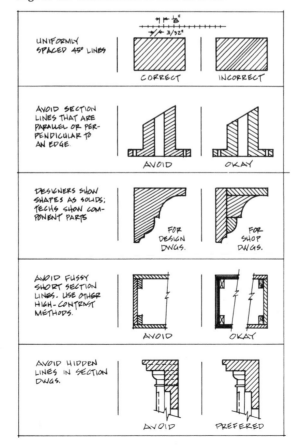

9.4 Types of Section Drawings

Full Section

When a cutting plane line is drawn across the entire object, the resulting drawing is a **full section.** The full section is often used to replace one of the standard views, since in most cases it more clearly describes the object. Both the cutting plane line and the resulting drawing must be clearly identified (fig. 9.4).

9.4. Side view with hidden lines vs. section view

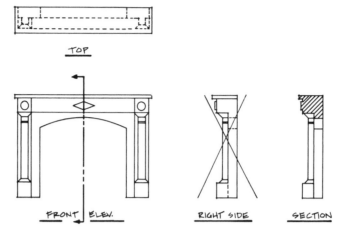

Half Section

When drawing a symmetrical object, the convention of a **half section** is often used. Similar to the half-view drawing introduced in chapter 6, the half section serves to reduce either the number or the complexity of required drawings. The half section uses the center line of the object as the cutting plane line and is a combination view, half elevation and half section (fig. 9.5).

9.5. Half sections

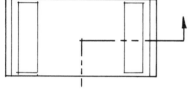

TOP VIEW

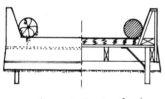

ELEV. / SECTION

Partial Section

While the half section could be considered a form of a partial section, the term is typically used in applications where a small detail or area of an elevation needs to be shown in section. The **partial or broken-out section** is indicated with a short break line, a thin freehand line. Applications in which this convention might appear are multiple levels (when stacked) and joinery details.

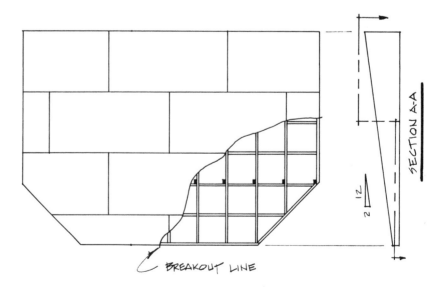

BREAKOUT LINE

9.6. Partial section

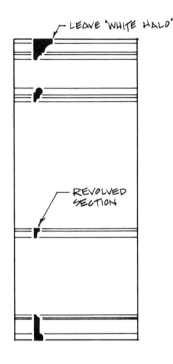

Revolved Section

Some rather complex forms, such as molding, are not well described when shown only in a front elevation. Using the convention of a **revolved section**, a section view is rotated 90° and placed directly on the elevation, making a comparison of the planes easy (fig. 9.7). The removed section should be given a small "halo" of white space to set it off from the background of the elevation.

Removed Section

When an irregular shape, such as a tree or rock, is drawn, a **removed section** is used to define the changing contour. A removed section is essentially a revolved section but drawn away from the original view. Multiple removed sections are used to indicate the profile changes and to develop full-sized templates of the needed shapes. Each removed section is clearly labeled using the reference letters from the cutting plane line.

9.8. Removed sections

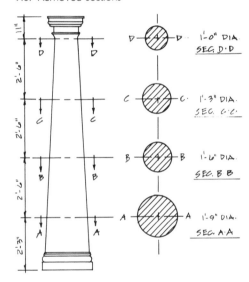

9.5 Problems

Worksheets 9.1, 9.2

Given two orthographic views of the objects drawn, draw the indicated section view. Observe carefully the conventions of line symbols and lineweights.

9.6 Checkpoints

√ A section view can replace or be part of one of the standard views of an orthographic projection.

√ Section drawings reduce the need for hidden lines.

√ All section views, except the ground plan, must be accompanied by a second view that clearly shows the location of the cutting plane line.

√ The location of the cutting plane and the type of section to be drawn are selected by the drafter to provide information in the clearest manner possible.

√ Planes that are cut by the cutting plane line are identified in the section view through the conventions of the section outline and cross-hatching (45° section lines).

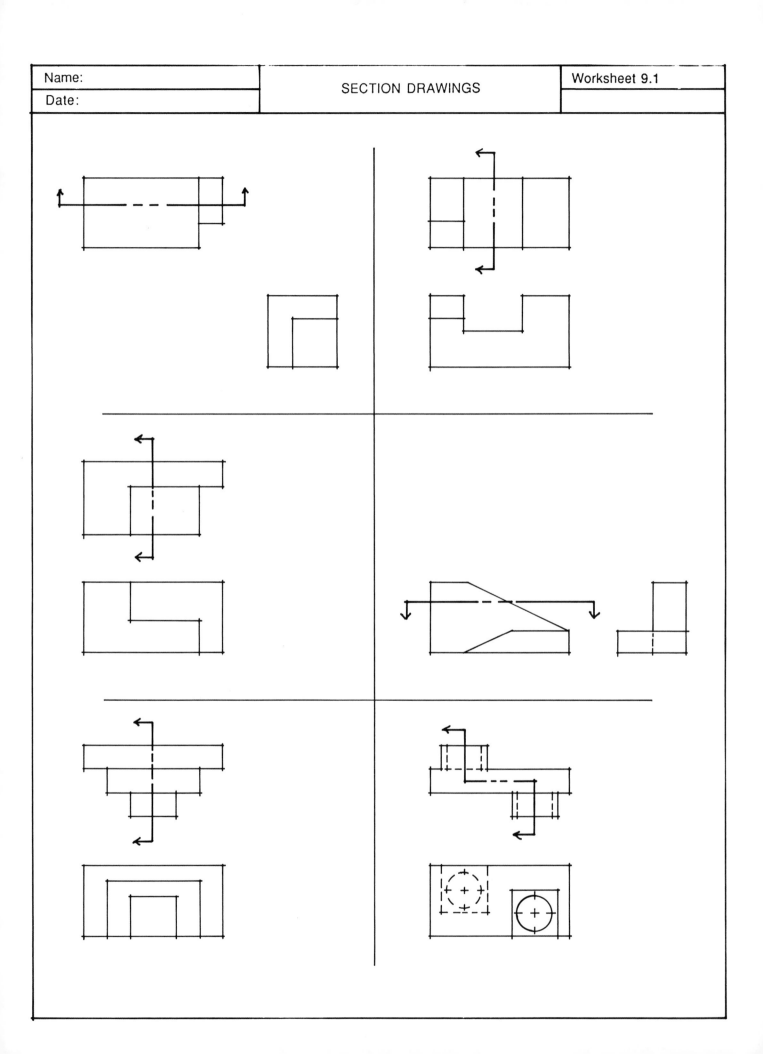

Name:	SECTION DRAWINGS	Worksheet 9.2
Date:		

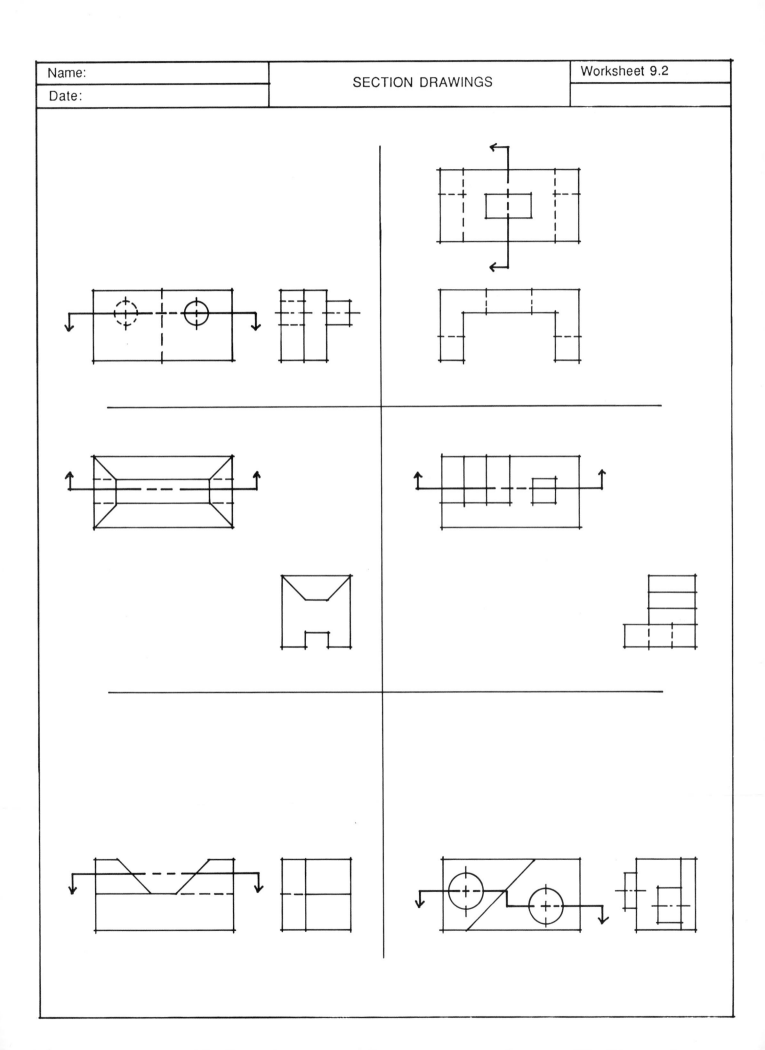

10   Auxiliary Views

10.1 Auxiliary Views

Some objects, such as a raked stage, have a surface that is not perpendicular to any of the principal planes of a multiview drawing. The condition is easily identified by the fact that the surface appears as an inclined or oblique line in two of the standard views. In the views where the oblique surface appears, the surface is seen foreshortened. Even though the dimensions of the surface can be readily determined from information shown in the standard views, it is usually necessary that the surface be drawn in its true size and shape. This can be done using standard drafting tools and conventions by modifying the rules of projection to produce a class of drawing known as the **auxiliary view.**

Typically the auxiliary view is drawn parallel to the oblique line (perpendicular to the oblique plane), and so the view appears askew on the drawing sheet. This condition, described in detail below, permits the view to be developed in the same manner as any standard view. Dimensions and notes specific to the inclined surface are attached to the auxiliary view rather than on a view that is neither true size nor true shape. Generally, hidden lines are omitted on auxiliary views, since the information needed is specific only to the oblique plane and not any surface beyond. The elimination of hidden lines helps to simplify the drawing and avoid possible confusion.

10.2 The Folding Line Concept

The logical construct of the auxiliary view is readily seen through the **folding line** concept. The auxiliary plane, P, is assumed parallel to the inclined surface, consequently the auxiliary view is perpendicular to the front plane of projection. This relationship is indicated in figure 10.1 by showing the inclined surface hinged to the front plane of projection. When the horizontal and auxiliary planes are unfolded to lie in same

10.1. The folding line method

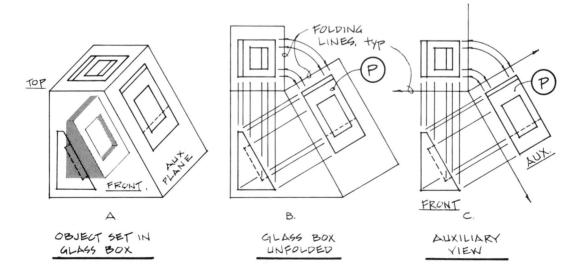

A.
OBJECT SET IN
GLASS BOX

B.
GLASS BOX
UNFOLDED

C.
AUXILIARY
VIEW

plane as the front elevation, the folding lines represent the hinge lines of the glass box planes. Only in the auxiliary view is surface P shown in true size and shape, the height dimension being projected directly from the front view and the depth dimension taken from the top view. Although the concept of folding lines is helpful, it is a concept only and not directly used in the construction of the auxiliary view. For this purpose, the most useful tool is a datum line, known as the **reference line.**

10.3 The Reference Line Method

The reference line method uses a datum plane to transfer distances obtained from another view, in this case, depth dimensions from the top view. The reference plane may be located in several positions. Figure 10.2 shows it congruent with the front surface of the object, A. If the object is symmetrical, it is useful to locate the reference line along the center line of the object, B. In fact the reference line can also be located at any intermediate point, its location dependent solely on its convenience as a datum line, C.

10.2. The reference line method

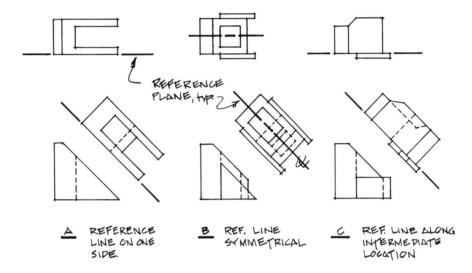

<u>A</u> REFERENCE LINE ON ONE SIDE.

<u>B</u> REF. LINE SYMMETRICAL

<u>C</u> REF. LINE ALONG INTERMEDIATE LOCATION

An auxiliary view is drawn using the following steps:
1. Given the front and top views, draw a line parallel to the oblique line at any convenient distance. The new line is the **reference line.**
2. Project construction lines from the front view, perpendicular to surface P, and passing beyond the reference line a distance greater than the depth of P.
3. Transfer depth measurements from the top view, using a compass, dividers, or tick strip.
4. Darken the needed profile to create the finished auxiliary view.

10.4 Locating the Auxiliary View

When either drawing or reading auxiliary views, convenience dictates drawing the reference line parallel to the oblique line. In this way it is easy to follow the source of projected lines, a significant aid to complete understanding of the drawing. At times, fitting the drawing into a desired location may be difficult, because the oblique layout requires a considerable area of sheet space. To make certain that sufficient room has been allowed, block out the needed space on a trial basis, using a second sheet of paper or some similar device. Allow room also for all notes and dimensions. In those situations where available space does not permit parallel orientation, the auxiliary view must be drawn as a removed view. When doing this, choose a location and orientation that facilitates referencing back to the oblique surface and clearly label the view as a "REMOVED AUXILIARY VIEW."

10.5 Partial and Half-Auxiliary Views

The only surface shown true size and shape in an auxiliary view is the oblique surface. A full auxiliary view shows surrounding surfaces foreshortened, which, in a way, simply reverses the situation that was initially the problem. For this reason, typically, a **partial auxiliary view** is drawn. This drawing shows only the oblique surface, but this time in true size and shape (fig. 10.3). Some drafters prefer to draw the full auxiliary view showing the entire oblique surface, using short break lines to leave only a hint of the surrounding areas. In either situation the resulting drawing should be clearly labeled as a "PARTIAL AUXILIARY VIEW."

10.3. Partial auxiliary view

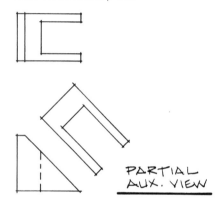

PARTIAL
AUX. VIEW

10.4. Half-auxiliary view

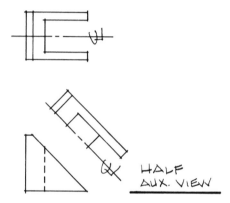

HALF
AUX. VIEW

If an auxiliary view is symmetrical, and space or time can be saved without sacrificing drawing clarity, consider drawing only half of the auxiliary view needed. Normally the half of the view nearest the oblique surface is the one drawn, but either side is acceptable. Clearly label the view as a "HALF-AUXILIARY VIEW."

10.6 Secondary Auxiliary Views

A **secondary auxiliary view** is required when the true shape of a surface cannot be shown on either the standard views or the primary auxiliary view. This happens when an object has an oblique surface that is not perpendicular to any of the principal planes of projection. The primary auxiliary view is first constructed so that it is perpendicular to the inclined surface and one of the principal planes. The secondary auxiliary view is then projected from the primary auxiliary view and is perpendicular to it (fig. 10.5). This condition can also be resolved using the true size and shape techniques discussed in chapter 11.

10.7 Auxiliary Sections

As the name implies, an **auxiliary section** is an auxiliary view drawn using the conventions of section drawings. Either a full or partial auxiliary view can be drawn, although the full view will provide a better understanding of the relationships between the object's component parts. Sections may be either removed, revolved, or drawn in the place of some standard view. Section lines are drawn at approximately 45° to the profile, regardless of the drawing orientation on the sheet.

10.5. Secondary auxiliary view

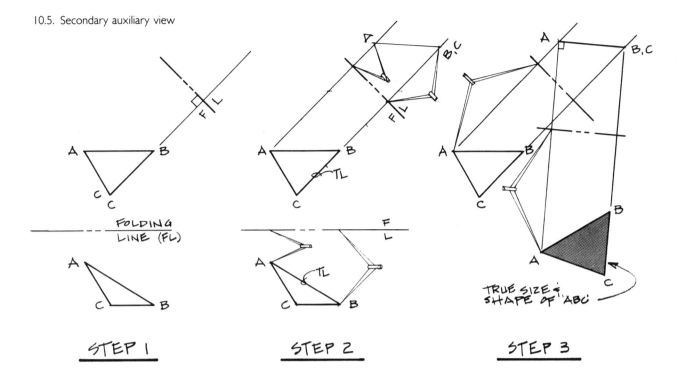

FOLDING
LINE (FL)

STEP 1

TL

STEP 2

TRUE SIZE &
SHAPE OF ABC

STEP 3

10.6. Auxiliary section

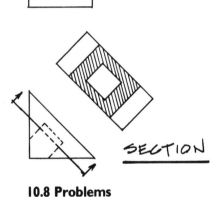

SECTION

10.8 Problems

Worksheet 10.1
Draw partial auxiliary views for each of the objects shown. Omit all hidden lines unless they promote drawing clarity.

Worksheet 10.2
In ½" scale, draw half-auxiliary views as needed of the doghouse roof. Dimension and label the drawings.

Worksheet 10.3
Given three views of the raked platform (⅛" = 1'-0"), draw a partial half-auxiliary view showing the true shape of the platform. Dimension and label the drawing. Having determined the overall size of the rake, divide it into stock platforms (4 × 8, 3 × 8, 2 × 4, etc.) as possible. Record the number and type of units in the "platform legend" provided. "Notes" should indicate whether the unit is stock or built. If more entries are needed than provided, add to the legend as required.

10.8 Checkpoints

√ Auxiliary view techniques are used to construct drawings of surfaces oblique to the standard planes of orthographic projection.

√ The orientation of auxiliary view drawings is normally parallel to the oblique line describing the plane.

√ Auxiliary view drawings are usually partial views and must be labeled as such.

Name:	AUXILIARY VIEWS	Worksheet 10.1
Date:		

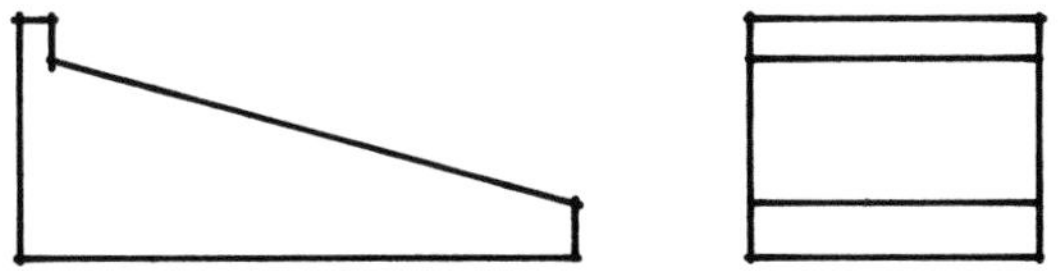

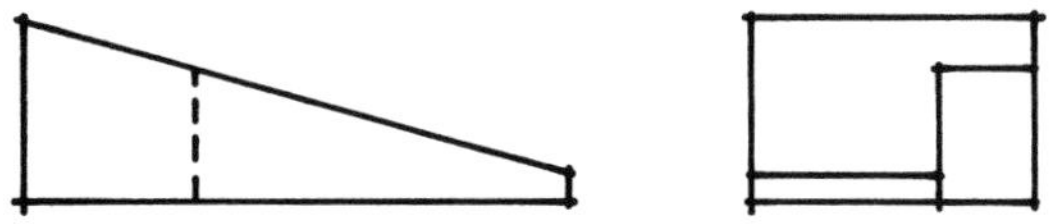

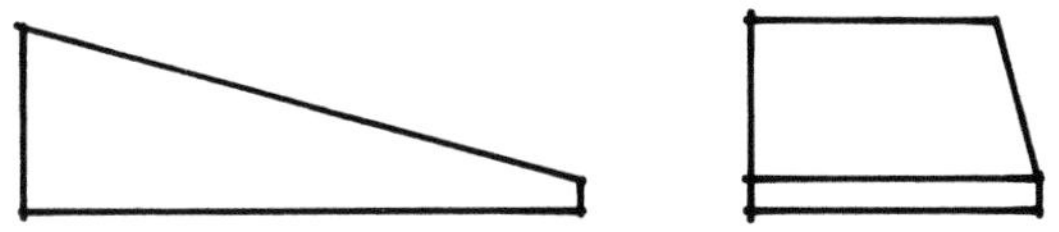

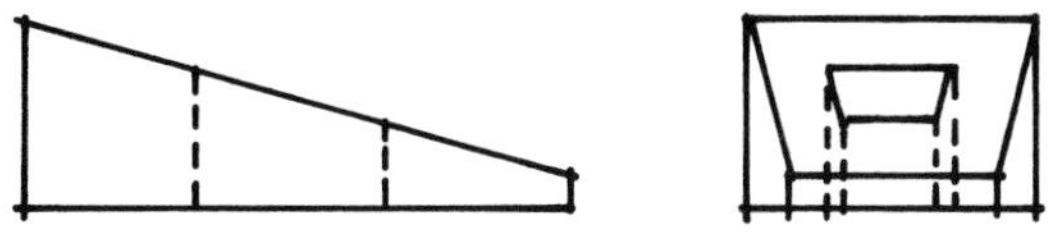

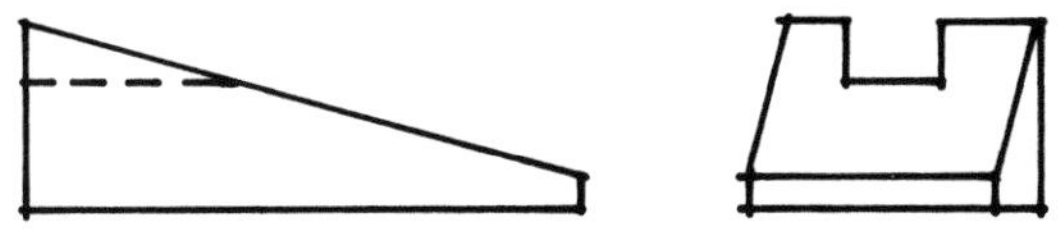

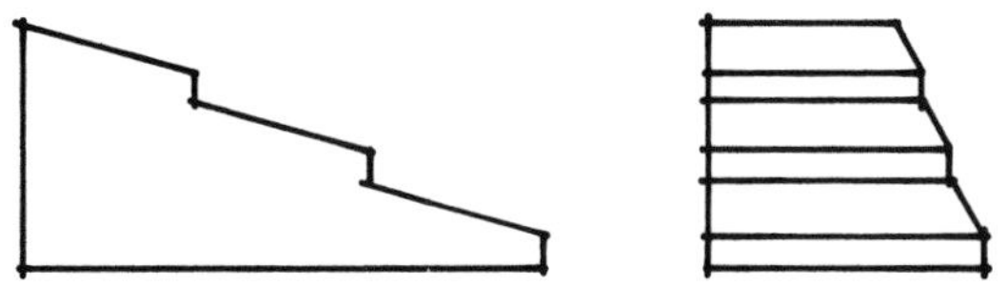

TOP

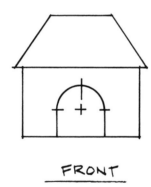

FRONT

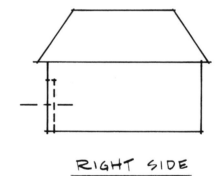

RIGHT SIDE

Name:	AUXILIARY VIEWS	Worksheet 10.3
Date:		

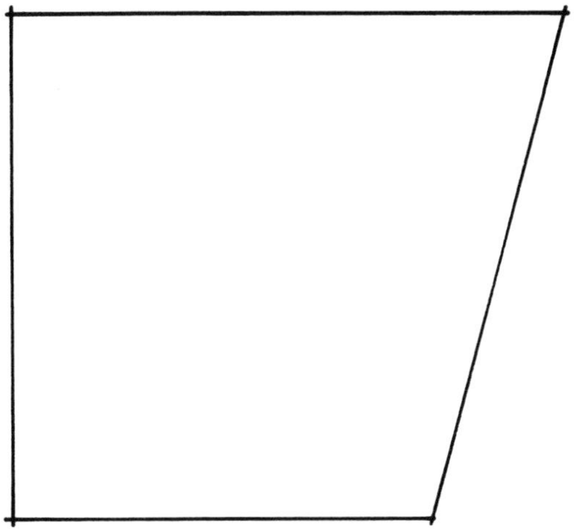

TOP

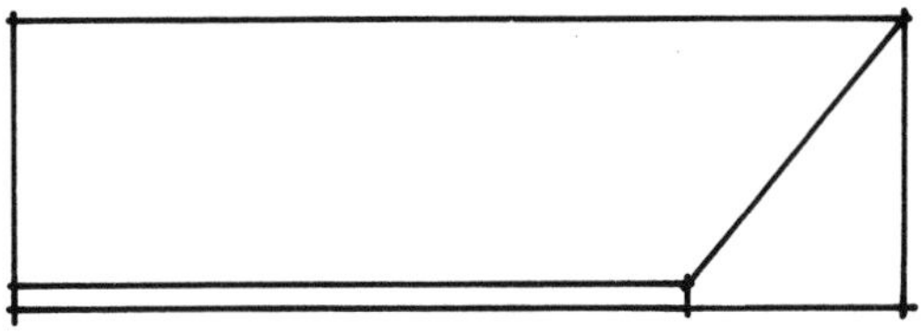

FRONT

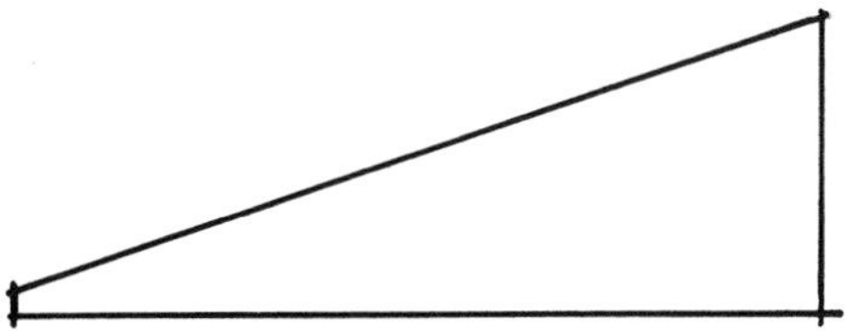

RIGHT SIDE

QUAN.	ITEM	DESCRIPTION	NOTES

11 True Size and Shape

11.1 True Size and Shape

If a technical drawing is to be of value to construction personnel, it must show an object in its true size and shape. Without true size and shape views, the builder will likely create a product that ultimately will be of little or no use. The loss of precious resources under such conditions is ample justification for making the considerable investment of time needed to develop accurate design and shop drawings.

Several tools have already been introduced to provide the drafter with the capability to produce drawings that are of true size and shape. The first objects studied in this text contained only flat or curved surfaces parallel to the six standard views of orthographic projection. Later, oblique surfaces were investigated. Because an oblique surface is parallel to at least two of the six views, it can be developed true size and shape by drawing its auxiliary view.

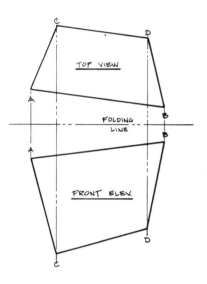

11.1. A projection screen oblique to both plaster and center lines

In this chapter, additional true-size-and-shape tools are introduced, techniques developed to produce technical drawings of objects containing surfaces that are not parallel to any of the six standard views. A projection screen that is hung at an angle to the stage floor and oblique to both center and plaster lines would be an example likely to be encountered in the theatre (fig. 11.1).

Although the procedure described is straightforward and easily followed, a word of caution must be given, since the process is tedious and fraught with the opportunity for error. Work with care, be patient, and use well-sharpened, hard-lead pencils and compass leads when developing true size and shape drawings.

11.2 Axioms of True Length

The graphic solution of any true-size-and-shape problem involves the application of descriptive geometry. Two such techniques are needed for this situation: 1) rotation and 2) triangulation. Triangulation is one of the geometric construction techniques introduced in chapter 5. Line rotation is an easily understood concept as well, involving the relocation of a line to a plane parallel with another plane, in this case the folding line (FL) in figure 11.2.

Finding the true length of a line begins by examining the information given in two or more views of the object being drawn. This requires the application again of the familiar concept of the folding line. For our purposes, the folding line represents the intersection of the top and front views. Given this arrangement, three axioms can be noted:

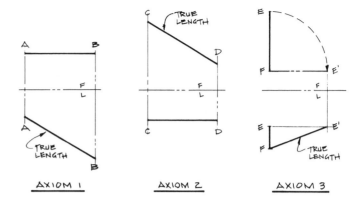

AXIOM 1   AXIOM 2   AXIOM 3

1. If a line is parallel with the FL (folding line) in the top (or plan) view , the line is shown in its true length in the front view.
2. The converse is also true, i.e., if the line is parallel with the folding line in the front view but oblique in the top view, then the top view is the true length.
3. If a line is perpendicular to the folding line in both front and top views, then the true length of the line will be found in the side view.

11.3 Rotating Lines for True Size and Shape

11.3. Rotating a line to find its true length

In the event that a line is oblique to the folding line in both top and front views, the principle of rotation must be applied to bring the line into conformity with one of the axioms. Figure 11.3 shows how the principle is applied to a single line. A simple theatrical example might be a pipe batten hung askew above the stage floor. Given the line AB, shown in both ground plan and front elevation:

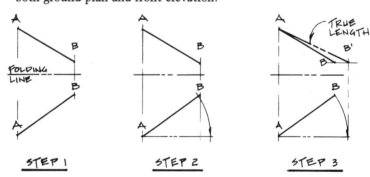

STEP 1   STEP 2   STEP 3

1. Examine both views to see if the line matches any of the situations described in the three axioms. In this case, the line is oblique to the plaster line (folding line) in both views, so the line must be rotated.
2. Keeping in mind that the operation is reversible, rotate the line in the plan view. Place the compass needle on A, adjust the compass to the length AB, then strike an arc as shown. With the T-square, draw a line that passes through point A and intersects the arc. The line AB is now parallel with the plaster line. Now, however, point B does not occupy the same position in both plan and front views. The plan view has been modified to create a condition where line AB fits one of the true length axioms; now line AB must be adjusted in the elevation to occupy the same space in both views.
3. At the point of intersection of the rotated point B, drop a

line to the front elevation equidistant from the plaster line as the existing point B. With the T-square, draw a line that passes through B and intersects the projected line. The true length of AB is shown in the front elevation and is the length of the line taken from point A to the intersection at point B'.

11.4 Rotating Planes for True Size and Shape

Once the true length of each line has been determined, any plane surface can be reconstructed using the process of triangulation. Given the triangle ABC, shown in both ground plan and front elevation:

11.4. Finding the true size and shape of a two-dimensional triangle

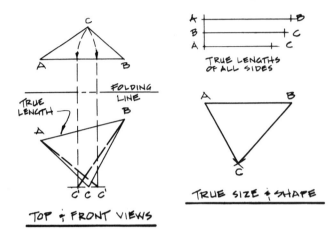

1. Examine the problem to see if any of the lines AB, BC, or AC already match any of the axiom conditions. In this example the line AB is parallel to the plaster line (folding line) in the plan view, so the true length of the line AB is found in the front view. The other two lines are oblique to the plaster line in both front and plan views and must be rotated.
2. A simple bookkeeping system is helpful in keeping the various lines straight, since the process is now more complicated. After finding the true length of each line, label each clearly and record it to the side.
3. Proceed to find all lengths using the rotation method. Once found, record the new lengths and use them to reconstruct the triangle. The resulting triangle is the only shape that triangle ABC can have; consequently, it is the true size and shape of ABC.

11.5 Finding the True Size and Shape of Polygons

Any polygon can be viewed as a series of triangles by the introduction of temporary diagonals. Each triangle is solved for true size by using triangulation and is combined with the next triangle to reconstruct the true size and shape of the polygon.
1. Find the true length of each side and the temporary diagonal (AC) using rotation.
2. Keep the orientation of the object the same as is shown in the front elevation, i.e., keep the bottom left corner the same in all views. Beginning with the bottom, construct the first triangle using the adjacent side and temporary diagonal. Note that the bottom line is drawn parallel to the line, as it is shown in the elevation.

11.5. Finding the true size and shape of a polygon (skewed quadrilateral)

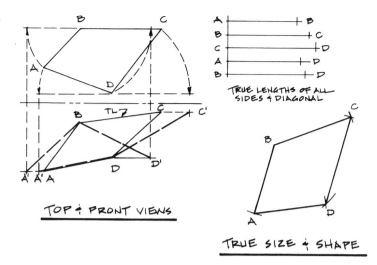

TOP & FRONT VIEWS

TRUE LENGTHS OF ALL SIDES & DIAGONAL

TRUE SIZE & SHAPE

3. Complete the polygon by adding the remaining two sides to the temporary diagonal.

11.6 Three-dimensional Objects

Thus far we have examined the approach to solving true-size-and-shape problems that involve single lines and then single plane surfaces. Most objects, however, have more than one surface, so it is necessary to apply the above techniques to three-dimensional objects. Begin by examining the regular and truncated square pyramids shown in figure 11.6.

The next example looks at a box set, enclosed with a raked ceiling. The technique is the same as before, breaking each polygon into a series of triangles through the use of temporary diagonals, rotating all lines not parallel to the folding line and finally reconstructing the shapes using triangulation.

The final example shows how to design an object with skewed surfaces in space. This is the most common approach taken by designers who wish to place such an object in elevation but then must determine the exact floor space required to produce the look. The steps illustrated show only the reconciliation of the two views. The determination of true size and shape of the surfaces is the same as before: rotation and triangulation.

11.7 Problems

Worksheet 11.1
Given the four problems on the worksheet, find the true size and shape of each line or object using rotation and triangulation.

Worksheet 11.2
Given the top and front views of two truncated pyramids, develop a true-size-and-shape pattern for each on individual B-size sheets. Hint: You may want to sketch out your ideas on tracing paper before you actually develop the final views.

11.8 Checkpoints

√ Surfaces that are oblique to all standard planes of projection are problems involving principles of rotation and triangulation.

√ Both end points of a line must coincide in each view.

√ The planes of a polygon and three-dimensional skewed objects are divided into triangles for the purposes of true-size-and-shape development.

11.6. Two examples of the development
of three-dimensional objects

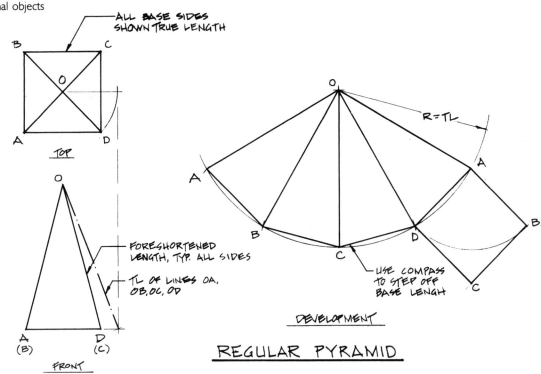

ALL BASE SIDES
SHOWN TRUE LENGTH

TOP

FORESHORTENED
LENGTH, TYP. ALL SIDES

TL OF LINES OA,
OB, OC, OD

FRONT

R=TL

USE COMPASS
TO STEP OFF
BASE LENGH

DEVELOPMENT

REGULAR PYRAMID

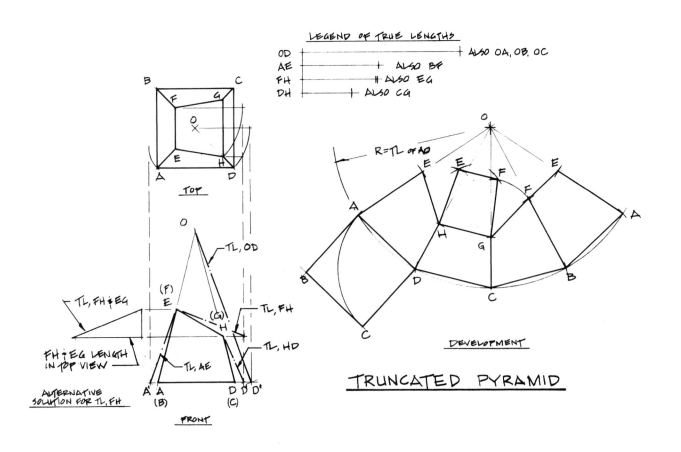

LEGEND OF TRUE LENGTHS

OD		ALSO OA, OB, OC
AE	ALSO BF	
FH	ALSO EG	
DH	ALSO CG	

TOP

TL, OD

TL, FH & EG

FH & EG LENGTH
IN TOP VIEW

TL, FH

TL, AE

TL, HD

ALTERNATIVE
SOLUTION FOR TL, FH

FRONT

R=TL of AD

DEVELOPMENT

TRUNCATED PYRAMID

11.7. Using true size and shape to determine the actual size of a ceiling piece

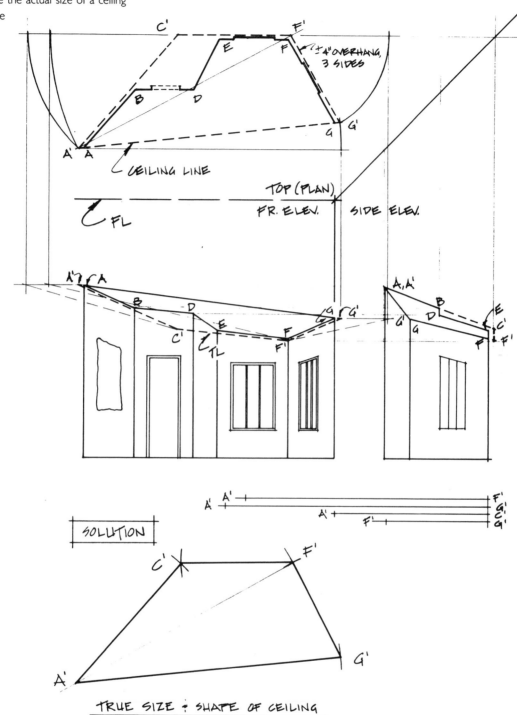

CEILING LINE

TOP (PLAN)

FR. ELEV.   SIDE ELEV.

FL

TL

±4" OVERHANG, 3 SIDES

SOLUTION

TRUE SIZE & SHAPE OF CEILING

11.8. Designing an object with skewed
        surfaces

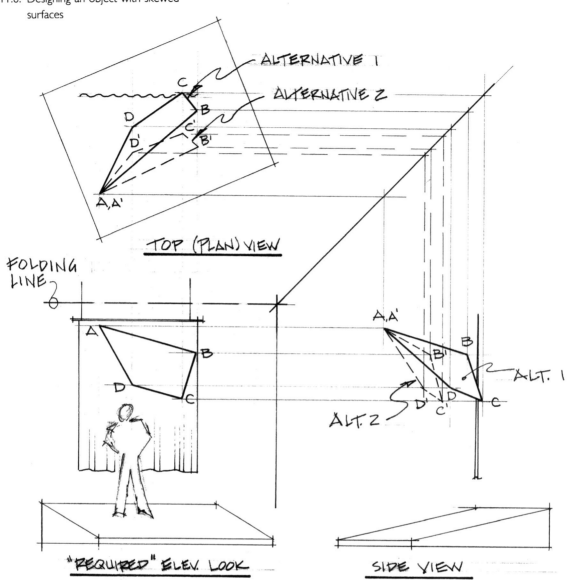

ALTERNATIVE 1

ALTERNATIVE 2

TOP (PLAN) VIEW

FOLDING
LINE

"REQUIRED" ELEV. LOOK

ALT. 1

ALT. 2

SIDE VIEW

1. LABEL THE TRUE LENGTH VIEW

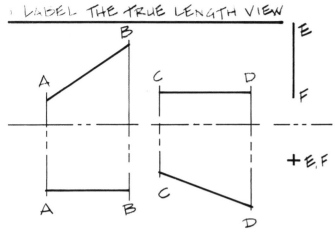

2. SOLVE FOR TRUE LENGTH

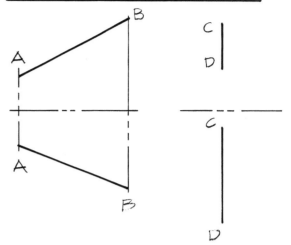

3. SOLVE FOR TRUE SIZE & SHAPE

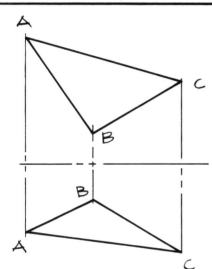

KEY

4. SOLVE FOR TRUE SIZE & SHAPE

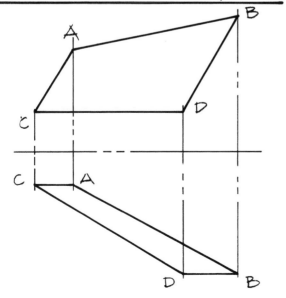

KEY

Name:	TRUE SIZE AND SHAPE	Worksheet 11.2
Date:		

1.

2.

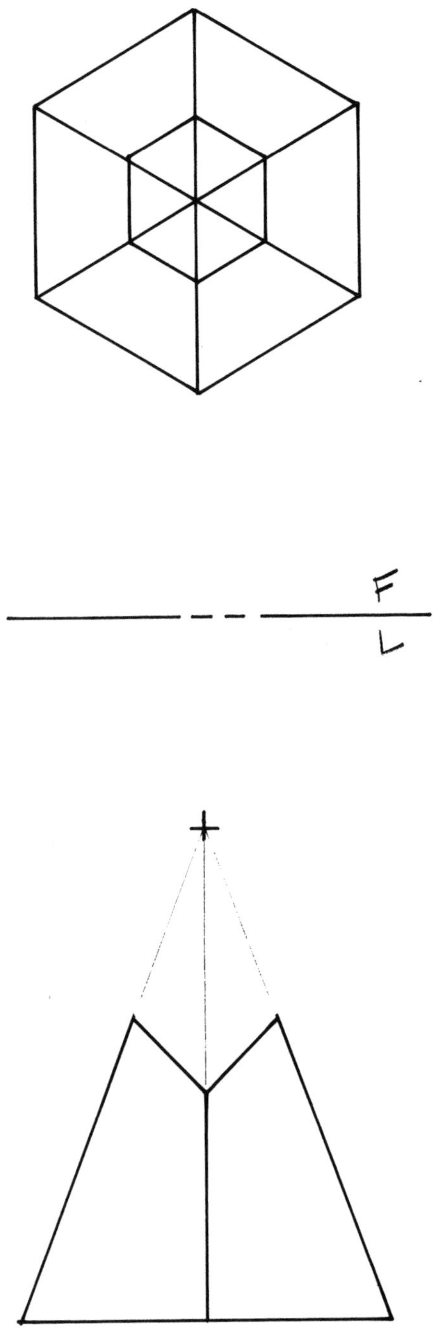

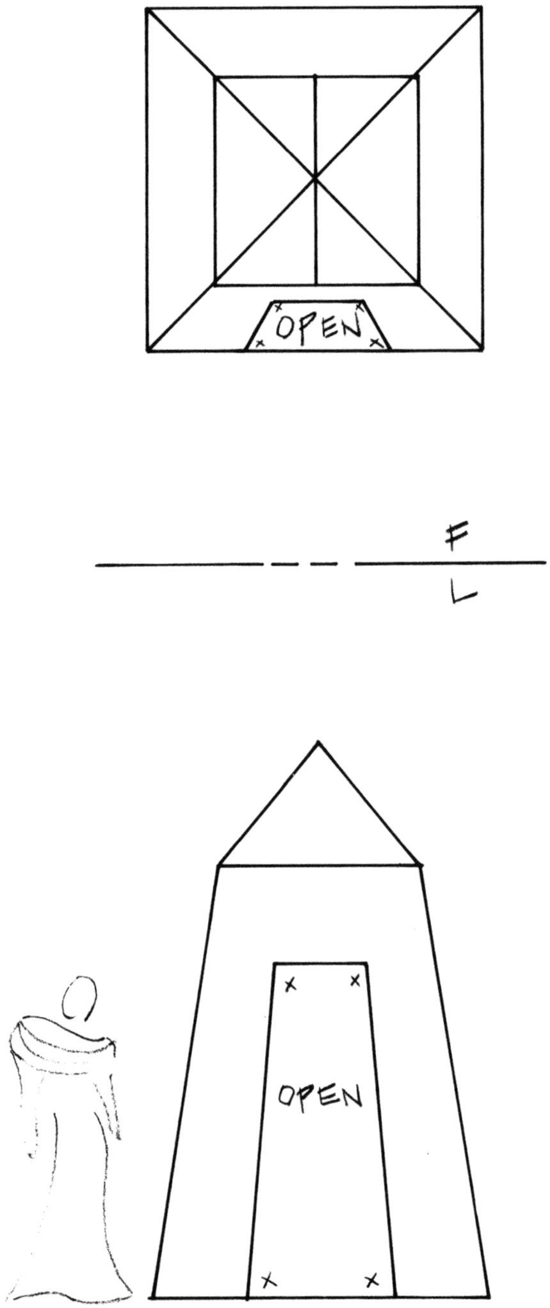

PART THREE

PICTORIAL DRAWINGS

12   Isometric and Oblique

12.1 Pictorials

Many persons not familiar with the conventions of orthographic projection find two-dimensional drafting difficult to understand. To these people, a sketch that shows an object in a more three-dimensional manner is frequently more useful. These so-called three-dimensional drawings are known as pictorials and are divided into two broad categories: those that can be scaled and those that cannot. Chapter 12 discusses those pictorials that can be scaled, and chapter 13 deals with perspective drawings, which, although more true-to-life, cannot readily be scaled.

12.1. Pictorials

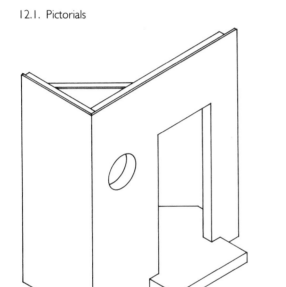

FRONT VIEW
OUTRIGGER ISOMETRIC

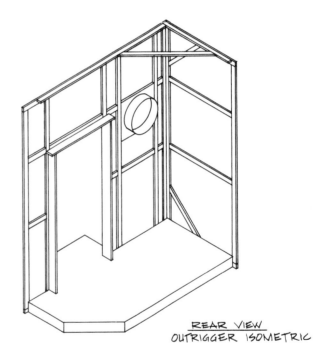

REAR VIEW
OUTRIGGER ISOMETRIC

12.2 Axonometric Drawings

Axonometric drawings provide a projected view in which the three surfaces of a rectilinear object are all inclined to the plane of projection. The projections of the three principal axes may be at any angle to each other than 90°, fitting into one of three principal forms: isometric, dimetric, trimetric. Only the isometric form is discussed in this chapter; however, all axonometric drawings are constructed using the same procedures and principles. All begin by establishing three principal axes.

Isometric: The most popular form of axonometric projection in which the three principal surfaces and axes are equally inclined to the plane of projection

Dimetric: Where two of the three principal surfaces and axes are equally inclined to the plane of projection

Trimetric: Where all three surfaces and axes make different angles with the plane of projection

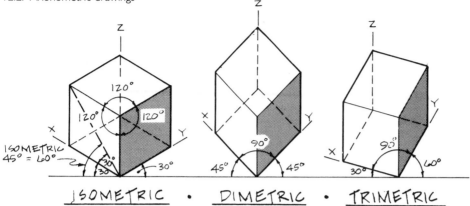

ISOMETRIC • DIMETRIC • TRIMETRIC

CHARACTERISTICS OF AXONOMETRIC DRAWINGS:
1. ALL VERTICAL LINES REMAIN VERTICAL
2. ALL PARALLEL LINES REMAIN PARALLEL
3. ALL LINES PARALLEL TO X,Y, Z AXES ARE DRAWN TO SCALE
4. ALL LINES NOT PARALLEL TO X,Y, Z AXES ARE NOT 'IN SCALE' ¢ ARE KNOWN AS "NON-ISOMETRIC" LINES

12.3 Isometric Drawings

12.3. The isometric cube

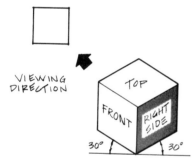

VIEWING DIRECTION

The three principal axes of an isometric drawing are a vertical line for the height dimensions and lines left and right, each at a 30° angle from the horizontal, for the width and the depth. The three faces seen in the isometric view are the same surfaces as would be seen in normal orthographic views: top, front, and side. Figure 12.3 illustrates the corner being viewed, the construction of the isometric axes, and a completed isometric cube.

The drawing of an isometric view can be visualized in one of two ways. In the first approach, the object is mentally treated as a number of sections, each section drawn one at a time in the proper relationship to each other. The second approach treats the object as being encapsulated within a box of the same overall height, width, and depth dimensions as the object. The parts of the box that are not part of the object are removed, leaving only the sections that form the finished object.

12.4. The section and box approaches

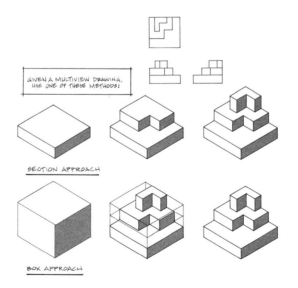

110

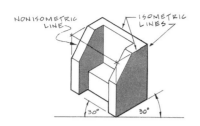

All lines on, or parallel with, the vertical and 30° axes are drawn true length and are known as **isometric lines.** Lines not parallel with the major axes are known as **nonisometric lines.** As the name implies, these lines are not drawn to their true length and therefore cannot be scaled. Nonisometric lines are drawn by locating their end points on isometric lines and connecting the end points with a straight line. **Hidden lines** are seldom used in pictorial drawings since they often only confuse rather than clarify.

12.4 Drawing Isometric Circles and Arcs

A circle drawn on any of the three isometric surfaces has the shape of an ellipse. There are three basic approaches to drawing isometric circles:

1. Use an **ellipse template** created specifically for this purpose. These templates feature 35°16' ellipses, the exact angle an object is tipped forward when drawn in isometric. Like circle templates, each ellipse has center line marks that locate the major and minor axes. The size given on the template indicates the size of the circle being drawn in isometric rather than the major dimensions of the ellipse.

12.6. A 35° 16' ellipse template

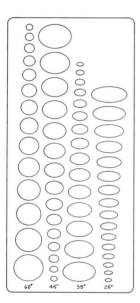

2. Employ a **grid system,** using the following steps:
   a. Draw a circle of the proper radius inscribed in a square.
   b. Overlay the circle with a grid; the tighter the grid, the more accurate the resulting ellipse.
   c. At the desired location on the isometric view, draw the same square and grid, using isometric lines
   d. Identify and transfer the points of tangency from the circle to the isometric grid.
   e. Using an irregular curve, adjustable curve, or working freehand, connect the dots to form the isometric circle.
   f. This system is also the best approach to drawing isometric irregular curves.

3. Construct a **four-center ellipse:**
   a. Draw an isometric square with sides equal to the desired circle diameter; then bisect the four sides, using a 30°–60° triangle, allowing the bisectors to cross.
   b. Using the obtuse-angled (120°) corners as centers, draw arcs opposite the corner, stopping at the points where the center lines intersect the square.
   c. Using points at which the bisecting lines intersect, draw arcs for the acute-angled sides of the ellipse, meeting the first arcs at their common points of tangency.
   d. This same system is used for drawing regular curves and arcs.

12.7. Drawing an ellipse, using a grid

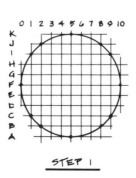

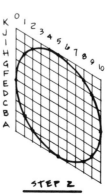

12.8. Drawing an ellipse, using four centers

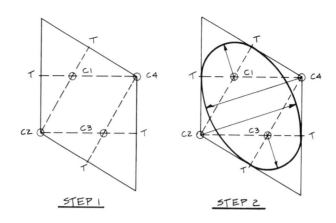

12.5 Isometric Sectioning

When a section view is drawn in isometric, the section lines are drawn at an angle of 60° off the horizontal. In half sections, the section lines are sloped in opposite directions, giving the appearance that they are wrapping around the object.

12.9. An isometric section

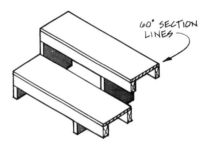

12.6 Dimensioning Isometric Drawings

At times an isometric drawing of a simple object may serve as a working drawing. In these instances, dimensions and specifications are placed directly on the drawing.

The two standard systems of dimensioning, aligned and unidirectional, apply to isometric dimensioning, but in both systems figures are read from the bottom of the drawing. In the aligned system, the extension lines, dimension lines, and lettering are all drawn in the isometric plane of one surface of the object. Lettering guidelines are drawn parallel to the dimension line, with the vertical component of the lettering parallel to the extension lines.

The unidirectional system is the preferred system of dimensioning isometric drawings. In this system, the extension lines and dimension lines are again drawn in the isometric plane. The lettering, however, breaks the convention. Figures are drawn parallel with the vertical axis of the object. In either system, notes are lettered parallel to the bottom of the drawing.

12.10. Aligned and unidirectional dimensioning

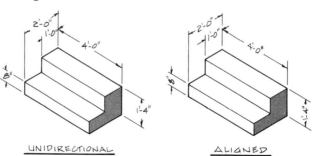

12.7 Oblique Projection

Pictorial drawings that place an object with one side parallel to the viewing plane are known as oblique projections. Typically the surface that is most complex or has the longest dimension faces the front, since this simplifies the drawing problem and produces the least distortion. Like the isometric, oblique projections use three principal axes, corresponding as before to the height, width, and depth of the object. The receding axes may be drawn at any angle, but 30°, 45°, and 60° are chosen frequently, since they are angles that are convenient when using triangles.

12.11. Cavalier and cabinet drawings

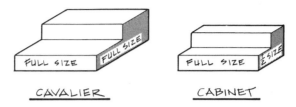

Two types of oblique projection are common: the **cavalier projection**, where all lines parallel with the axes are drawn to their true length; and the **cabinet projection**, where the lines of the receding axes are drawn proportionally. Cabinet projections are normally understood to use a 1–2 ratio, although it is possible to employ a different ratio. Clarity can be aided by further identifying the ratio of the drawing as a 1–2 cabinet drawing (½ size) or a 3–4 cabinet drawing (¾ size). The ratio employed refers to the amount by which the receding dimensions are divided. The front view of a cabinet drawing always remains full size.

Most of the drawing and dimensioning techniques used for isometric drawings apply also to oblique projections. The most notable exception is the construction of curved surfaces on the receding face. Whenever possible the surface of the object having circles or arcs should face the front. When this is not possible, the resulting ellipse can only be drawn using the point-plotting system described earlier.

12.8 Problems

Problem 12.1

Given the orthographic projection of the stair unit (fig. 12.12), develop a fully dimensioned isometric drawing on an A-size sheet.

12.12. Stair multiview drawings for problems 12.1, 12.2

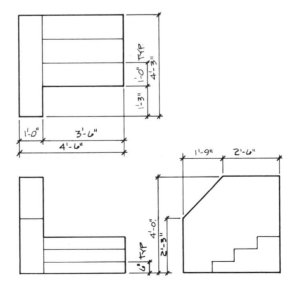

Problem 12.2

Given the same orthographic projection of the stair unit (fig. 12.12), develop a fully dimensioned 1–2 cabinet drawing on an A-size sheet.

12.9 Checkpoints

√ Axonometric drawings project a view in which front, top, and side views are all inclined to the plane of projection.

√ Isometric drawings utilize 30° angles for the receding lines of width and depth.

√ Oblique drawings place one side of an object parallel with the viewing plane and utilize any convenient angle for receding lines.

√ The unidirectional system is preferred when dimensioning isometric and oblique drawings.

13   Mechanical Perspective

13.1 As Seen by the Human Eye

Although a thorough knowledge of perspective is most useful to theatre designers, theatre technicians also need to understand basic principles of perspective, since a significant amount of scenery is constructed in either **true** or **forced** perspective. **Forced perspective** is the term used when the converging lines do not meet at correctly defined vanishing points. Perspective techniques are also commonly used in scene painting.

The perspective form of drawing produces an image that in many ways resembles a photograph. The technique is used by illustrators, designers, and architects as a proposal-making tool. A colored perspective sketch or rendering shows a client precisely how the final product will appear, from a specific location, in advance of construction. Photographs, of course, are not possible, since the object being considered does not yet exist.

13.1. Perspective drawing: The cone of vision

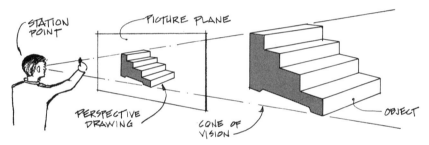

13.2 Definitions

Figure 13.2 illustrates the principal elements of a perspective drawing. Although much of this discussion focuses on stage applications, the principles and elements of perspective drawing are the same whether the drawing is used for theatrical, architectural, and interior design or for other similar purposes.

Picture plane: An imaginary vertical plane of projection, PP

Station point: The position of the observer's eye, SP (also commonly known as OP, observation point)

Horizon line: The edge view of the horizon plane (horizontal), an imaginary reference usually set at the eye level of the observer, HL

Ground line: The edge view of the horizontal ground plane on which the object being drawn will rest, GL

Vanishing point: A point or points on the horizon line where all receding lines (width and depth) converge, VPC (vanishing point center), VPL (vanishing point left), VPR (vanishing point right)

Measuring line: A line dropped perpendicular from the picture plane to the groundline, at which point the height (vertical dimension) of an object is true size and can be scaled; most perspective drawings can have multiple measuring lines, ML1, ML2 (not shown)

13.2. The elements of a perspective
drawing

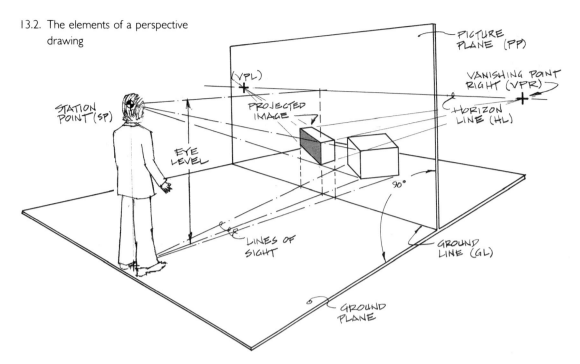

13.3 Variables within the Perspective Drawing

Although there are typical placements for the various points and planes previously defined, each can be varied resulting in a different perspective view. Extreme changes in station point location can result in significant distortion of the object being drawn. Subtle changes in location, however, can result in distortions useful for stage purposes, although given the wide range of theatrical styles and approaches, it is conceivable that almost every distortion could be useful regardless of how extreme it might be.

Location of the Station Point

The station point (SP) is usually located along the center line of the proscenium arch (or set) and at a distance far enough back so that the cone of vision from the observer's eye to the extreme edges of the proscenium (or set) is approximately 30°. An acceptable range in the angle of the cone of vision is considered to be 30° to 60°. Beyond 60° the image produced will contain considerable distortion; much less than 30°, the object becomes flat and uninteresting. Thus 30° is an ideal choice, since the distance from the proscenium to the SP is easily determined using the 30°– 60° triangle. Shifting the SP to the left or right of center will, of course, produce an image altogether different. A similar effect can be achieved by modifying the angle of the object as seen in figure 13.4.

13.3. Moving the station point alters the cone of vision

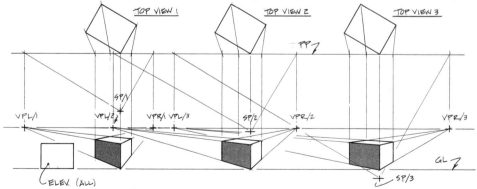

13.4. Orientation of object to picture plane

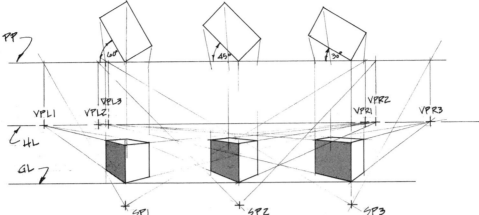

Location of the Picture Plane

The picture plane (PP) is usually the plaster line or a similar datum line near and parallel to the proscenium arch. If the object being drawn is located on the picture plane, it is true size and shape. As the object is moved behind the PP (upstage), the object will appear to diminish in size; if placed in front of the PP (downstage), the object will appear to be larger than true size.

13.5. Moving the picture plane alters the apparent size of an object

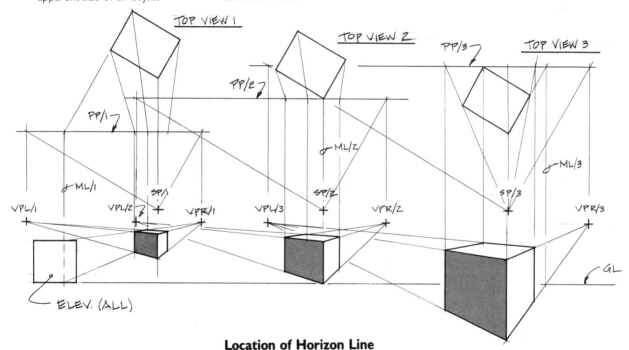

Location of Horizon Line

The horizon line (HL) represents the curvature of the earth and is drawn at the eye level of the observer, taken relative to the groundline. The groundline is taken as being stage level. The normal horizon line is set at a distance of 5'-0" to 6'-0" above the groundline. If the object is placed above the horizon line, it is above the level of the eye (SP) and will appear as seen from below. Likewise, if the object is below the horizon, it will appear as seen from above. Object lines located on the horizon line are parallel to the groundline.

13.6. Moving the horizon line gives either a bird's-eye or a worm's-eye view

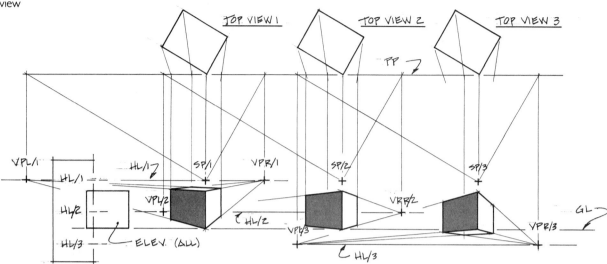

13.4 Types of Perspective

13.7. The three types of perspective

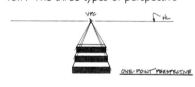

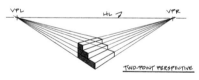

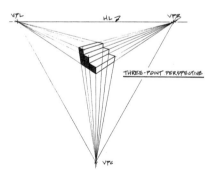

13.5 Circles in Perspective

One-Point (Parallel) Perspective
This type of perspective is drawn with one surface of the object parallel to the picture plane and is similar to an oblique drawing, except that all receding lines converge at one point on the horizon. The view is easiest to draw if the front surface is located directly on the picture plane, allowing that surface to be drawn true size and shape.

Two-Point (Angular) Perspective
Placing the object to be drawn so that the depth and width surfaces are not parallel with the plaster line will produce a two-point perspective drawing. This type of drawing is similar to axonometric drawings, except that all receding lines converge to two vanishing points located on the horizon. Vertical (height) dimensions remain parallel with the picture plane; the lines forming the width and depth recede.

Three-Point Perspective
In three-point perspective, the object is placed so that no principal surfaces are parallel to the picture plane. The result is that each of the three principal surfaces will have a separate vanishing point. Consequently all lines—height, width, and depth—recede from the picture plane, leaving no lines vertical. This type of perspective drawing is seldom used in theatre work, except perhaps in those situations that call for heightened or forced perspective. The application of three-point perspective can enhance a sense of distance or absurdity.

If a circle is parallel to the PP, its perspective is a circle. If the circle is inclined to the PP, its perspective may be any one of the conic sections, but in most cases an ellipse. The surface containing the circle is drawn as a perspective square, grided, points plotted, and the points joined by using a flexible curve, irregular curve, or freehand. Arcs are handled in the same manner.

13.8. Circles in perspective

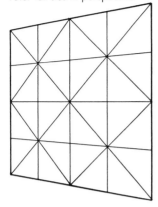 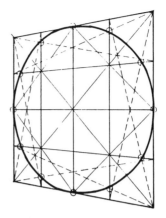

STEP 1: DIVIDE A PERSPEC-
TIVE SQUARE INTO 16 PARTS
USING DIAGONALS.

STEP 2: DRAW DASH LINE
DIAGONALS. ENCIRCLED IN-
TERSECTIONS FORM CIRCLE.

STEP 3: CONNECT POINTS
TO DRAW AN APPROXIMATE
PERSPECTIVE CIRCLE.

13.6 Guidelines for Creating a Simple Perspective Drawing

The following set of directions will assist the beginner in developing a basic mechanical perspective drawing of a simple geometric shape. Follow along with a pencil in hand and use this opportunity to be reintroduced to the various elements of a two-point perspective drawing.

1. Using a "to scale" floor plan of the stage as an underlay, tape down a sheet of tracing paper large enough to cover the ground plan and provide an equal amount of paper below. Draw the plaster line and label it PP (picture plane).
2. Extend the center line of the stage into the auditorium space, a distance approximately twice the width of the proscenium opening.
3. Place the 30° tip of the 30°–60° triangle along the center line and slide it along the line until the two sides of the triangle touch the extreme edges of the PP/plaster line. Mark the location of the 30° angle along the centerline as SP (station point).

13.9a. Establishing the cone of vision (PP and SP)

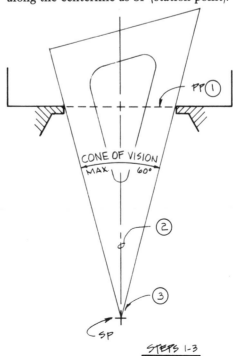

4. Position the object to be viewed on the ground plan of the stage in its playing position.
5. Slightly above the SP, draw a horizontal line, parallel with the PP; label it GL (groundline).
6. Draw a second horizontal line approximately 5'-0" to 6'-0" in scale above the GL; label it HL (horizon line).
7. Using the GL as the base line, construct either an elevation or measurement line, in scale, containing all the heights of the object(s) to be drawn. The extreme right side of the drawing beyond the proscenium opening is a useful location for this information.

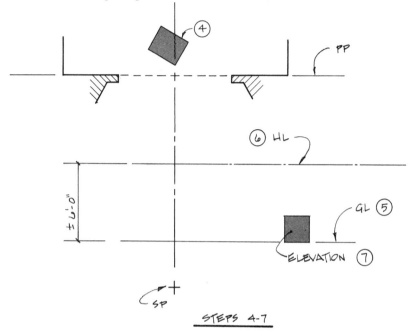

13.9b. Establishing the horizon line (HL)

8. Locate the right vanishing point by drawing a line that is parallel to the right side of the object and that passes through the SP and intersects the PP. At the point of intersection with PP, drop a perpendicular to the HL; mark this intersection as VPR. Reverse and repeat this procedure to find VPL. Clearly mark and label both vanishing points.
9. Locate ML1 (measuring line 1). If the object touches the PP, the point of intersection can serve as the ML. If the object is entirely behind the PP, extend one side until it touches the PP. For either case, drop a perpendicular to the GL to form the ML.
10. Using a straightedge, draw a construction line from each corner of the object to the SP. Normal practice is to actually draw the lines only between the corners and the PP. Label each intersection clearly, so it can be readily identified during the drawing of the perspective.

At this point, all the preparation steps have been completed; now the actual perspective drawing can be produced. As with all other types of line drawings, the simple rule is, First, determine the overall size of the object, then begin to fill in the interior details.

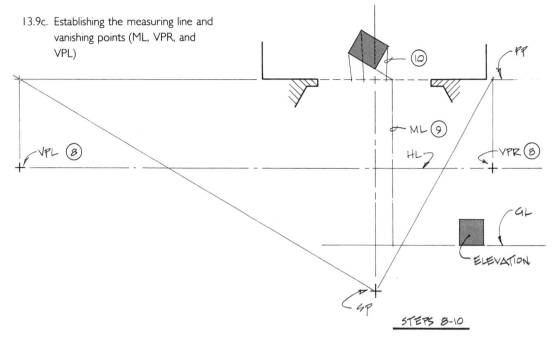

13.9c. Establishing the measuring line and vanishing points (ML, VPR, and VPL)

11. Assuming that the object does not touch the PP, connect the top and bottom points on the ML to the VP of the surface that was extended to created the ML.
12. Drop perpendiculars from the two corners forming the surface to be drawn. Heavy up the top and bottom lines. This is the surface as seen in perspective.
13. Ignore the ML, and connect the top and bottom points of the near edge of the surface to the opposite VP. Drop a perpendicular from the PP to the GL to form the upstage edge of this surface.
14. Because the HL is above the top surface of the object, it is possible to see the top. To draw it, connect the top corners to the appropriate VP. Heavy up all lines. The object is now complete.

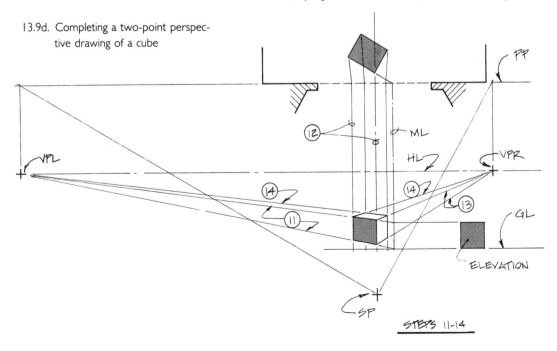

13.9d. Completing a two-point perspective drawing of a cube

The directions above are complete to the extent that they cover only simple shapes. The object we chose to draw was a simple cube; had there been more objects, each arranged in a different orientation to the PP, with none of their surfaces parallel, the problem would have been a good deal more involved.

13.7 Basic Rules of Perspective

1. All parallel lines that are not parallel to the picture plane (PP) vanish to a single point. If these lines are parallel to the ground plane, the vanishing point will be on the horizon.
2. Each surface has its own vanishing point; two-point perspective drawings may have many more than two vanishing points. Each object will have its own VPR and VPL, determined in a manner exactly as described above.
3. Vertical lines that are parallel to the picture plane (PP) remain parallel and do not converge toward a vanishing point (the exception is three-point perspective).
4. Choose a ML that contains as much information as possible. Failure to do this will mean an almost never-ending series of vanishing points back and forth until you reach the proper plane. When the drawing has many planes of depth, it is usually easier to use a corresponding number of vanishing points.
5. Use the opportunity of multiple MLs to check the accuracy of your drawing. The same solution should be reached using alternative approaches.

13.8 Perspective Aids

Creating a drawing by using mechanical perspective can be laborious and time-consuming, as seen from the described process. For most artists, once the theories of mechanical perspective have been mastered, it is time to look for alternative methods. Given the space and focus limitations of this text, only the subject of perspective grids is discussed. Beyond this, there exist a variety of special tools and equipment designed specifically to create perspective drawings. Computer software is by far the most sophisticated, although other less costly tools are available. By a wide margin the perspective grid is the most popular choice of theatre artists. Two types of grids are common:

Commercial grids: Standardized perspective grids can be purchased for use as underlays or in preprinted nonreproducible blue on drawing media. Such grids of course do not allow for the variables discussed earlier and in this sense are limiting.

Homemade grids: Drafters can construct a perspective grid specific to a particular theatre space and incorporate the cone of vision and horizon line of choice. Typically, designers make identical grids in both ¼" or ½" scale. The homemade version of perspective grid will provide the same underlay information as the standardized ones, and perhaps more.

For both systems the desired sketch is developed through the process of interpolation. Some lines will fall directly on the lines of the grid; the majority will be approximated, but the grid provides a degree of accuracy impossible for most people to achieve drawing freehand. For many users, the perspective grid is a significant drawing aid, allowing them to work quickly and accurately with sufficient time left to perhaps develop alternative sketches. A system for developing a perspective grid is shown in figure 13.11.

13.10. A commercially available perspective grid. Courtesy Graphicraft

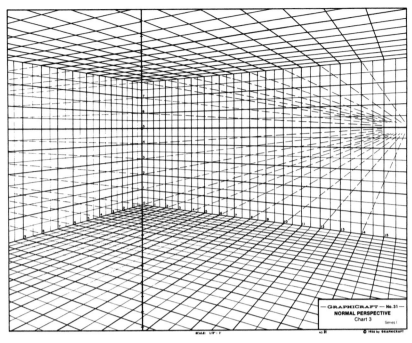

13.11. Developing a perspective grid

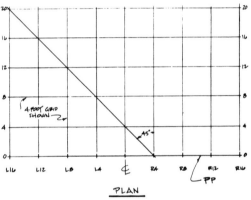

PLAN

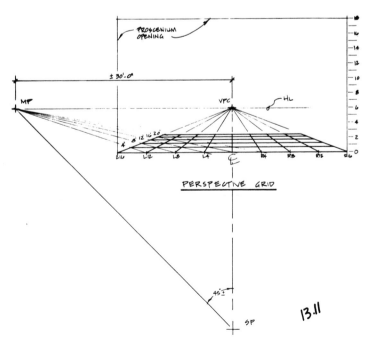

PERSPECTIVE GRID

13.11

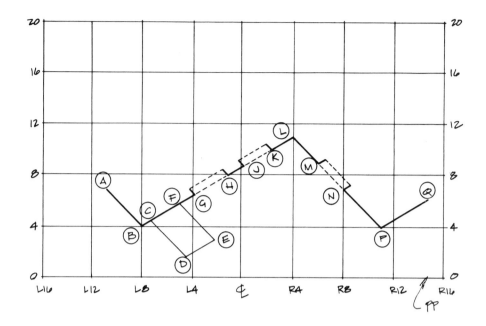

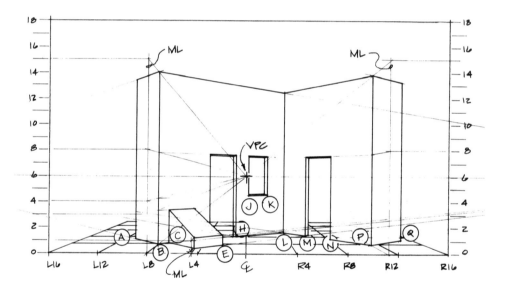

13.9 Less Well Known Approaches to Perspective

The techniques discussed in this chapter have been traditional ones. They are systems that are not particularly easy to grasp, are tedious to use, and are fraught with the opportunity for error. Users of perspective are continually searching for simplified methods. For some the computer has been the solution. For those, however, who do not yet have access to three-dimensional CADD software, there are yet some other interesting and useful approaches.

Paul S. Hoffman has refined a mathematical approach to perspective rendering.[1] His system is based on a centuries-old awareness that there ex-

[1]Paul S. Hoffman, "Perspective Rendering by Hand-Held Calculator," *Theatre Design and Technology* (Winter 1978): 5–12. See also Hoffman, "Deriving Precise Measurements from Scenic Sketches," *Theatre Design and Technology* (Summer 1979): 4–8.

ists a geometric relationship between the object viewed and its perspective sketch. The basis of this procedure is similar triangles, as shown in figure 13.13. The system requires paper no larger than the size needed for the finished drawing, an engineer's scale, a groundplan of the set and either an elevation of a list of the unit heights. A distinct advantage of this system is that it works in both directions. Not only can the drafter use it to develop a perspective sketch, but the system works conversely to derive precise measurements from a sketch to aid in preparation of the corresponding ground plan and elevation.

13.13. Perspective using a calculator. Courtesy Paul S. Hoffman

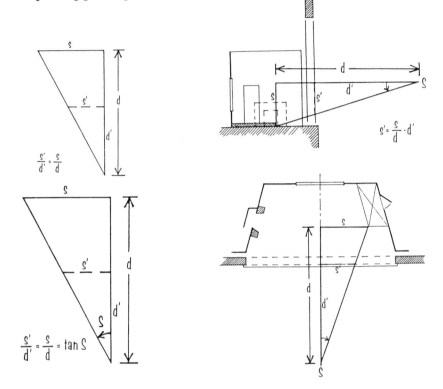

The dilemma of most scene designers when using perspective is the multiple axes needed to achieve the correct proportions of the set walls and furnishings. Tim Palkovic describes the use of an eleven-point perspective technique[2] that makes it possible to approximate these orientations with a significant degree of accuracy. Too lengthy for discussion here, Palkovic's system offers yet another resource to designers looking for a quick non-CADD procedure.

The techniques mentioned above, as well as the more traditional methods, are also useful when employing forced perspective, a modification of the rules of perspective often used on the stage. Figure 13.14 shows an application of forced perspective in foreshortening a three-dimensional set piece.

13.10 Problems

Worksheet 13.1
Given the picture plane (PP), station point (SP), groundline (GL), vanishing points left and right (VPL, VPR), and the object to be drawn, develop the resulting perspective drawing.

[2]Tim Palkovic, "Eleven Point or Six Axis Perspective," *Theatre Design and Technology* (Fall 1984): 5–11.

13.14. Creating forced perspective for the stage

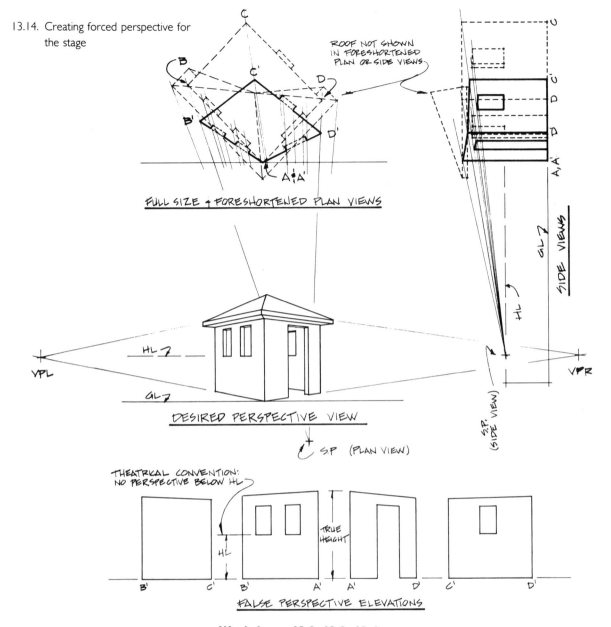

FULL SIZE & FORESHORTENED PLAN VIEWS

ROOF NOT SHOWN IN FORESHORTENED PLAN OR SIDE VIEWS

SIDE VIEWS

DESIRED PERSPECTIVE VIEW

S.P. (PLAN VIEW)

S.P. (SIDE VIEW)

THEATRICAL CONVENTION: NO PERSPECTIVE BELOW HL

TRUE HEIGHT

FALSE PERSPECTIVE ELEVATIONS

Worksheets 13.2, 13.3, 13.4

Given three copies of a small stage set, develop a two-point perspective drawing of each. Locate each drawing in the space below the plan view and above the station point. Although the ground plan and partial section remain the same in each version, the location of the picture plane and station point change, resulting in three sketches of differing sizes and viewing angles.

13.10 Checkpoints

√ Perspective drawings produce an image that resembles a photograph and shows how a design will look from a specific location when realized.

√ Changes in the location of the various points necessary for the construction of a perspective drawing can result in useful distortions for theatre design.

√ The step-by-step process of developing a perspective drawing may be aided through the use of a commercial or homemade grid.

Name:	MECHANICAL PERSPECTIVE	Worksheet 13.1
Date:		

TOP VIEW, COLUMN 3
TOP VIEW, COLUMN 2
TOP VIEW, COLUMN 1
PICTURE PLANE
VPL + VPL ARE THE SAME FOR ALL BLOCKS. EACH ROW HAS A DIFFERENT MEASURING LINE; INDICATED AS 'ML'. DRAW ONLY ROWS 1-3 FOR COLUMN 1; DRAW ROWS 1-4 FOR COLUMNS 2&3
ML, ROW 4
ML, ROW 3
ML, ROW 2
SP
ML, ROW 1
ELEV.
VPR
GL, ROW 2
VPL

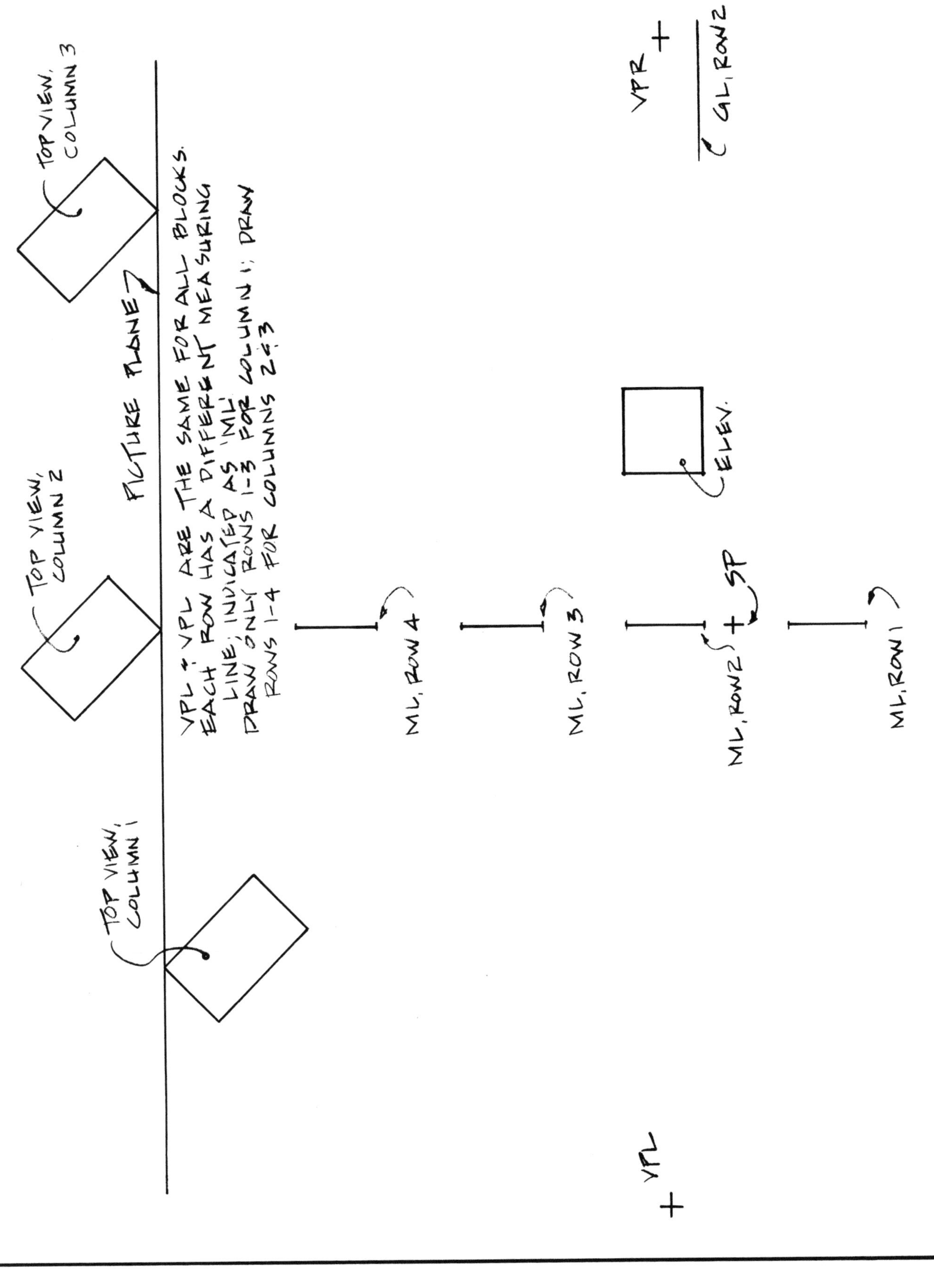

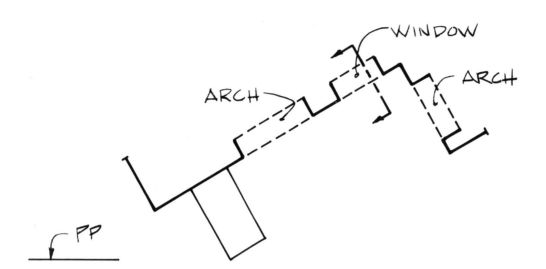

PP

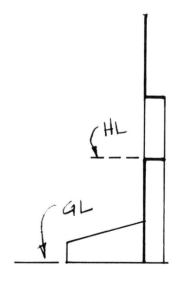

+ S.P.

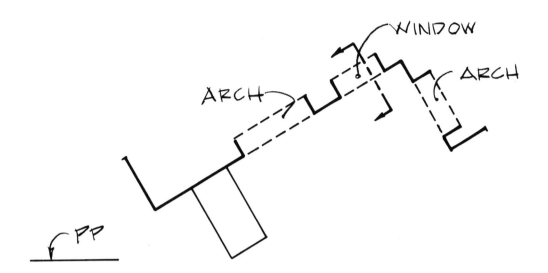

ARCH

WINDOW

ARCH

PP

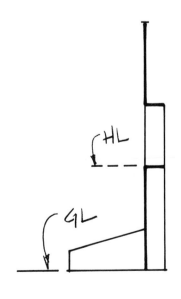

HL

GL

+ S.P.

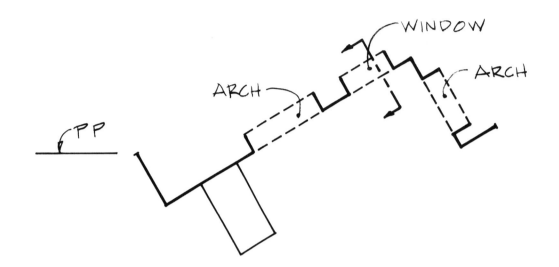

WINDOW

ARCH

ARCH

PP

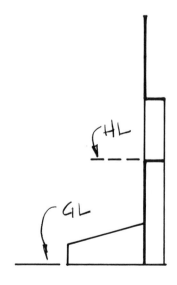

HL

GL

+ SP

PART FOUR

SPECIALIZED TECHNIQUES

14   Transfer and Enlargement

14.1 Tools for the Theatre Researcher

Because theatre is an art form that draws heavily upon historical research, theatrical designers and technicians are often called upon to enlarge, transfer, or modify drawings and other visual images. Often the scale of the material chosen needs modification; in almost every instance, the information needs to be transferred from one medium to another. To fully realize the designer's artistic vision, transfers are used extensively in the development of original images, design elevations, and in the construction and painting phases of a production.

Transfer and enlargement needs may be met by a variety of techniques. Some of the more common methods are discussed in this chapter. Since no single technique is convenient or suitable for all circumstances, drafters should be familiar with several options. The choice of which transfer and enlargement method to use should be based upon a) the nature and quality of the original image; b) the resources at hand, including time, equipment, and talent; and c) the finished product needed.

14.2 Techniques That Transfer Only

The following techniques permit the transfer of an object from one location or medium to another but will produce a final image of the same dimensions as the original.

Triangulation
The basics of triangulation were covered earlier in chapter 5 (geometric construction) but are included here again as a refresher. Triangulation is a method that can be used to transfer any polygon. The given polygon is simply divided into triangles, and then each component triangle is transferred as shown in figure 14.1.

14.1. Triangulation

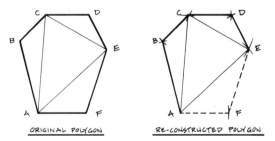

ORIGINAL POLYGON   RE-CONSTRUCTED POLYGON

Given triangle ABC, set off any side, such as AB, in the new location. With the ends of line AB as centers and the length of the other sides (AC and BC) of the given triangle as radii, strike two arcs to intersect at C. Join C to A and B to complete the triangle.

Rectangular Transfer
Any given polygon can be inscribed within a rectangle. Once the original material is enclosed, draw an identical rectangle in a new location. Lo-

cate the vertexes of the polygon by marking points A, B, C, etc., at the points they intersect the original rectangle. Next use a divider, compass, tick strip, or scale ruler to transfer these intersections to the new rectangle. Join the points to complete the figure.

14.2. Rectangular transfer

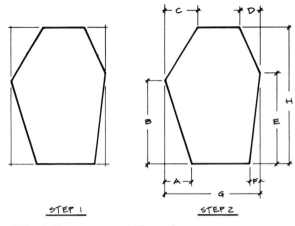

Offset Measurement Transfer

Offset measurements are useful when it is necessary to exactly transfer free curves. The figure to be transferred is enclosed in a rectangle. The sides of the enclosing rectangle are then used as reference for locating points along the curve. A congruent rectangle is drawn in the new location and the reference points are transferred. The transferred points are then joined either freehand or with the help of irregular curves.

14.3. Offset measurement transfer

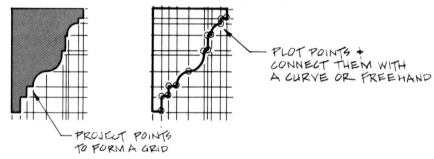

Radial Arc

For the direct transfer of a given object, use a compass to develop intersecting points. Establish a base line upon which the center points of the arcs are marked. The compass is then used to transfer corners of the object by using intersecting arcs (triangulation again). This method is conceptually identical to the rectangular transfer method but does not require the use of T-square and triangles.

14.4. Radial arc transfer

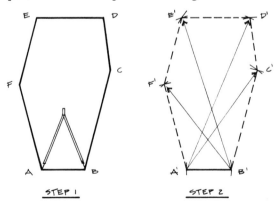

Prick-Point Freehand Method

Place a sheet of tracing paper over the drawing to be transferred. Use a sharp pencil to make a small dot directly over each important point on the drawing. (Encircle each dot so as not to lose it.) Remove the paper and position it over the new location. Using a needlepoint, such as a compass point, prick each dot. When finished, remove the tracing and connect the resulting points with a pencil to complete a duplicate image. This system, although very low-tech, is quite useful in freehand sketching.

14.5. Prick-point transfer

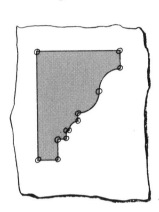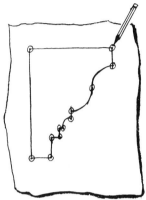

For circles, only the center and one point on the circumference are necessary to transfer the information, since a compass may then be used to complete the drawing. A freehand curve is transferred by selecting as many points as desired.

Tracing Methods

Place a sheet of tracing paper over the original and a make a line tracing of the image, using a soft-lead pencil. Reposition the finished tracing under drafting paper and make another tracing to complete the transfer.

If the object to be transferred is symmetrical, the tracing can be placed face down on top of drafting paper and the lines burnished onto the new surface by rubbing a pencil over the back of the traced lines. A faint graphite image will result that should then be darkened to complete the transfer. This technique works well for quick transfers in a reverse and repeat situation.

14.6. Tracing transfer

14.3 Manual Transfer and Enlargement Techniques

Radial Line

This technique involves the drawing of radial lines from one corner of a rectangle that fully encloses the object to be reduced or enlarged. Figure 14.7 illustrates a very simple application in the enlargement of a rectangle. More complex shapes may be reduced or enlarged using this same basic technique. Place the original drawing underneath a sheet of tracing paper, then inscribe the object to be enlarged within a rectangle. Next draw a rectangle of the size desired for the finished item. Project radial lines to the profile of the new rectangle.

Only points that are located on the enclosing rectangle of the original can be accurately projected to the enclosing rectangle of the enlargement or reduction. All interior points must be projected, first, to points on the original rectangle and, then, to the respective locations on the enlarged (or reduced) rectangle.

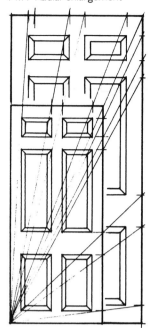

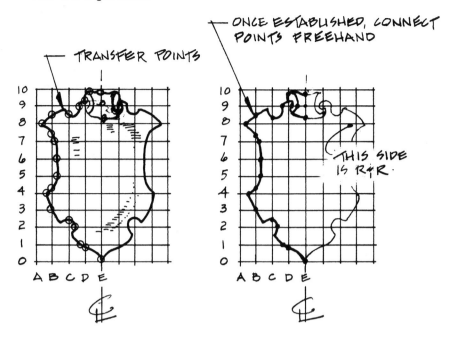

Grid-to-Grid Transfers

For complex transfers, a superimposed grid is often used. Begin by drawing a grid of an appropriate size over the original to be transferred. Then draw a grid of equal-sized squares at the new location. Transfer the points of intersection by inspection, and complete the transfer by connecting the dots. To facilitate finding the proper location, it is suggested to label one set of lines with numbers and the other set with the alphabet. Using this system the intersections can be easily identified as A3, B7, C9, etc.

This method is very valuable for the transfer of scaled designs, from the painter's elevations to full-scale scenery. The original grid is drawn in scale and the transfer grid is drawn full size. The result is an accurate transfer of details to the larger format. Should one or two squares need additional points of intersection to transfer complex details, add diagonals or fill in the area with another grid using smaller squares.

Tick Strip or Unit Card

A sectioned tick strip can be used to establish and maintain accurate proportional relationships (fig. 14.9).

14.9. Using a tick strip

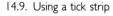

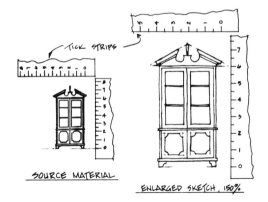

SOURCE MATERIAL

ENLARGED SKETCH, 150%

14.4 Machine-aided Transfer and Enlargements

Projection Transfers

Projection equipment is probably now more commonly used for the successful transfer and enlargement of designs than any of the graphic methods discussed above. Although accuracy is not always assured, proportions are nearly always more true. Several major types of equipment are used. An **opaque projector** accepts opaque media and projects it onto any surface. Standard **35-mm photographic slides** may be taken, developed, and then projected onto work surfaces. **Transparencies** may be made from design originals by using a photoduplication machine. These may then be projected with an **overhead projector.** All three methods work well, but all require a room large enough for appropriate throw distances as well as a darkened environment. These space and light requirements limit their practical use in some situations.

Photoduplication

Machines that enlarge and reduce original material at the touch of a button have revolutionized the design and graphic communication worlds. Original material of practically any size (the full range of paper sizes A to E) may be made larger or smaller depending on application requirements. With practice, accurate full-scale patterns may be developed from even the smallest original. Used as an intermediate step, the photocopy machine can prepare transparencies and opaque media for later projection. Standard reduction and enlargement percentages are shown in figure 14.10.

14.10. Photocopying ratios

Computer-aided Graphics

With the aid of digitizers and optic scanners, graphic media may now be transformed into electronic media and manipulated. Image size, shape, location, and density are just a few of the elements that can be modified. Once in the desired configuration, the new image can be retrieved and printed in either an opaque or transparent medium. At this point it could stand alone or be used as the source material for one of the projection systems discussed above. Chapter 17 is devoted to the subject of CADD systems.

14.5 Problems

Problem 14.1

Given the drawing of the door shown in figure 14.11, use one of the drawing methods discussed in this chapter to enlarge its height to 7'-6" in

14.11. Enlarging a door, problem 14.1

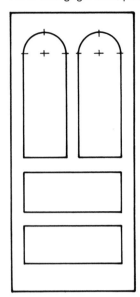

½" scale. Show all construction lines and heavy up the final outline. Include a title block in the bottom-right corner. Use an A-size sheet.

Problem 14.2
Given the cornice molding shown in figure 14.12, use one of the drawing methods discussed in this chapter to enlarge it to a piece that is three times the given height by 7" wide. Show profiles at each end and show all construction lines. Include a title block in the bottom-right corner. Use an A-size sheet.

14.12. Enlarging a cornice, problem 14.2

14.6 Checkpoints

√ Transfer and enlargement techniques are used in developing and transferring images for theatre use from outside sources.

√ A variety of methods are available, ranging from low- to high-tech; choose the method that best suits the resources available.

√ Transfer and enlarging techniques are useful both at the drafting table and in the scenic studio.

15   **Sketching**

15.1 Sketching

Freehand sketching, although generally not associated with mechanical drafting, is a significant and often vital part of the drafting process. Sketching provides the freedom necessary to express less than fully developed thoughts. When these fragile thoughts are sketched out and become a refined idea or solution, **ideation** has taken place. Ideation is the process that commits thoughts to paper and allows for their refinement and clarification. Design and technical solutions that are arrived at through ideation greatly improve the quality of final drawings.

The freedom of the sketch helps overcome our fear of the blank piece of drawing paper taped down in front of us and allows us to quickly solve problems. Sketches can be either accurate representations of objects or conceptual abstractions. Both enhance the thought process and save time at the drafting table. By "working the problems out on paper" in the free environment of sketching, one is not confined by convention nor slowed down by proper tool use.

Sketches are also used to explain thoughts to other people. A quick sketch of a design or technical solution provides a common frame of reference and helps everyone involved to visualize and, it is hoped, to understand the desired effect. Sketching improves visual thinking ability: mentally seeing problems and solutions in three-dimensional form. Visual thinking is the tool by which great designers are made.

15.2 Bubble Diagrams

Sketching should not be limited to drawing realistic objects. Sketching is used very effectively to express abstract concepts and relationships. The bubble diagram is a valuable conceptual tool and is useful in defining problems. Bubble diagrams are used by architects in planning the relationships between rooms of a building in the programming phase of construction. These simple sketches serve as a foundation for the layout of facilities within a building footprint.

15.1. A bubble diagram

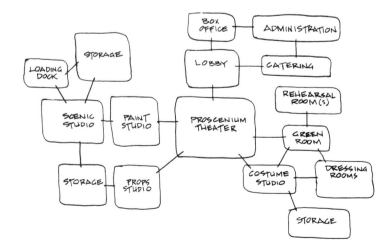

139

15.3 Using Geometric Shapes

The keys to sketching an object accurately are proper line technique and maintaining proportion throughout your sketch. When sketching a view (or views) of an object, first lightly sketch the overall size as a rectangle or square. Break objects down into simple geometric shapes: squares, rectangles, triangle, and circles. Combine these basic shapes until the outline of the object is established. The detail lines of the shape can now be added. Finally, heavy up the final outline and details necessary to portray the object.

15.2. Block sketching

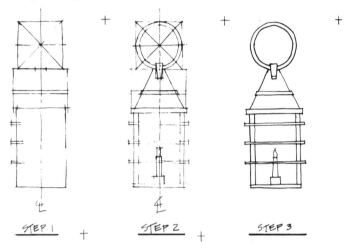

STEP 1   STEP 2   STEP 3

15.4 Line Technique

Straight Line

Horizontal lines are drawn working from left to right; vertical lines are best drawn with a downward stroke. Use a fairly soft lead—HB, F, or H. Sketched lines are made up of a series of short segments approximately 1″ in length. Greater line quality control is obtained through the use of these shorter segments. When drawing inclined straight lines, it may be helpful to shift the paper slightly to compensate for the desired angle.

Long straight lines are some of the most difficult lines to sketch. This task may be made easier by marking the ends of the line with light dots. Working lightly, move the pencil back and forth between the dots in long sweeps, constantly eyeing the dot toward which the pencil is moving. Once the path of the line is lightly established between the two dots, the final line may be darkened using short, crisp strokes.

15.3. Sketching straight lines

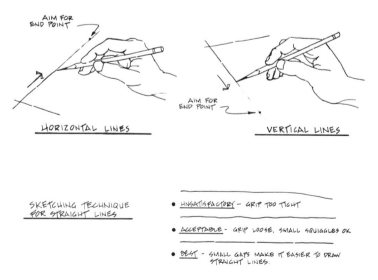

HORIZONTAL LINES   VERTICAL LINES

SKETCHING TECHNIQUE FOR STRAIGHT LINES

- UNSATISFACTORY – GRIP TOO TIGHT
- ACCEPTABLE – GRIP LOOSE, SMALL SQUIGGLES OK
- BEST – SMALL GAPS MAKE IT EASIER TO DRAW STRAIGHT LINES.

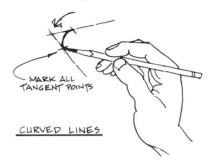

15.4. Sketching small curves

MARK ALL TANGENT POINTS

CURVED LINES

Curved Lines

Small circles and arcs can be easily sketched using one or two strokes, but large circles require more preparation.

One method is to first lightly sketch a square that completely encloses the circle. Midpoints of the side are then marked as points of tangency. Next, diagonals are drawn from the corners of the square and points of intersection are drawn. Finally the points of intersection and tangency are connected with smooth arcs forming the completed circle.

Another method that works especially well for large circles is the use of a tick strip. The center point of the circle is established and a tick strip is marked with the approximate radius of the circle. The strip is then used to mark from center as many points as desired. The points are connected with arcs to form the completed circle.

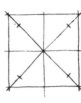

USING A SQUARE

15.5. Sketching large curves by using a square or a tick strip

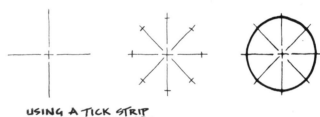

USING A TICK STRIP

Methods of sketching arcs are adaptations of those used for sketching circles. In general, arcs are more easily sketched with the hand and pencil on the concave side of the curve. In sketching tangent arcs, always keep in mind actual geometric construction practices and carefully approximate all points of tangency.

15.5 Maintaining Proportion

The most important rule in freehand sketching is to keep the sketch in proportion. The relative proportions of the height to the width must first be carefully established. From this first proportional relationship all other lines are based. The more sketching you do the easier this will become, but there are some techniques that may aid the process.

Pencil Comparison

Proportional relationships may be established by using a pencil as a unit of measure. This technique is useful when sketching large objects. Holding the pencil at arms length, by inspection determine how many pencil units tall something is, compared to how many units wide. This relationship may then be transferred to established units on your drawing papers and relative proportions maintained.

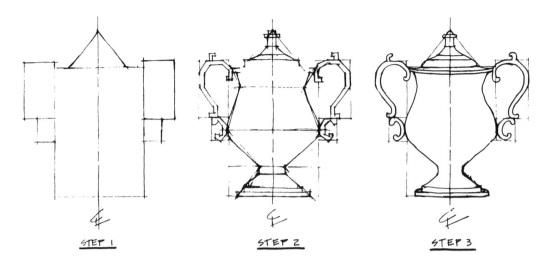

STEP 1   STEP 2   STEP 3

15.6. Blocking in irregular shapes

The Blocking-in Method

This technique is preferred when sketching irregular shapes. The steps for blocking in and completing the sketch of an irregular object are demonstrated in figure 15.6. As always, attention is first given to establishing the overall proportions of height and width. Next the general size and direction of flow of the curved shapes are established. Finally the lines are darkened to form the completed sketch.

Graph Paper

Graph paper can be a real aid to sketching, as the paper is already divided into defined units. Ratios can more easily be maintained, and the graph lines serve as guides for straight lines. A variety of commercial graph paper is available with many different grid sizes. Sketching may be done directly on the paper, or an overlay sheet may be placed on top of the graph paper. A manila folder filled with an assortment of graph paper samples is a handy tool to have in your drafting studio.

15.6 Rendering Techniques

Burnishing

Burnishing cards have a raised texture that is transferred to a drawing by placing the card under the drawing and rubbing, or "burnishing," over the surface with the side of your pencil. These cards are sold in a variety of textures and patterns that can be used rapidly to add considerable detail to drawings. Although rarely used in construction or shop drawings, burnishing cards can greatly enhance design drawings and sketches.

Shading

Subtle changes in elevation, positive-versus-negative space, and curved surfaces are sometimes difficult to draw in the two-dimensional media of drafting. One technique used to clarify these difficult-to-draw situations is shading. Shading gives life to a drawing and provides very valuable information to the reader. Shading is commonly done on the back side of a drawing, so as not to interfere with or muddy the lines drawn on the top side. A dull, soft-lead pencil held at a slight angle to the paper is rubbed lightly over the area to be shaded. Excess lead is erased from unwanted areas with an eraser and a shield. A kneaded eraser also works well for picking up the excess graphite left on the drawing.

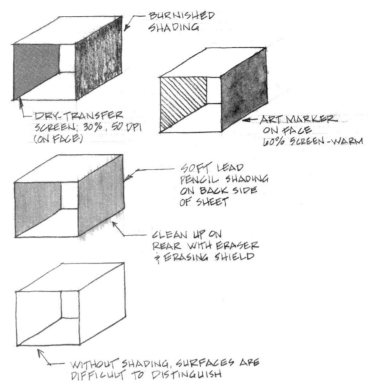

- BURNISHED SHADING
- DRY-TRANSFER SCREEN; 30%, 50 DPI (ON FACE)
- ART MARKER ON FACE 60% SCREEN - WARM
- SOFT LEAD PENCIL SHADING ON BACK SIDE OF SHEET
- CLEAN UP ON REAR WITH ERASER & ERASING SHIELD
- WITHOUT SHADING, SURFACES ARE DIFFICULT TO DISTINGUISH

15.7 Problems

15.8. Geometric isometrics, problem 15.1

Problem 15.1

Given the isometric drawings of some geometric shapes in figure 15.8, sketch three views of each object, using ¼" graph paper. Allow two grid spaces between views and a minimum of four spaces between objects.

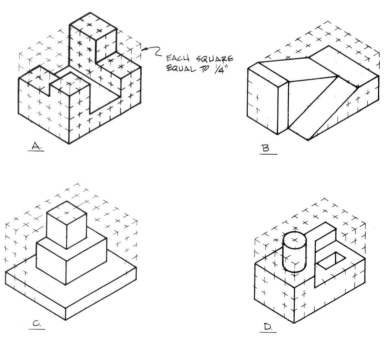

EACH SQUARE EQUAL TO ¼"

A.

B.

C.

D.

Problem 15.2

Given the isometric drawings of furniture in figure 15.9, sketch three views of each object, using ¼″ graph paper provided. Allow two grid spaces between views and a minimum of four spaces between objects.

15.9. Furniture isometrics, problem 15.2

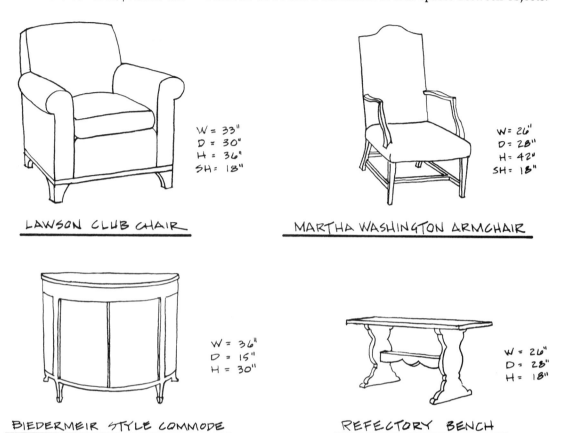

W = 33″
D = 30″
H = 36″
SH = 18″

LAWSON CLUB CHAIR

W = 26″
D = 28″
H = 42″
SH = 18″

MARTHA WASHINGTON ARMCHAIR

W = 36″
D = 15″
H = 30″

BIEDERMEIR STYLE COMMODE

W = 26″
D = 28″
H = 18″

REFECTORY BENCH

15.8 Checkpoints

√ Sketching is useful in graphic problem solving and in establishing drawing layout.

√ Use short, crisp strokes to create quality lines.

√ Use visual guides to help maintain proportion when sketching.

16   Simplified Drafting

16.1 Drafting as a Means to an End

As stated earlier, drafting for the theatre is a graphic means to communicate ideas that will be translated into a theatrical production. To that end, every effort should be made whenever possible to reduce the time necessary to create drawings, as long as the drafter is still able to produce a product that meets the standards for quality reproduction and provides information that is complete and meets the needs of the user.

One way to speed the creation of drawings without loss of clarity is to utilize what are commonly called simplified drafting techniques. Simplified drafting involves the use of acceptable shortcuts that decrease the amount of time spent at the drafting table while at the same time maintaining high graphic standards and efficient communication.

16.2 No Extraneous Views or Information

To avoid redundancy, never draw a view of an object unless it provides necessary information that is not shown elsewhere. This practice is already accepted when drawing flats. Only front and rear views are usually drawn because side and top views would add nothing to the overall shape description. Taking this elimination of unnecessary views one step further, a drafter can, through the use of a center-line reference, eliminate half of a symmetrical object.

16.3 The Useful Center Line and Phantom Line

Center lines are used as extension lines for dimensioning purposes, eliminating the need for writing an "on center" note. The center line can also be used to locate redundant objects like gates under a raked platform. The details of the rake necessary for construction would then be provided in another view. Symmetrical objects are divided by the center line and drafted with differing information about the object on each side of the center line. This technique is just one of the many forms in which the "reverse and repeat" (R&R) concept can be used.

Repetitive patterns and highly elaborate details should be drawn only once. Additional use of these complex details are indicated through the use of a phantom line.

16.4 A Picture Is Worth . . .

Although they say a picture is worth a thousand words, sometimes words and numbers are much more effective communicators than fully developed drawings. Both general and specific notes can clarify as well as eliminate the need for additional drawings.

Tables and lists of standard parts or stock scenery communicate very efficiently. Tables can serve the scenic studio as checklists for pulling of assigned materials or mass production of parts. A table of information when viewed in conjunction with a small scale sketch of the object is very effective.

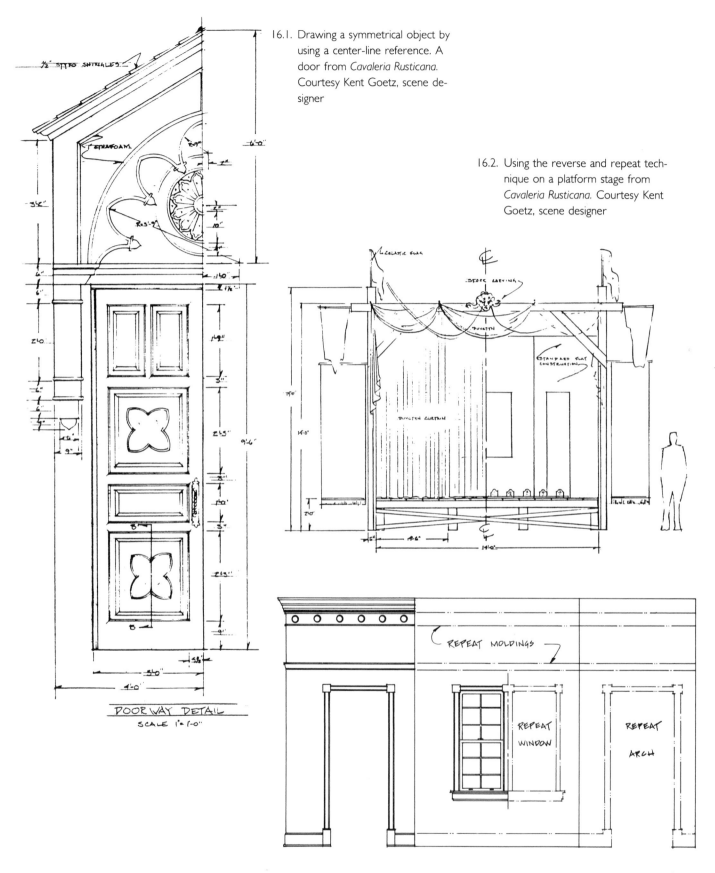

16.1. Drawing a symmetrical object by using a center-line reference. A door from *Cavaleria Rusticana.* Courtesy Kent Goetz, scene designer

16.2. Using the reverse and repeat technique on a platform stage from *Cavaleria Rusticana.* Courtesy Kent Goetz, scene designer

DOORWAY DETAIL
SCALE 1"=1'-0"

REPEAT MOLDINGS

REPEAT
WINDOW

REPEAT
ARCH

16.3. Using phantom lines

16.4. A lamppost from *Spokesong*. Courtesy Dana Kenn, scene designer

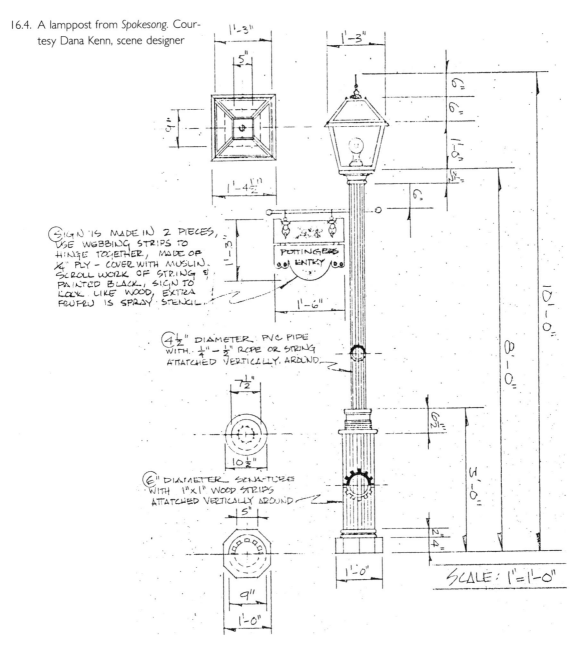

SIGN IS MADE IN 2 PIECES, USE WEBBING STRIPS TO HINGE TOGETHER, MADE OF ¼" PLY - COVER WITH MUSLIN. SCROLL WORK OF STRING & PAINTED BLACK, SIGN TO LOOK LIKE WOOD, EXTRA FRUFRU IS SPRAY STENCIL

PUTTINGERS ENTRY

4½" DIAMETER PVC PIPE WITH ¼" - ½" ROPE OR STRING ATTACHED VERTICALLY, AROUND

6" DIAMETER SONA-TUBE WITH 1"x1" WOOD STRIPS ATTACHED VERTICALLY AROUND

SCALE: 1"=1'-0"

16.5. Using a summary table

SHOW: 'ON BORROWED TIME'					STOCK		COVER		STIFF/BR.	
DES.	DESCRIPTION	No. UNITS	COMPONENTS		Y	N	N	O	Y	N
A	10'-0"H × 12'-0"W	3	4×10' FLATS		✓		✓		✓	
B	10'-0"H × 12'-4"W	1	5×10' "		✓		✓		✓	
		1	4'×10' "		✓					
		1	1'-8"R SWEEP			✓				
C	10'-0"H × 3'-0"W	1	3'×10' FLAT		✓			✓		✓
D	10'-0"H × 6'-0"W	2	3'×10' "		✓			✓		✓
E	10'-0"H × 4'-0"W	1	4'×10' "		✓			✓		✓
F	14'-0"H × 4'-0"W	1	4'×10' "		✓		✓		✓	
		1	4'×4' △ FLAT			✓				
G	14'-0"H × 6'-0"W	1	6'×8' FLAT		✓					

16.5 Templates and Symbols

Hardware items such as hinges, hanging irons, and casters can be located through the use of an appropriate symbol. Standardized symbols for many theatrical hardware items have been developed as part of the USITT Graphic Standards. When confronted with a need for a symbol that is not part of the graphic standards, the drafter should create one. The new symbol must, however, be identified both by a specific note and by inclusion in a "key" on the drawing that defines all the symbols used.

Symbols not only are used to directly identify hardware but also are recommended as a means to assist in the easy identification of any scenic elements. Consistent use of symbols from ground plan to construction to load-in and strike greatly enhances the flow of communication. Most symbols are drawn by using a template. These stamped plastic sheets are great time-savers, and because of the wide variety of templates available, the number of symbols available for use by the drafter is almost unlimited.

16.6. Symbol use

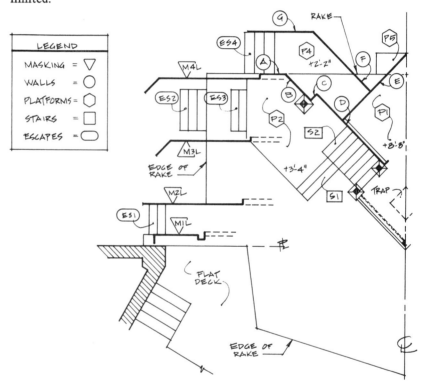

16.6 Labor-saving Approaches to Drafting

Sketches and overlays of tracing paper can greatly aid in the development of final drawings. A torn piece of tracing paper and a soft-lead wooden pencil are not nearly as intimidating as a clean sheet of vellum taped to the drafting board and a mechanical pencil in hand. Problems are uncovered and solutions are discovered through the process of making full-scale sketches and scaled tracings. Once satisfied with the result, the drafter should place these "rough" drawings under the vellum and trace these images, this time using drafting tools for greater accuracy and improved layout. Although with this approach the drafter admittedly draws many objects twice, the problem-solving benefits far exceed the value of the extra time spent.

In situations where the same information is to be used in many drawings, **intermediates** such as sepias and mylars should be used. Intermediates may be drawn on directly, a process that is made even easier if "reverse prints" are used. This process places the copied information on the back side of the print; to do this the original was printed face down rather than face up. The working side of the intermediate is then unmarked and ready to be drawn upon. The original information on the rear can be removed by either scraping, bleaching, or erasing.

Intermediates are also used to provide a "second set of originals" so that printing of additional blue-line prints can take place in more than one location. These drawings are especially helpful in situations where the designer is not in the same location as the production staff. Paper sepias are the least expensive intermediate choice, followed by mylar slicks and matte-surfaced mylars.

Many of the drawings required for theatre involve multiple layers of detailed information. The application of **pin graphics** can be an excellent time-saver in the combining and drawing of these various layers. Prepunched plastic film along with a standard "pin bar" taped to the top of the drawing table is used as a registration system to align the several sheets of drawings. This mechanically positive system takes the guesswork out of overlaying drawings and assures exact registration of each sheet.

Layers of information can therefore be drafted on different sheets of paper and arranged in a logical order with the help of the pin registration. Commercial blueprint companies can then take these pin-registered drawings and produce a composite with all the various layers on one sheet. These layered drawings also allow many people to be working on different aspects of the same project, which are then combined in the final printing. Pin graphics works well for drawing composite ground plans and provides a means for saving drawing time for the technical director, lighting designer, stage manager, and others. The concept is simple: do not draw anything more than once.

16.7. Pin-drafting flow chart

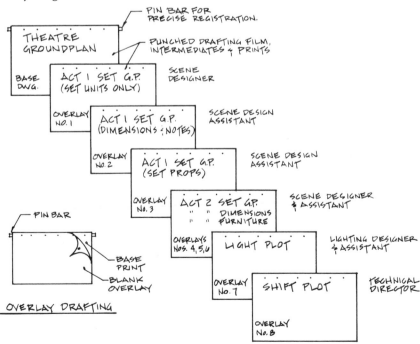

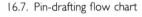

With the addition of **large format photo duplication** technology, original drawings no longer all need to be prepared on the same sheet. Cutting and pasting drawings from different originals and reproducing them with a photo duplication machine can be a real time-saver, one already familiar to many drafters, although perhaps not in a scale the size of most drawing sheets. Source material, typewritten notes, as well as details in various scales can easily be combined into one drawing without retracing by simply use this "cut-and-paste" approach.

One of the last things added to a drawing is the lettering. Lettering large amounts of information onto drawings can be extremely time-consuming. A product that has been in use in architectural drafting firms for several years is **adhesive-backed, transparent transfer film.** Information may be typed directly onto the film, although photocopying works best. Once the sheet is ready, the backing paper is removed and the block of information positioned on the drawing. For repetitive notes, as well as a large block of general notes, so-called **sticky back** is an excellent time saver. This technique is not recommended for specific notes, as the cutting and pasting necessary is too time-consuming.

In addition to notes, sticky back copies are often used for the insertion or paste up of entire drawings in large format documents. Because of the high degree of opacity achieved through the photo duplication process, sticky-back transfers to transparent media like vellum or mylar produce drawings that can be copied at a considerable cost savings as standard diazo prints. If run at slow speeds, it is possible to produce prints that show no evidence of the paste-up techniques used by the drafter.

16.7 Problem

Using the units shown in figure 16.8, develop a photocopied ½" scale enlargement on a B-size sheet. The final product should include figures with labels (arranged in numerical order), border, and title block. Use the title block provided but modify the scale, date, and drafter information to suit current needs.

16.8 Checkpoints

√ Never draw more views of an object than necessary.

√ Utilize notes, symbols, and tables wherever possible.

√ Intermediates and pin graphics allow multiple users access to the same original material.

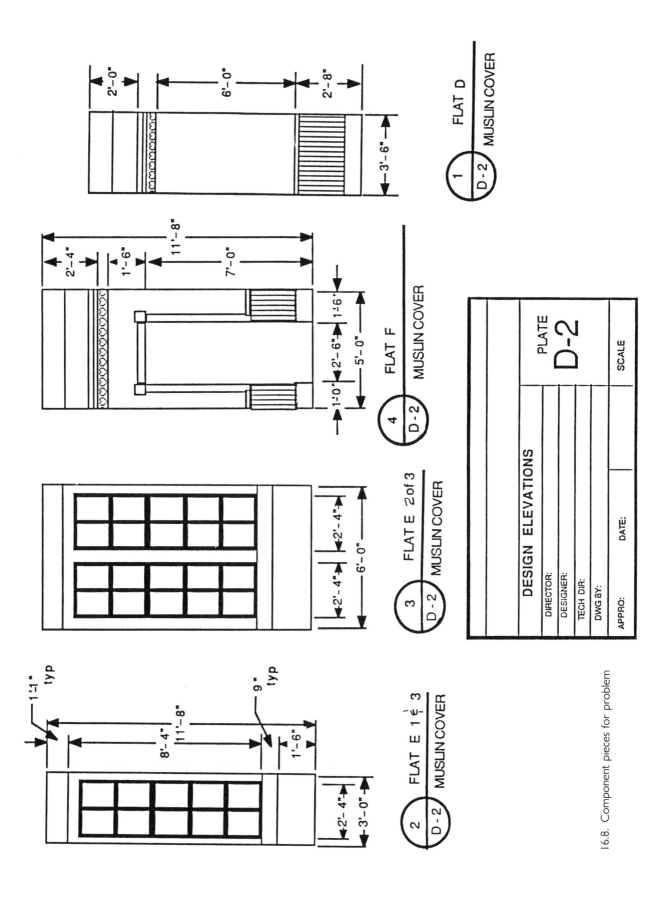

FLAT D
MUSLIN COVER
1 / D-2

FLAT F
MUSLIN COVER
4 / D-2

FLAT E 2 of 3
MUSLIN COVER
3 / D-2

FLAT E 1 of 3
MUSLIN COVER
2 / D-2

DESIGN ELEVATIONS

DIRECTOR:
DESIGNER:
TECH DIR:
DWG BY:

APPRO: DATE:

PLATE
D-2

SCALE

16.8. Component pieces for problem

17   Computer-aided Drafting and Design

17.1 From Mainframes to Micros

Once computers were built that had the capacity to handle the large amount of information needed to create even the simplest of drawings, the development of computer-aided drafting and design (CADD) software quickly followed. Early programs were awkward to use, required an enormous amount of memory, and needed expensive and bulky hardware. Despite these drawbacks the computer was recognized almost immediately as a drawing tool capable of relieving drafters from long hours of tedious and repetitive work.

Large memory requirements limited the use of early CADD software to mainframe computers, large, complex systems designed to handle and process enormous amounts of information. By the early 1980s CADD programs became widely available for use on microcomputers. Priced to be affordable to both small businesses and to the individual consumer, micros can perform most of the functions of a mainframe but on a reduced scale. A rule of thumb often applied to computers is that microcomputer-based software is capable of delivering 80% of the functions of a mainframe but at only 10% of the cost.

17.2 CADD: What It Could Mean to the Theatre

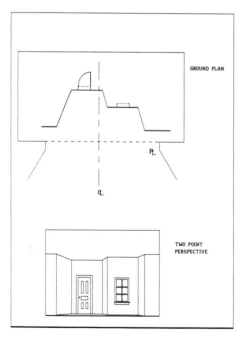

17.1. Two-point perspective and ground plan. Courtesy Autodesk, Inc.

As noted earlier in this text, the principal function of the technical drawings used in theatre drafting is to communicate in a clear and concise manner the design and construction needs of a production. To this end, CADD is a tool identical in purpose to the T-square and pencil used in traditional forms of drafting. While CADD will not replace the drafter, the computer has the capacity to make the individual significantly more productive, while the final product is likely to be more attractive and guaranteed reproducible. Beyond these very pragmatic concerns, CADD offers a spiraling array of potential uses for the performing arts (fig. 17.1).

For the **scene designer,** CADD brings the opportunity to explore a design almost endlessly. For several years already, CADD programs have permitted an object, once created, to be rotated and therefore studied from many angles to find an observation point for the audience that maximizes the potential of the design features. But this feature seems simple in comparison to many of the features now available.

Already some of the more powerful programs allow the CRT screen to be divided into quadrants, each containing related information about a single object. One area shows the object in plan view, another in front elevation, yet another in side elevation, and the final quadrant shows the object in two-point perspective. A line change in any quadrant will result in a corresponding change in the other three views. This split-screen feature goes hand in hand with a feature permitting the designer to plot a path that pictorially walks observers around (and even through) the object. Such features permit both designer and director the opportunity to observe the concept together, then discuss and utilize a design in a way that optimizes its visual and spatial effectiveness. In addition some programs also permit the creation of color renderings, an opportunity enhanced by the many color and shade combinations that can be quickly produced for comparison.

To the **lighting designer** CADD offers relief from the monotony of drawing the same symbols repeatedly. Beginning with the very ground plan and section of the theatre, the location of the lighting positions, perhaps even standardized features such as the legend, title block, and first electric configuration, to name a few, the lighting designer's time is spent designing, not drawing. Several CADD programs devised specifically to aid the lighting designer also permit the integration of graphics and data management, where the equipment in the plot is checked against the available inventory and sorted as required to create the various forms of paperwork needed, such as electric hookup, focus charts, magic sheets. This integration significantly reduces the chances for error.

Technical directors and **scenery drafters** will find CADD equally useful. CADD permits the ultimate layering possibilities (see §16.6) and, therefore, a significant saving of time for those members of the production team who must work off the drawings of others. For example, layer 1 might be the outline of a unit; layer 2, the framing details; layer 3, the dimensions; and layer 4, the notes. The result is a composite of drawings that precisely and even more accurately achieves the goals of pin graphics.

Even the **costume shop** will find CADD a useful tool, since it is ideal for the creation of clothing patterns. Imagine the nearly endless possibilities that exist when basic period patterns can be stored in the computer and simply altered to match the measurements of the individual actor. The pattern can be modified in small scale on the CRT, then printed full size, complete with instructions, ready to be given to the costume-cutting crew.

Although still very much a vision, it seems nearly a certainty that eventually the scheme outlined above will be commonplace. Marvelous as it may seem, however, this flexibility will not come without some steep costs, in terms of both equipment and patience. Initially a drafter can draw much faster by hand, but given time to learn the intricacies of use, a drafter using a well-developed CADD package can substantially reduce the amount of time required at the drafting table.

17.3 Microcomputer Systems

At present the most commercially successful microcomputer systems are the PC family manufactured by IBM and the Macintosh series of micros produced by Apple Computer, Inc. (fig. 17.2). The Mac is very user-friendly and can be used in much the same fashion that a person would work at a desk. All the essential directions are available to the user through pull-down menus located along the top of the screen.

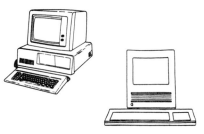

17.2. The IBM-PC and Apple Macintosh

IBM has produced a text-oriented system that requires the user to memorize commands and processes. While not as user-friendly as the Mac, the PC enjoys the position of being the favorite of business and technical users. A faster operating speed and a more flexible architecture have made the PC the dominant system to date. Consequently many more CADD programs exist that have been written for the IBM and its clones than currently exist for the Mac. Chief among these is AutoCADD®, a product of Autodesk, Inc. This software has captured a major part of the CADD software market and serves as the benchmark against which all other software is measured. Versions of AutoCADD are currently available for both the PC and the Macintosh, making it almost universally recognized in the micro world. Because of this prominence within the CADD field and, in truth, its accessibility to the authors, AutoCADD was chosen for the simple demonstration that follows. Most CADD programs are organized in a very similar manner, so regardless of the software selected for personal use, the logic shown here should appear very familiar.

17.4 Getting Started on CADD

Numerous books have already been written that exhaustively address the subject of computer-aided design and drafting. Anyone really interested in gaining more than a cursory knowledge of CADD would be well advised to choose one of these many references as a guidebook. The purpose here is to simply provide readers an introduction and overview of the subject of CADD-generated drawings. To demonstrate the applicability of this phenomenal tool to the needs of the theatre, an object familiar to all is used.

Begin by booting the program. If using AutoCADD, after several prompt screens, you will be looking at the screen shown in figure 17.3. This is known as the **editing screen** and is the screen in which all drawing is done. At the top-left corner is the **layer number,** conceptually identical to pin graphics. Top center are the **x, y coordinates,** given in either decimal, metric, or feet and inches. To the far right of the screen is the **main menu,** a list of available commands. In the bottom-left corner, at the bottom of the **prompt area,** is the **command line.** It is on this line that the user has the most direct interaction with the program. In the **drawing area,** two intersecting perpendicular lines (cross hairs) will appear. At the point where these two lines cross, the drafter can affect the screen using one of several input devices.

17.3. AutoCADD's editing screen. Courtesy Autodesk, Inc.

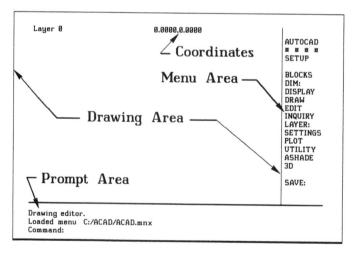

Input devices fall into two broad categories: **keyboard** and **pointing devices.** The keyboard is the most basic tool, workable but slow. The pointing devices are generally faster. The principal types are shown in figure 17.4 and defined below. Units are listed in descending order regarding ease of use.

17.4. Common types of pointer devices

Digitizer

Mouse

Track Ball

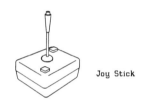
Joy Stick

Digitizer: An electronically sensitive plate used in combination with a paper- or plastic-laminated template and light pen. The template covers the entire working surface of the digitizer, usually 11″ × 11″ in size, and is divided into squares each representative of one of the commands available. In the center of the template is a large blank area, representative of the screen. The drafter uses the light pen to select commands and draw in the blank space. Most drafters prefer the tablet to other input devices, since the logic and order of working is very similar to traditional methods of drafting.

Mouse: A hand-held box that contains motion sensors and several buttons. The user moves the mouse, which in turn moves the screen indicator a proportionate amount. Once the indicator is in the right location, the user selects the desired command by using one or more of the buttons.

Track ball: A box that contains an inset ball and several buttons similar to those on the mouse. The drafter places a hand on the ball and rolls it to move the indicator to the needed location, then selects the command using the buttons.

Joy stick: A box equipped with the standard buttons and with a lever that pivots from the center of the box. When the lever is moved, the screen indicator moves in the same direction. Once the indicator is in the right location, the drafter selects the needed command with the buttons.

17.5. The AutoCADD digitizer template, version 10. Courtesy Autodesk, Inc.

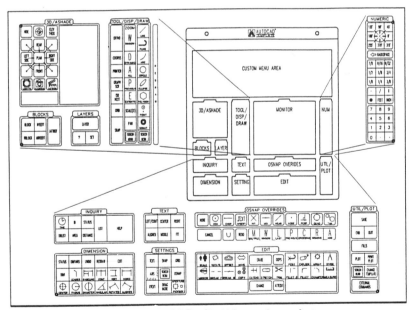
The AutoCAD digitizer template

17.5 Drawing a Flat in AutoCADD

The object selected for this example is a simple stage flat. The size is small, chosen so that the entire object can be drawn in ½″ scale and be contained comfortably within one screen without scrolling. A shop drawing (rear elevation) has been chosen as the subject rather than a design drawing (front elevation), since the rear view contains considerably more detail and offers the opportunity to demonstrate additional features plus notation and dimensions.

1. To begin, chose the DRAW option from the menu. This will change the menu to the drawing menu. Next select the PLINE (Polyline) option. This option specifies the width of the line and should be used to define the outline of any object (fig. 17.6).

17.6. The PLINE menu. Courtesy Autodesk, Inc.

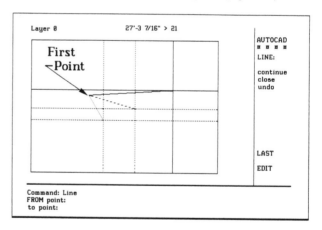

2. Pick the location of the lower-left corner of the flat on the screen, using the pointer device.
3. Draw a line using one of two methods:
a. Drag the line to the desired location, using the pointer. Select the desired location with the pointer button. The length and angle of the line are now determined, and the next point can be chosen. The coordinates will indicate the distance of the cross hairs from the previous point (fig. 17.7).

17.7. Drawing with a pointer. Courtesy Autodesk, Inc.

b. Type in the command @ *distance < degree.* To draw the first line of the flat, the command would be *@8'-0"<90.* This will draw a vertical line 8'-0" long, beginning at the first point. Draw the second and third lines in the same manner. The commands would be *@4'-0"<0* and *@8'-0"<270* respectively. To close the frame, select the CLOSE option from the menu. This will connect the first and last points (fig. 17.8).

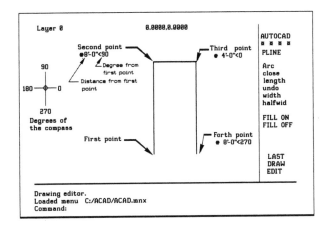

4. Next create the gussets (corner blocks , straps, and keystones). These are objects that will be used repeatedly. CADD provides a way with the BLOCK option to avoid drawing these items each time they are needed. Blocks are shape descriptions that can be stored in the memory and used as often as desired.

   To create a block, draw the object in the same manner as described in step 3. Once complete, select the BLOCK option from the main menu and follow the instructions at the bottom of the screen. When the steps have been completed, the object will disappear (fig. 17.9).

17.9. The BLOCK menu. Courtesy Autodesk, Inc.

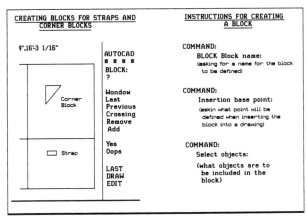

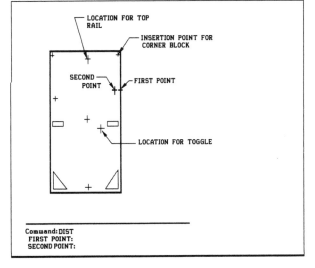

17.10. Using the DIST command. Courtesy Autodesk, Inc.

5. Locate the positions of the corner blocks and straps by typing DIST on the command line. The statement "first point" will appear on the command line. Use the pointer to pick the point on the frame from which the distance would be measured. The statement "second point" will appear next on the command line and the coordinates will change to indicate the distance of the cross hairs from the first point. When that point is chosen, a set of small cross hairs will appear at that point. Use this method to locate all the corner blocks and straps (fig. 17.10).

6. Position the corner blocks and straps using the INSERT command from the BLOCK menu and follow the directions at the bottom of the screen. Blocks can be placed anywhere on the screen and can be rotated to fit.
7. Use the DIST command to locate the remainder of the lines (rails, stiles, toggles, and braces) that will complete the flat. Use the LINE option from the DRAW menu to complete the flat. Mistakes can be easily erased by choosing the ERASE option from the EDIT menu (fig. 17.11).

17.11. Finishing the flat. Courtesy Autodesk, Inc.

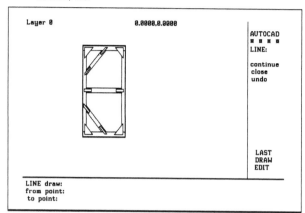

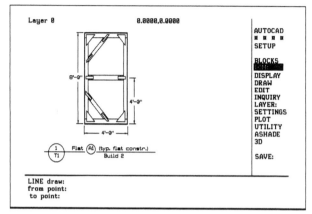

17.12. Using the DIM and TEXT commands. Courtesy Autodesk, Inc.

8. Dimension the unit by choosing the DIM option from the main menu. Notation is inserted using the TEXT option from the DRAW menu (fig. 17.12).

17.6 Working with Existing Drawings

The efforts of past experience will continue to assist the drafter in the daily routine, in the form of "existing drawings." These are drawings that have been created in a different editing session and imported or copied into the present editing session. These drawings can take many forms, from blocks to full ground plans or sections that can be copied into the present drawing in a matter of moments.

A great deal of time can be saved by drawing the standard border and title block once and importing it into each new drawing. The ground plan and section of any theatre can be copied as often as needed. Commonly used flats or other stock units can be used repeatedly with little effort. Symbols such as the USITT Graphic Standards for scenery and lighting can be drawn once and stored for future needs.

Objects that have already been drawn using CADD may be modified in a variety of ways. CADD software allows the drawing sheet to become fluid. Unlike traditional paper and pencil methods, where information frequently needs to be erased and redrawn, once information is placed in the computer, it can be easily manipulated without the worry of poor erasures or smudging the paper original. The commands listed below are common to most CADD software.

1. **COPY** an object to another location on the screen.
2. **INVERT** the object to create a mirror image.

3. **ROTATE** the object to any orientation.
4. **RESIZE** allows an object to be enlarge or reduced.
5. **RESHAPE** changes the proportion of an object.

These features can be used quickly and easily, eliminating the need for the drafter to redraw the same or a similar object repeatedly (fig. 17.13).

17.13. Manipulating a drawing. Courtesy Autodesk, Inc.

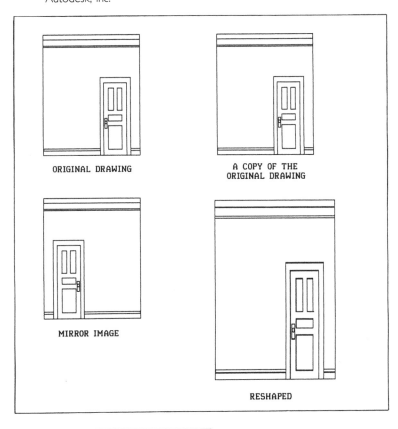

ORIGINAL DRAWING

A COPY OF THE
ORIGINAL DRAWING

MIRROR IMAGE

RESHAPED

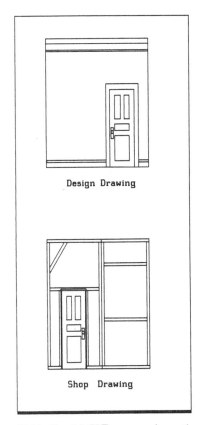

Design Drawing

Shop Drawing

17.14. The INVERT command: creating a mirror image of a design drawing to develop the shop drawing. Courtesy Autodesk, Inc.

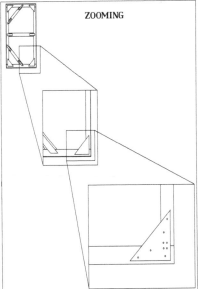

ZOOMING

17.15. The ZOOM command. Courtesy Autodesk, Inc.

One example of how useful these operations can be in theatre graphics is the reversing of a design drawing (front elevation) to create a shop drawing (rear elevation). The technical director need only use the INVERT command to create a mirror image of the outline and then begin to fill in all the construction information (fig. 17.14). Many CADD packages will allow the text to be separated from the line work, so that while the lines will be seen mirror image, the dimensions given by the designer will remain readable.

One problem inherent to all CADD programs is how to make an entire 24″ × 36″ drawing fit onto a relatively small 9″ or 13″ CRT screen. To address this problem, AutoCADD and others provide a ZOOM command. This allows the user to magnify a portion of the screen so that very fine detail can be shown (fig. 17.15). While this feature is helpful, it does not really solve the problem of not being able to view an entire D-size drawing on a single screen without scrolling.

17.7 Putting It on Paper

Once the drawing is complete, it must be transferred to paper media (hard copy). There are four common methods of producing a hard copy of graphic work.

Dot matrix printer: Very quick with text but inconsistent with graphics. In general of poor quality, since it must segment non-90° lines.

Plotter: The plotter is designed for graphics. It uses pens to draw on a sheet of paper. The more expensive models have automatically interchangeable pens to provide a variety of colored lines and/or line widths.

Laser printer: Similar in operation to a standard copy machine in that the image is photographed onto the page. The information is sent from the computer to the printer as a batch; the printer then regenerates the picture and photographs it. The first drawing takes awhile to create, but additional copies are produced rapidly (approximately eight pages per minute).

Laser plotter: Functions much the same as laser printers but is designed to handle large sheets of paper, typically 36″ wide by almost any length.

17.8 The Final Word

CADD can be frustrating to learn. For many users, it is often a process that involves learning simultaneously both the program and how to handle the computer and its many functions. This is usually a very time-consuming process; there are many times when it would be much faster to draft the object by hand rather than to figure out how to make the machine perform the desired task.

In addition, computer equipment is expensive to purchase and to maintain and can breakdown without warning. CADD software is among the most expensive software on the market, a significant purchase in its own right. Exercise caution when purchasing, since not every package will be applicable to the type of drafting done in theatre. Purchase equipment and software carefully. Talk to people who have used them for theatre jobs before. And ask to see everything demonstrated before purchasing it.

Like it or not, CADD is the next level of drafting tools for the theatre. As new generations of CADD software are created, programs will become ever easier to use and even more flexible than today's models.

But while it can significantly improve the productivity of a drafter, CADD cannot replace the drafter. As with hand drafting, the speed and quality of the product created is dependent on the proficiency of the drafter. Whether using traditional or CADD methods, the drafter needs to understand what is being drawn. The better that understanding the quicker and better the drawing will be. There is no substitute for practice and patience.

17.9 Problems

Problems 17.1, 17.2
Using whatever CADD resources available, draw in ½″ scale both front and rear elevations of the units shown in figure 17.17. Include dimensions, labels, and notation.

17.16. Scenic units, worksheets 17.1, 17.2

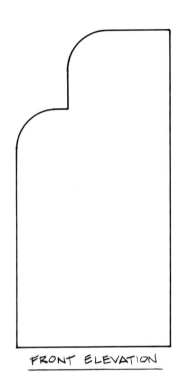

FRONT ELEVATION

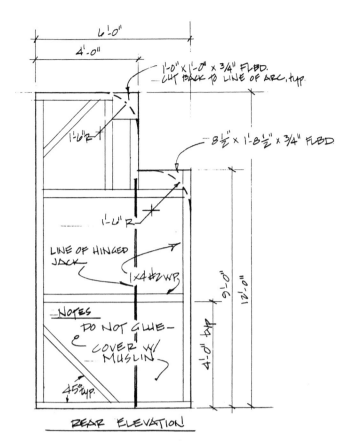

REAR ELEVATION

17.10 Checkpoints

√ CADD is a tool to aid the drafter. Its many advantages include:
   Speed
   Layering
   Image modification
   Stored symbols and information blocks

√ CADD produces revisions easily, quickly, and cleanly.

√ Whether using traditional or CADD methods, the drafter needs to understand what is being drawn. There is no substitute for practice and patience

PART FIVE

THEATRE APPLICATIONS

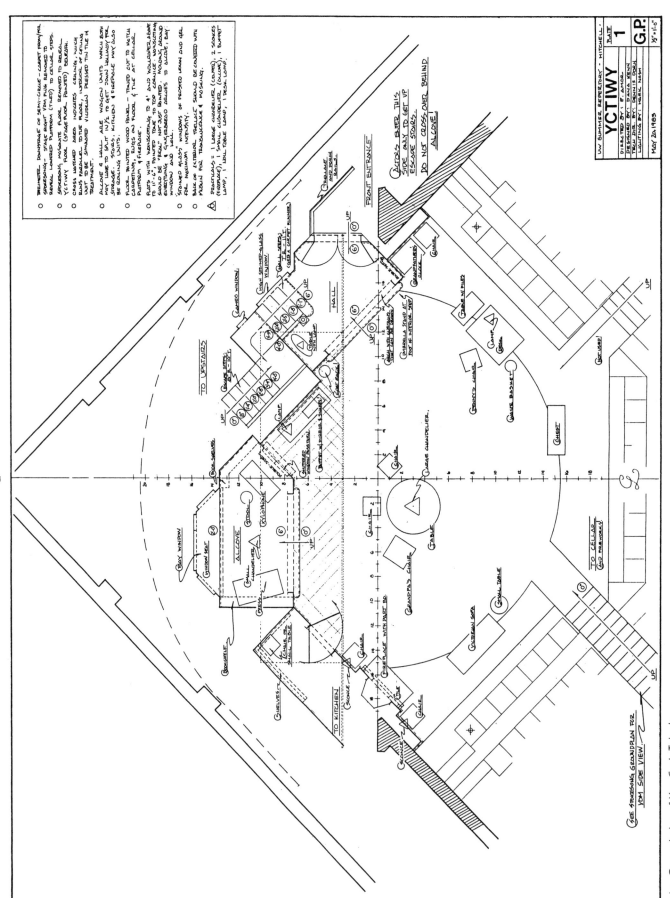

18.1a. Ground plan of *You Can't Take It with You*. Courtesy Dana Kenn, scene designer

18   Scene Design Drawings

18.1 What Does It All Look Like?

The scene designer's drawings are to the scenery construction process what an architect's drawings are to the building trades. These drawings are the means by which the images previously captured by the designer in sketch or rendering form become translated into finite objects having specific dimensions and shapes.

Besides describing the look and dimensions of a production, design drawings specify where scenery is to be located, what units hang from the rigging system, which units move, and how the scenery is to be stored when not in use. Throughout the development of the production this information will direct the efforts of many members of the production team including the director, stage manager, lighting and sound designers, technicians, and craftspersons. The quality, accuracy, and completeness of the information contained within these drawings are vital to them all.

Many of the examples shown in this chapter use drawings prepared for a production of *You Can't Take It with You,* produced by University Theatre at the University of Wisconsin-Madison. Figures 18.1b and 18.1c show the designer's pencil rendering and ¼″ scale white-paper model.

18.2 Ground Plan Types

One of the first drawings to be completed by the designer and the most basic is the **ground plan.** The ground plan views the stage floor and the scenery on it from above and is typically drawn in ½″ = 1'-0″ scale. This drawing is actually a conventionalized horizontal offset section. The cutting plane moves about usually at a height between 4–0″ and 10'-0″ above the stage floor. Any wall unit that sits directly on the stage floor will be cut through by this cutting plane.

The cross section of most flat-framed scenery is 1″ or less in thickness, therefore flats are indicated by a thick line. Doors, windows, and other such objects that are standard in shape are indicated through the use of symbols. Figure 18.2 shows symbols approved by USITT as well as some other recommended symbols for items not yet covered by USITT. Any objects on the ground plan, such as chandeliers, beams, borders, and flown scenery that are located above the cutting plane, are drawn using a long-dash line symbol. By convention, stairs, platforms, furniture, and fireplaces are shown in top view.

Several types of ground plans are used in theatre drafting, although not all types are needed for every production. The ground plans vary primarily in the amount of detail shown; each is tailored for a specific application. The most complex of ground plans is known as the **composite plan.** This plan is developed by the designer when a multiset show is being produced. The composite plan shows the location of the scenery in all acts in both playing (onstage)and storage (offstage) positions. Each act and

18.1b. Pencil rendering of *You Can't Take It with You.* Courtesy Dana Kenn, scene designer

18.1c. Photo of ¼″ scale model of *You Can't Take It with You.* Courtesy Dana Kenn, scene designer. Photo by Linda Essig

18.2. Ground plan standards

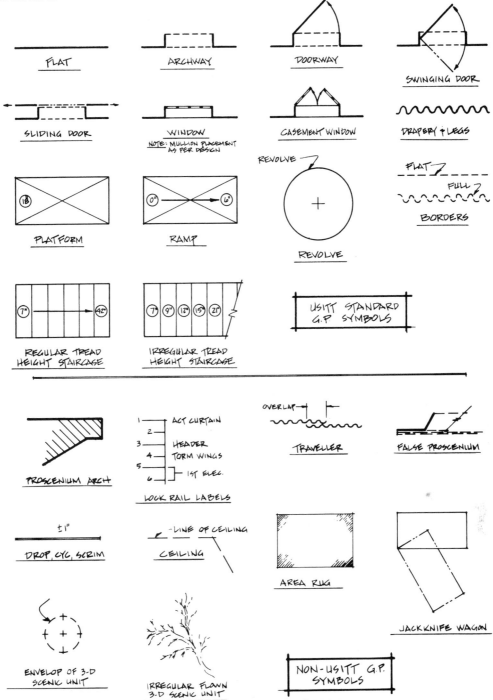

FLAT

ARCHWAY

DOORWAY

SWINGING DOOR

SLIDING DOOR

WINDOW
NOTE: MULLION PLACEMENT AS PER DESIGN

CASEMENT WINDOW

DRAPERY & LEGS

PLATFORM

RAMP

REVOLVE

REVOLVE

FLAT

FULL

BORDERS

REGULAR TREAD HEIGHT STAIRCASE

IRREGULAR TREAD HEIGHT STAIRCASE

USITT STANDARD G.P. SYMBOLS

PROSCENIUM ARCH

1 ACT CURTAIN
2
3 HEADER
4 TORM WINGS
5
6 1ST ELEC.

LOCK RAIL LABELS

OVERLAP

TRAVELLER

FALSE PROSCENIUM

±1"

DROP, CYC, SCRIM

LINE OF CEILING

CEILING

AREA RUG

JACKKNIFE WAGON

ENVELOP OF 3-D SCENIC UNIT

IRREGULAR FLOWN 3-D SCENIC UNIT

NON-USITT G.P. SYMBOLS

167

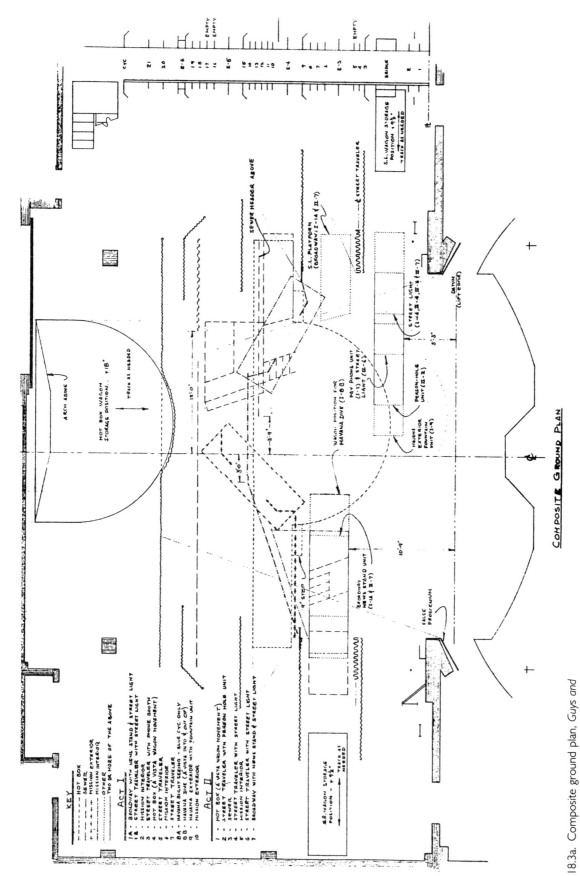

18.3a. Composite ground plan, *Guys and Dolls.* Courtesy Daniel Proctor, scene designer

use of a piece of scenery is coded by an appropriate line symbol. Several layers of such information are drawn on a single sheet. While often difficult to read, a composite plan indicates how all stage space will be used throughout a performance and readily indicates potential spatial problems.

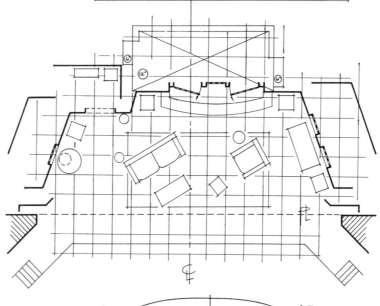

18.3b. Furniture plot ground plan

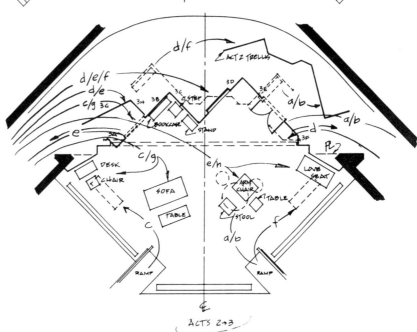

18.3c. Shift plot, *The Importance of Being Earnest*. Courtesy Daniel Crump, scene designer

The various layers of information from the composite plan, when separated, serve as the foundation for other ground plan types. **Furniture plots** (½"= 1'-0" scale) indicate the basic outline of the set with few dimensions and specify furniture location and size. A **shift plot** (¼"=1'-0" scale) shows traffic patterns and storage locations of scenery during scene and act shifts. This plan is similar to the schematic plans used by coaches to draw out plays for athletes. The lighting designer prepares a ground plan, known as the **light plot** (½" = 1'-0" scale), that shows the scenery only in enough detail to indicate acting areas, scenery to be lighted, any special lighting considerations, and obstructions in the theatre space. (See chap. 22 for illustrations and details.)

Stage managers use a much-simplified version of the ground plan during the rehearsal process. The **stage manager's plan** is drawn in ⅛" = 1'-0" or smaller scale; only wall and furniture layout is shown, and the drawing is not dimensioned. Multiple copies are placed in the promptbook to facilitate blocking notation. (A scaled reduction sized for a single page of the promptbook may easily be developed through the use of the reduction techniques discussed in chap. 14.)

18.3d. Stage manager's ground plan for inclusion in promptbook

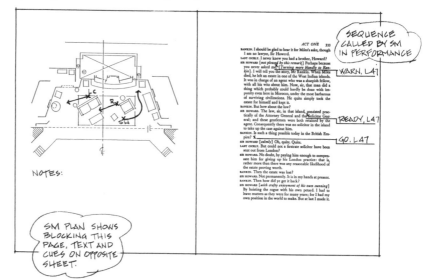

18.3 The Reference Lines of a Ground Plan

A set for a given play is often used in more than one theatre, therefore the basic reference points for ground plans must not be dependent on a specific theatre space. To compensate for various stage sizes, three basic reference or datum lines are used to develop ground plans. A pair of these lines forms an X,Y axis from which all wall intersections and key placement points are referenced.

The principal horizontal or X axis is formed by the **plaster line.** The plaster line is the connection of the upstage corners of the proscenium wall. An alternative X axis is the **set line.** The set line of a "box set" is formed by the connection of the downstage corners of the set. In a "non-box set," the set line may be any convenient datum line identified by the designer and used consistently to reference dimensions.

The vertical or Y axis is the **center line** of the stage. The center line is the perpendicular bisector of the plaster line. When scenery is loaded into the theatre, the appropriate datum lines are marked on the stage floor, usually with a chalk line, so that the designer's specifications for scenery placement can be followed exactly.

18.4 Dimensioning Ground Plans

A variety of methods are used to dimension the layout of the scenery on the stage floor. The method selected is based on the amount of detail to be shown on the ground plan and the level of accuracy desired. The most accurate method is through the use of standard extension and dimension lines. Intersections of flats where a change of direction occurs, corners of platforms, and two points on all furniture are dimensioned. As per the

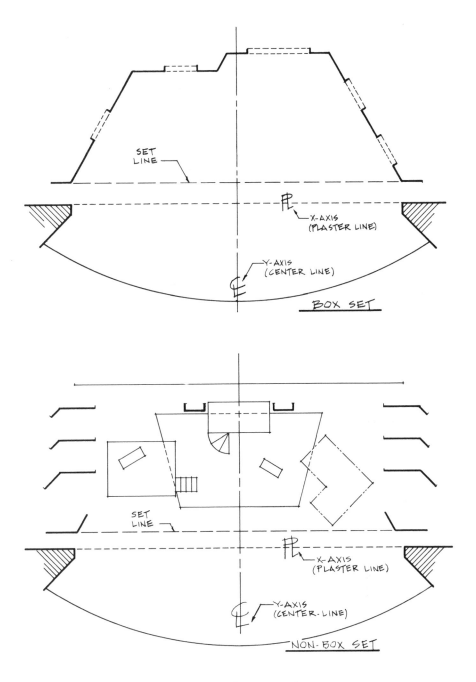

rules of dimensioning, dimension and extension lines are not to cross one another. On the ground plan of a set having only a few required dimensioned points, this rule can be readily followed. On more complicated designs, avoiding crossed dimension and extension lines becomes very difficult.

An alternative technique that eliminates the need for dimension and extension lines uses basic algebra as its foundation. For each point needing dimensions, a set of X,Y coordinates is established by the axis formed by the center line and the plaster, or set, line. This combination of numbers is enclosed in parentheses and placed adjacent to the point referenced, using a leader line if necessary. A reference key is always included on the ground plan to explain this technique to the reader. The X,Y designations should be less confusing than the array of intersecting lines that result from the addition of extension and dimension lines.

E = 5'

18.5. Two types of dimensioning

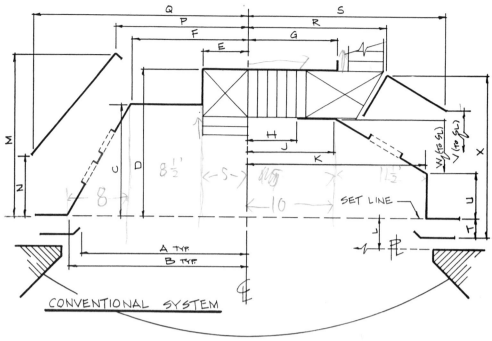

CONVENTIONAL SYSTEM

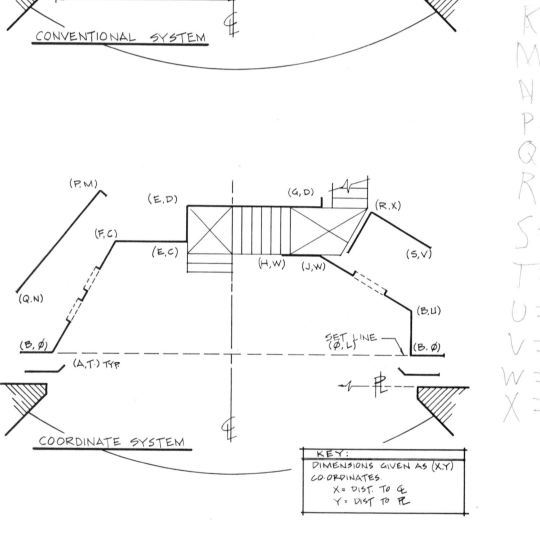

COORDINATE SYSTEM

KEY:
DIMENSIONS GIVEN AS (X,Y) CO-ORDINATES.
X = DIST. TO ℄
Y = DIST TO ℄

A =
B = 2 1/2'
C = 13'
D = 19'
E = 5'
F = 13 1/3'
G = 10 1/2' 11° 12'
H = 8 1/2'
J = 10'
K = 2 1/2'
M = 21'
N = 7'
P =
Q =
R = 18'
S =
T =
U = 6'
V =
W = 11'
X = 19'

172

Two other dimensioning techniques are used on ground plans where only approximate locations of acting areas and furniture placement are required. The first method involves the use of scales placed on or near the center and plaster datum lines. It is a technique more common to light plots than scenery ground plans, although certainly useful in both instances. On a ½" scale drawing, scale marks usually appear on every foot, with a tick mark indication of the 6" point in between; on a ¼" scale drawing, only foot markings are drawn. Regardless of the scale used, label only the even-numbered foot ticks; labeling every tick makes the scale difficult to letter and confusing to the reader. The horizontal scale is drawn along the plaster line and is numbered to the left and right of the center line. The vertical scale is drawn along the center line and is numbered above and below the plaster line. Use positive numbers only, despite mathematical conventions (fig. 18.1c).

Furniture plots introduced the idea of creating a grid to indicate proportions. A grid of small squares will be very confusing, so, typically, grids with squares 2'-0" in scale are drawn, using the plaster line and center line as base lines. The grid system aids the director and stage manager when laying out furniture or similar pieces of scenery or props during rehearsal and is useful to even the casual reader in determining the spatial relationships between the various scenic elements (fig. 18.3b).

18.5 Labels and Sightlines

The ground plan identifies all scenic units and establishes the labels to be used for their identification in future design, construction, and load-in references. Often the label is placed within a geometric figure, making it a symbol and therefore more easily identified. Proper notation such as unit identification, including an accompanying legend or key, is a must for a ground plan to be truly effective. (See chap. 8.)

The horizontal sightlines of the audience are to be indicated on the designer's ground plan. The extreme seats of the auditorium are identified by use of a circle and set of cross hairs (bull's-eye). Thin, lightly drawn lines are extended from these seat locations to the various openings on

18.6. Set labels and sightlines

the set; these lines indicate the unobstructed view of the audience and help to assure the designer checking the plan that audience members are able to see all the action of the play. To alter the natural sightlines of a given theatre space, pieces of masking are frequently installed. The location, size, and effect of the masking on sightlines are to be determined by the designer and shown on the ground plan. Making these decisions early in the planning assures an enhanced design for the audience and ensures the early installation of the masking elements in the theatre.

18.6 Section Drawings

The second major drawing developed by the designer in the drafting process is the **center line section,** sometimes known as the **hanging section.** The section view details the height of objects onstage and the hanging trim of masking elements. This information is critical to the overall look of the production and directly responsible for many of the choices made by the lighting designer regarding equipment selection and placement.

In developing this view, the center line serves as the cutting plane line. Figure 18.7 shows the section drawn as seen from stage right looking toward stage left. Frequently the view shown is that as seen from stage left; however, there is no standard stating which view is preferred. Often the decision as to which view is drawn is determined by the master drawings for the theatre in which the production is performed. Ideally the decision should be determined by the view that provides the majority of the critical information. For designs that are very complex, separate section drawings may need to be drafted showing both views. Use two distinct drawings, do not try to combine the two views through the use of dotted lines or similar conventions.

Section drawings are dimensioned to indicate overall heights of scenic elements. Dimension and extension lines are drawn using the stage floor as the base line. Vertical sightlines as well and horizontal masking hanging over the stage (borders) are indicated, using the same symbol and line of sight discussed under ground plans. All objects hung from battens are shown and a trim height for each in its playing position (in trim) provided. Trim heights are usually given as the distance from the stage floor to the bottom of the unit, but this practice may vary.

18.7. Center line section of *You Can't Take It with You,* looking stage left. Courtesy Dana Kenn, scene designer

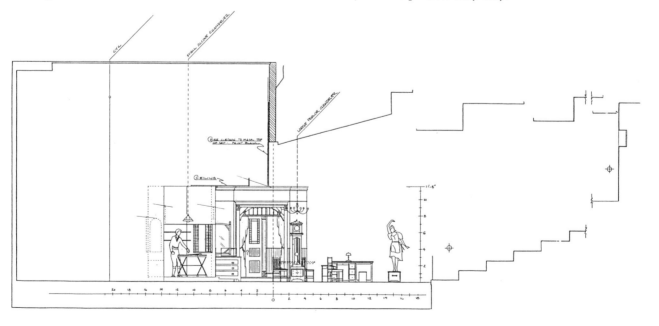

18.7 Compositional Elevations

Once the ground plan and section have been completed, the designer needs to finalize the image of set as seen in elevation. Given the extensive number and size of standard elevations, many designers prepare a set of small detailed drawings known as **compositional elevations** or **thumbnails.** Compositional elevations are usually drawn in ⅛″ = 1′-0″ scale, making it possible to work quickly and proportionally. Compositional elevations do not separate adjacent wall sections but show them attached. By doing this the designer can cut them out when done and fold the walls along the wall divisions and create a small three-dimensional model.

These small drawings show all dimensional detail and items of set dressing located directly on the surfaces as well as elements like furniture and platforming, which sit on the stage floor but visually affect the final composition of the elevations. Like furniture plots, compositional elevations can be grided to aid in determining proportion, although the inclusion of a 5′-9″ tall human figure is the most helpful in providing a sense of scale.

18.8. Compositional elevations of walls from *You Can't Take It with You.* Courtesy Dana Kenn, scene designer

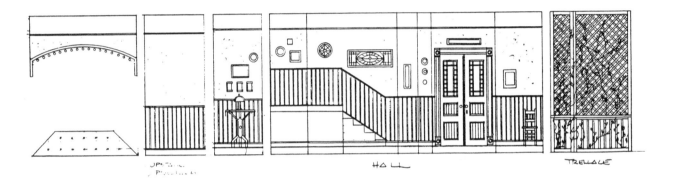

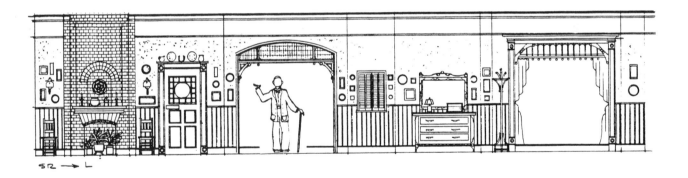

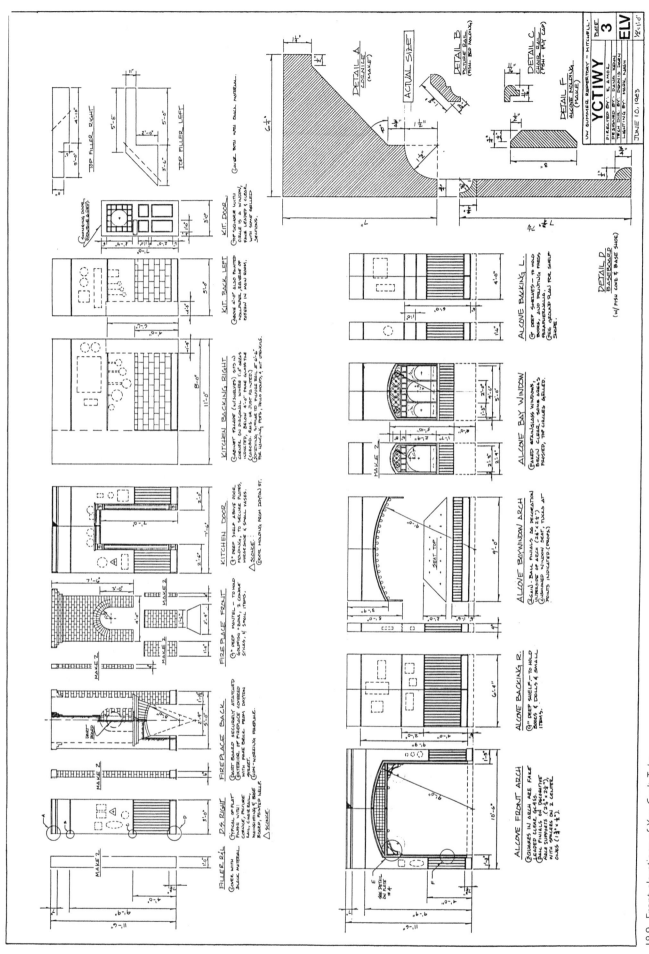

18.9. Front elevations of *You Can't Take It with You*. Courtesy Dana Kenn, scene designer

18.8 Elevations

Once the "look" and space of the set has been determined through the ground plan, section drawing, and compositional elevation, the designer is ready to begin the task of creating **working drawings.** These are typically **elevation and section views.** Several approaches are used, the choice dependent upon the complexity of the individual scenic unit. The most commonly used scale is ½" = 1'-0", the same as the ground plan and section. All units are labeled using the designations assigned on the ground plan. Units are usually drawn as distinct pieces, although it is not uncommon to see design drawings in which adjacent units are drawn attached to each other.

18.9 Two-dimensional Units

With simple scenic units such as flats, sufficient detail can be shown with only a **front elevation** of each piece. Height and width dimensions are shown as well as shallow thickness pieces such as door and window reveals, which are usually called out through the use of local notes. Within the profile that is drawn using a thick outline, the elevation view must also show the location of all dimensional features such as moldings, curtains, paneling, or similar pieces. These items are drawn with a thin, light line and are often given a "screened" look by lightly lifting the lead on the sheet though use of a kneaded eraser. Movable set-dressing elements such as pictures, brackets, and lighting fixtures are frequently drawn with dotted lines, since these items are conventionally supplied by another department than the carpenters. All dressing elements should be shown by the designer, however, so that the carpenters can provide sufficient structural support for attachment during load-in.

18.10 Break Lines

The location of "break" lines between individual flat frames forming a large wall is often determined by the technical director, although it is preferable that the designer assume this task. This way, the resulting seam will be more likely to blend into the lines of the design. In those cases when the need to segment a unit is determined during the construction phase, the more specific the information regarding finish, the more likely the TD can determine an appropriate location for the break. The "break" line is typically indicated with a dotted line and a local note specifying the method of attachment and finishing, when necessary.

18.11 Three-dimensional Units

Complex pieces of scenery require a set of views rather than the single front elevation. Multiview drawings including **plan, elevation, and section views** are used to describe the unit. The three views are used in a consistent orientation. The front elevation is the top left, the section is to the right, and the plan is drawn directly below the elevation. Two section views have been chosen to replace the standard orthographic top and right-side views, since the section drawings more clearly reveal the variety of planes involved in the piece of scenery. Additional section views may be needed when a scenic unit is particularly complex. For reasons of clarity all views must be carefully labeled and placed in a logical alignment with the front elevation. The fireplace shown in figure 18.10 illustrates this technique.

18.12 Detail Drawings

In those instances when ½" = 1'-0" scale drawings do not provide sufficient detail or do not allow enough room to accommodate ⅛" high dimensions or notation, enlarged scale drawings known as **details** are required. Typical scales used are 1" = 1'-0", 1½" = 1'-0", 3"= 1'-0", half size, and full size. Detail drawings are usually needed for moldings, doors, balustrades, intricate joinery, and similar nonstandard construction assemblies. Detail

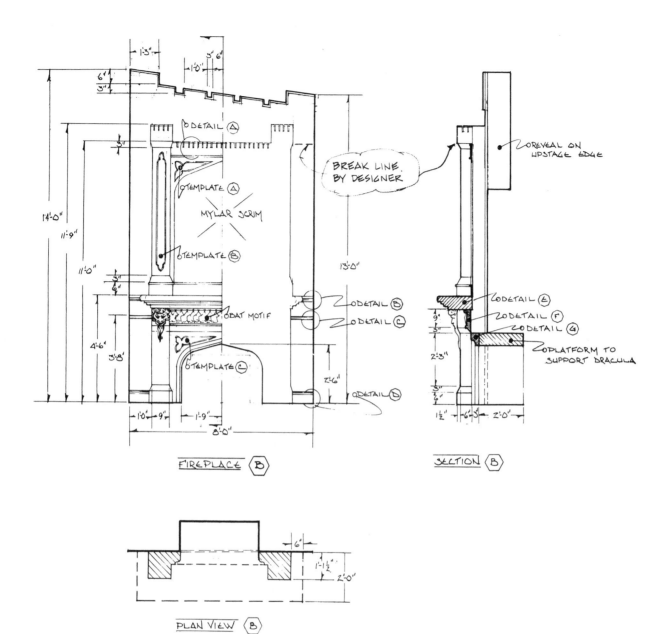

FIREPLACE (B)

SECTION (B)

PLAN VIEW (B)

Labels within figure:
DETAIL (A)
TEMPLATE (A)
MYLAR SCRIM
TEMPLATE (B)
BAT MOTIF
TEMPLATE (C)
BREAK LINE BY DESIGNER
REVEAL ON UPSTAGE EDGE
DETAIL (B)
DETAIL (C)
DETAIL (D)
DETAIL (E)
DETAIL (F)
DETAIL (G)
PLATFORM TO SUPPORT DRACULA

18.10. Three-view drawing of a three-dimensional unit, including break lines, *Dracula*. Courtesy Kent Goetz, scene designer

drawings can be done as a separate plate; however, they are more helpful when they appear on the same sheet of drawings as the ½" elevations. In such cases details must be prominently labeled and the scale noted. When a variety of scales is used on a single drawing, the scale box in the sheet title block contains the word "Varies."

18.13 Prop Drawings

The designer can provide prop drawings in a variety of ways, although generally they appear in variations of one of three forms: multiview drawings, isometric drawings, or photo copies. Regardless of the form in which the information appears, it is desirable to include prop drawings as part of the set of design drawings, but drawn on sheets separate from the scenery and numbered sequentially following the set drawings. The most common scale for prop drawings is 1" = 1'-0", but larger scales may become necessary as the degree of detail increases.

Anything being built from scratch, and having a significant amount of

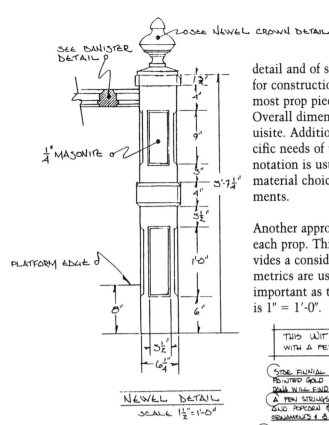

detail and of specific dimensions, requires standard multiview drawings for construction. Simple props may require just a front elevation, but most prop pieces will need two or more views to fully describe them. Overall dimensions for each prop, i.e., width, height, and depth, are requisite. Additional dimensions may also be required depending on the specific needs of the prop. Regardless of the drawing style used, extensive notation is usually needed to provide prop builders with information on material choices, finishes, painting, handling, and operational requirements.

Another approach for prop description is to sketch an isometric view of each prop. This approach shows the prop in a pictorial fashion and provides a considerable amount of artistic license for the prop builders. Isometrics are used when the interior dimensions of the object are not so important as the overall "look" and proportions. Again, the desired scale is 1″ = 1'-0″.

NEWEL DETAIL
SCALE 1½″=1'-0″

18.11. Detail drawing of a newel post, *Dracula.* Courtesy Kent Goetz, scene designer

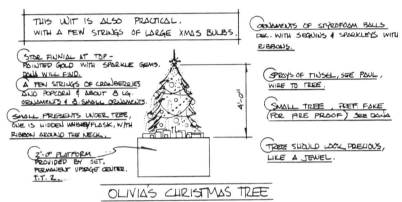

OLIVIA'S CHRISTMAS TREE

18.12. Prop drawings, *Twelfth Night.* Courtesy Dana Kenn, scene designer

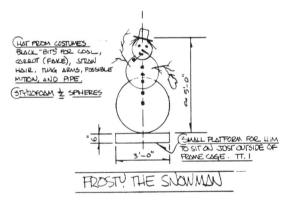

FROSTY THE SNOWMAN

A photocopy of the source material researched by the designer can be very useful to the prop crew. In those instances when the object is to be found, rather than built, a marked-up photocopy is all that is required. The photocopy, however, should be prepared in a manner that allows the image to be contained easily within the set of design drawings. This means photocopying onto "sticky back" material and placing the cutout image onto a larger sheet of vellum or film. Notes and overall dimensions may be lettered directly on the sheet or may have been included prior to photocopying the sticky back. Alternatively, the designer may prepare sketches similar to compositional elevations. These are most helpful if grouped as to the visual arrangement that will appear on stage as shown in figure 18.13.

18.14 Paint Elevations

Scenic artists require additional information over what has been provided on standard design drawings. **Paint elevations** show a front elevation of each section of the set, painted precisely as the designer wishes. Typically drawn in ½″ = 1′-0″ scale, each view shows the lining, colors, blending, and shading desired. These drawings often are notated with instructions to the scenic artist regarding painting techniques. Most paint elevations are drawn on white illustration board, although heavy paper or even blue-line paper can be used. Once complete, the painter's elevation is wrapped in plastic (clear acetate) for use in the scenic studio. The plastic cover prevents damage to the original and allows paint testing and color matching directly on the elevation.

Most paint elevations are just what the name suggests: painted. An exception is shown in figures 18.14 a and 18.14b. These are paint elevations that are actually line drawings. They show the line work required by the designer, while the color toning, etc., are shown only on a relatively small paint sample. This technique saves the designer from hours of work painting surfaces that are essentially patterns. Tonal values in corners still need to be defined, but the designer can determine specific patterns without having to paint each brick or plank.

18.15 Checkpoints

√ Design drawings include ground plans, sections, elevations, details, and prop drawings.

√ Design drawings provide complete information as to what the scenery and props will look like to the audience.

√ Notes and dimensions are used extensively to enhance prop detail drawings.

18.14a. Painter's elevation, *You Can't Take It with You.* Courtesy Dana Kenn, scene designer

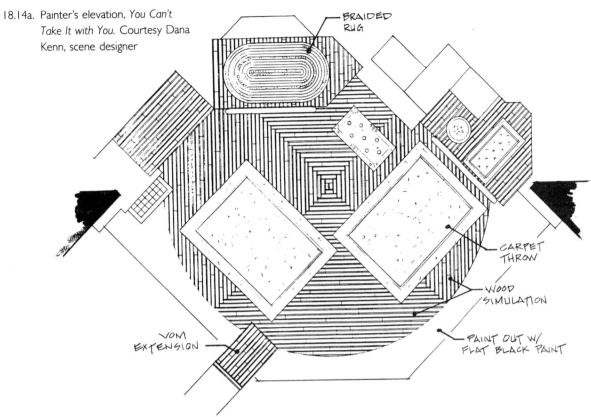

18.14b. Painter's elevation, *Dracula.* Courtesy Kent Goetz, scene designer

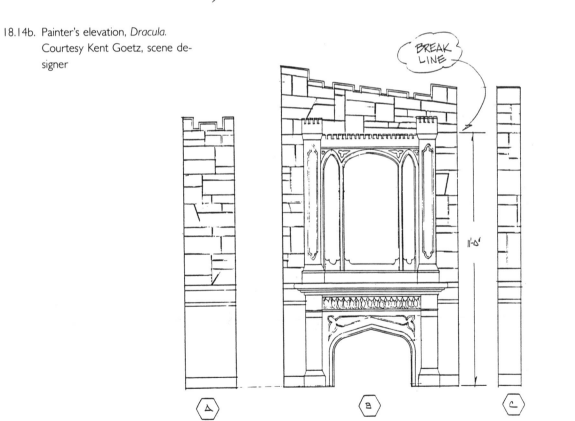

19   Shop Drawings: Flats

19.1 How Are We Going to Build That?

Shop or construction drawings approach scenery from the inside out. These drawings identify the construction techniques to be used to create the designs as prepared by the designer. Shop drawings indicate joinery, materials, hardware, covering, and finishing notation and are accurately dimensioned typically in ½″ = 1′-0″ scale. Details are drawn in a larger scale.

The technical director has the responsibility for the preparation of shop drawings. For any given piece of scenery, as many views as necessary to clearly convey the desired construction techniques are drawn. In the preparation of drawings, decisions are made that will ultimately speed the construction process and identify potential problems. One of the goals in the preparation of shop drawings is to make as many decisions as possible at the drawing table and limit the decisions required of the carpenter on the scenic studio floor.

Occasionally shop drawings are not prepared, and scenic carpenters are asked to build scenery directly from design elevations. With experienced carpenters this system can be satisfactory, but in most educational and regional theatre situations, shop drawings are considered desirable and necessary.

Every shop drawing must identify the standards to be used in construction, unless the scenic studio has a specified "standard" that all carpenters are required to use. Specifications can be provided in one of three ways, listed here in order of preference.

1. Local notes, using leader lines
2. General notes, located in a conspicuous location on the sheet and referencing the specific units to which the note applies
3. A separate set of written or graphic instructions specifying materials and assembly techniques, i.e., a "shop standard"— the least desirable, since it is physically not part of the shop drawing, not always specific to a unit, and requires the carpenter to assume information

19.2 The Regular Flat

The simplest and most basic unit of scenic construction is the regular flat. Almost all other constructed pieces of scenery are based on the design of this traditional scenic element. Figure 19.1 identifies the component parts of a standard flat frame.

While the design elevations provide the overall outline of a given flat, along with indications of finish and color, the framing of each unit is de-

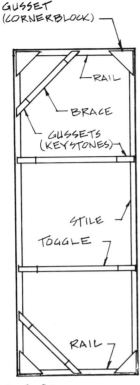

GUSSET
(CORNERBLOCK)

RAIL

BRACE

GUSSETS
(KEYSTONES)

STILE

TOGGLE

RAIL

19.1. The parts of a flat

termined by the technical director at the drafting board. Here are a few rules of thumb that can assist in determining the best layout for a flat.

1. Establish the perimeter of the unit first. Next draw in the rails, then the stiles; then establish the top and bottom edges of interior openings (doors and windows) with toggles; the sides with interior stiles.
2. Place toggles no farther than 4'-0" apart from each other. Add toggles as needed to support decor such as moldings, pictures, and lighting fixtures when indicated in the design elevations.
3. Draw diagonal braces with ends mitered at 45°. Locate one end of the brace as close to the center line of the rail as possible and attach the other end to the stile. No angle label is necessary. Diagonal braces are necessary on flats 4'-0" or wider. Always draw diagonal braces attached to the same stile.
4. Support the bottom toggle of a window opening with an interior stile located on the center line of the opening.
5. Use 90° angles in framing layout whenever possible.
6. Use 1 × 3 or 1 × 4 framing, ¼" ply gussets, muslin, canvas, or some 4 × 8 panel material if a hard surface is necessary. Draw all framing members actual dimension in scale. Place toggles and interior stiles at locations to support all seams of the hardcover material.

19.3 The Four Standard Flats

19.2. Five standard flats

Flat frame techniques are based on four standard flat frames: the simple or regular flat, the door flat, the window flat, and the arch flat. Check the illustrations of these frames to see how well the rules of thumb have been followed. Note that two different styles of the arch flat are shown.

SIMPLE FLAT

OPEN

SILL IRON

DOOR FLAT

OPEN

WINDOW FLAT

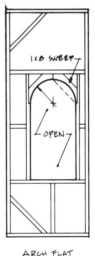

1×8 SWEEP

OPEN

ARCH FLAT

OR

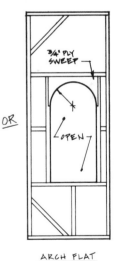

¾" PLY SWEEP

OPEN

ARCH FLAT

When drafting rear elevations of flats, do not draw gussets (keystones and corner blocks) or label each piece of the flat. This type of information is typically not included on shop drawings. A basic assumption is made that scenic carpenters are familiar with both component names and gusset attachment techniques. Should some unusual joinery be necessary, however, then it would be wise to draw the gussets to clarify the desired construction.

19.4 Required Information

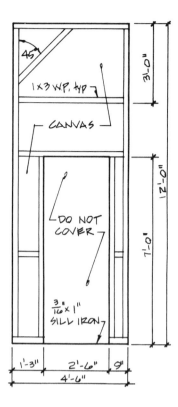

19.3. Shop drawing of a flat

19.5 Getting Them All Together

19.4. Rear elevation of a bifold flat

Shop drawings always require more information than shown in the simplified examples of figure 19.2. Flats must be fully dimensioned, and all construction materials identified. Specific notes with arrows are used. Most drawings feature several flats that are to be built using the same material specifications. These notes are given only once and are followed by the abbreviation "TYP" (which stands for typical). When the carpenter sees the TYP designation, then all similar applications are to use the same material unless otherwise noted.

Not only should the framing materials be identified, but the covering of the flat frame should be identified as well. This information can also be indicated with a specific note or may be spelled out in the general notes if all of the flats drawn on a given plate are to be covered in the same manner. Within specific door and window flats those areas that are not to be covered are notated as well. "Open" and "Do Not Cover" are the common notations used.

Dimensioning of a shop drawing should be so complete that a carpenter could build the flat from the drawing without the use of a scale rule. The overall dimensions, the dimensions of any openings such as doors and windows, the location of toggles and interior stiles, are all drawn. The location of all critical framing members must be clearly identified.

Omit dimensions for a framing member whose location is not critical to the structure or appearance of the flat. An example of this rule of thumb is diagonal braces. Unless their location is critical, braces are installed so that they come as close to the center line of the flat as possible and are cut at a 45° angle. If a specific location and angle are necessary for the diagonal brace placement, then this information is supplied in full.

How flats are to join to each other is also determined at the drawing board. While the designer's ground plan identifies adjacent flats, there is no indication of their joinery. This results in the need for hardware locations to be drawn on construction drawings. To speed the drawing of hardware the USITT Graphic Standards are used. Although these and any other symbols are intended to be universally understood, drawings that make use of symbols should also contain a key, identifying the specific symbols used.

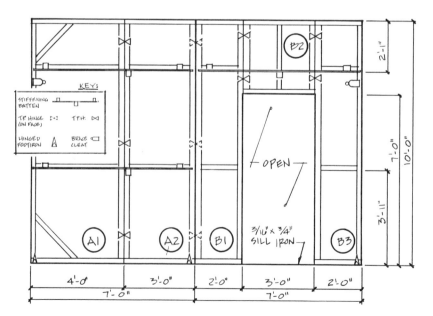

Should stock flattage be available to combine with built flats for the bifold unit shown, the rear elevation can be greatly simplified. The stock pieces need to be identified, as well as the joinery and stiffening, but framing outlines are omitted.

19.5. Rear elevation of a bifold flat, using stock flats

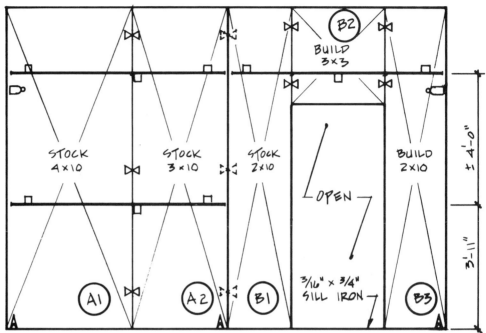

Although it is said that "a picture is worth a thousand words," at times a table conveys information more clearly. Tables use terse language and serve to clarify, not confuse. If stock flat frames are to be used for a set unit and their joinery is standard, a table can quickly provide the shop with the information necessary to pull and prepare the flats.

19.6. A table for using stock flats for a bifold flat

UNITS	FLATS	SIZE (W×H)	NOTES
A	A1	4'-0" × 10'-0"	TPH ON REAR
	A2	3'-0" × 10'-0"	STIFFEN ON REAR
			BRACE CLEAT (+7'-0"), NON-HINGED EDGE
			2 FOOT IRONS ON BOTTOM RAIL (HINGED)

* TPH 'A' TO 'B' ON FACE BEFORE COVERING AS SINGLE UNIT W/ MUSLIN

UNITS	FLATS	SIZE (W×H)	NOTES
B	B1	2'-0" × 10'-0"	SAME AS 'A' EXCEPT:
	B2	3'-0" × 3'-0"	1 FOOT IRON ONLY, NON-HINGED EDGE
	B3	2'-0" × 10'-0"	

19.6 Cost/Cut Lists

Shop drawings serve as the basis for the carpenter in the scenic studio to construct a given flat frame. From these drawings, cut lists are prepared to further speed construction. A cut list identifies like-sized framing members and determines the most efficient process to cut them.

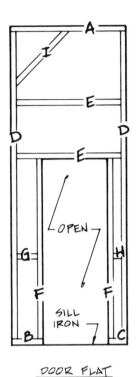

DOOR FLAT

	SCENIC CONSTRUCTION CUT LIST					

Show: CUT LIST EXAMPLE   Plate No. 19.3   Prepared by: D-

Date: AUG. 18   Unit Description DOOR FLAT

Comments: NOTE EXAMPLE OF DIAGONAL BRACE (PL. 'I') FORMULA

Unit Label	Piece Label	Stock	Qty.	Length	Notes	Done
FIG 19.3	A	1x3	1	4'-6"		
	B		1	1'-3"	3/16" X 3" NOTCH FOR SILL IRON	
	C		1	9"	— SAME AS ABOVE —	
	D		2	11'-7"		
	E		2	4'-1"		
	F		2	6'-9½"		
	G		1	10"		
	H		1	4"		
	I	↓	1	2'-10⅝"	LENGTH GIVEN IS LONG SIDE	

$$\text{BRACE} = \frac{\frac{54"}{2} - 2.5"}{(.707)} = \frac{27" - 2.5"}{(.707)} = \frac{24.5"}{(.707)} = 34.65"$$

FRACTIONAL CONVERSION PROCESS:

$$\frac{65}{100} \text{ INS.} = \frac{X}{16} \text{ INS}$$

$$X = \frac{65 \times 16}{100}$$

$$X = 10.4$$

$$\frac{10.4}{16} \text{ INS.} \approx \frac{5}{8}"$$

THEREFORE THE BRACE LENGTH IS: $34\frac{5}{8}"$ OR

$$\boxed{2'-10\frac{5}{8}"}$$

Unit label: Identifies the entire flat by using the designation from the design ground plan.

Piece label: Identifies the individual parts of the flat by using a shop-added designation, usually a letter or a number code.

Stock: Nominal dimensions of the stock that is to be used.

Qty. (Quantity):   Number of pieces of a given size that need to be cut.

Length: Lengths of pieces determined by using basic flat construction formulas. All formulas rely on actual rather than nominal dimensions.

Rails = the width of the flat

Stiles = the height of the flat less 2 x the width of the rails

Toggle = the width of the flat less 2 x the width of the stiles

$$\text{Brace}^* = \frac{(\text{length of rail} / 2 - \text{width of stile})}{\text{sine of } 45° (.707)}$$

*Formula determines long side, assuming brace meets center line of rail and all dimensions used in formula are expressed in inches.

Notes: Indicates special circumstances like bevels, miters, and rabbets.

Done: A check is placed in this column as each piece is cut.

A cut list can also serve as a base for very accurate cost estimations. Because all pieces of an individual flat frame are identified in the cut list, all costs for these items can be determined. Line costs are found by multiplying the quantity × the length × the unit price. All length measurements are rounded to the nearest 6" increment for ease of multiplication. For example, two 1 × 3 toggles @ 4'-7" long would be rounded to two pieces at 5'-0". When rounding, always round to the next highest unit, never the lower.

To assure accuracy in the estimate, all components of the finished flat such as gussets, sill irons, covering materials, hardware, and overhead items (glue and staples) are included. Gussets are counted and the cost of the necessary plywood is added. Sill irons are listed with current steel prices reflected. Soft covering is figured using total yardage. Hard covering figures full sheet use.

19.8. A cost/cut list

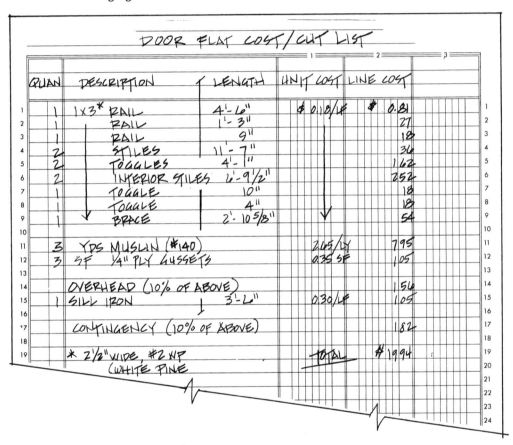

Hardware and overhead costs are determined through the use of a percentage of the total lumber costs. A 10% overhead charge is adequate in most situations. To provide enough financial resources to meet unforeseen problems, a contingency is also added. The standard contingency for familiar construction is 10% of the total materials bill. For complex or unfamiliar construction techniques that might require research or experimentation, a 15% figure provides a more appropriate cushion.

19.7 Problems

Worksheets 19.1, 19.2

Given the outlines of the four standard flat frames—the simple or regular flat, the door flat, the window flat, and the arch flat—draw the shop drawing for each. Fully dimension, note, and label each flat. Your focus will be to clearly convey all of the needed information for the construction of these flats. Ask yourself the question, "Could I build this flat with only the information provided?"

Worksheet 19.3

Prepare a cost/cut list for the window and arch flats (C and D) from worksheet 19.2, using the form provided. Check with your instructor or local vendors for the unit costs needed. Be thorough and do not forget to include overhead and contingency entries.

19.8 Checkpoints

√ Typical shop drawings are rear elevations drawn in ½″ = 1′-0″ scale and provide all of the information necessary for the accurate construction of a piece of scenery.

√ Shop drawings allow for decisions to be made at the drawing table rather than on the scenic studio floor.

√ Graphic conventions such as symbols, TYP, and tables help make drawings more clear.

√ The shop drawing is the basis for a cost/cut list, used to speed estimation and construction

B

A

D

C

FLATS 'C & D'
CUT/COST LIST

	QUAN	DESCRIPTION	LENGTH	UNIT COST	LINE COST		
1							1
2							2
3							3
4							4
5							5
6							6
7							7
8							8
9							9
10							10
11							11
12							12
13							13
14							14
15							15
16							16
17							17
18							18
19							19
20							20
21							21
22							22
23							23
24							24
25							25
26							26
27							27
28							28
29							29
30							30
31							31
32							32
33							33
34							34
35							35

20 Shop Drawings: Weight-bearing Scenery

20.1 Holding It All Up

Flat frames such as those discussed in the previous chapter are designed to simulate interior and exterior walls and are rarely called on to support much weight other than their own. These frames use construction materials in the face direction which is essentially a "two-dimensional" orientation. On the other hand, weight-bearing structures such as platforms, stairs, wagons, and stud walls rotate these framing materials 90°, using them in the "on edge" position. This rotation increases the moment of inertia of the material, with the result being an increase in the structural capacity of the material.

Numerous materials with potential structural properties can be found in the average scene shop, subsequently, a wide range of alternative construction techniques for weight-bearing structures has evolved. For most theatre technicians there is no single preferred technique, no "one right answer," rather a variety of alternate systems, each having advantages and disadvantages. Choices of technique are based on the unit's desired appearance, use, and handling.

Examining all these numerous alternatives here would be impossible and inappropriate, since this text is devoted to drafting, rather than engineering, principles. So while the drafter will be introduced to a few basic engineering concerns, the focus must remain on how these concepts are to be communicated in "typical" theatre drawings. Remarks are focused on the nature and depth of the detail required to produce a drawing useful to the scenic studio. The drafter, although typically not the person who will build the unit, must know and understand the basic principles behind such construction in order to produce useful drawings.

20.1. Platforms, stairs, wagons, and stud walls

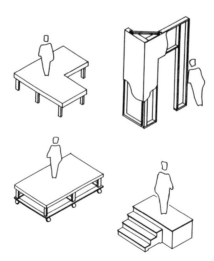

20.2 "Hollywood" or "TV" Flats and Stud Walls

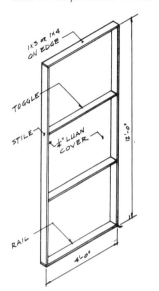

20.2. A Hollywood or TV flat

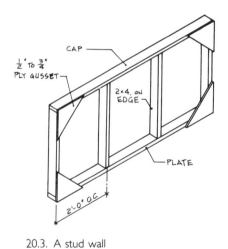

20.3. A stud wall

20.3 Platforms

Board lumber is significantly stiffer when placed "on edge" than when used in the face direction. This increased stiffness is the engineering principle behind the construction of the Hollywood/TV style flat. As the name indicates, this flat is utilized extensively in the television and film industries, and is characterized by its light weight, rigid frame, and rapid construction. Placing the frame "on edge" eliminates the need for the addition of stiffeners, making the unit ideal for situations requiring hard-cover applications. Rear elevations of hollywood flats are more difficult to draw than standard frames, since the ¾" dimension of the frame is very narrow in ½" = 1'-0" scale. Framing principles remain the same, except that members must be placed on modules to accommodate the 4 × 8 modular sheets used to cover them. Exterior plywood gussets and internal diagonal braces are often used to keep the walls in square. Typical specifications include the frame material (typically 1 × 3 or 1 × 4), fasteners, along with covering and joinery details.

Borrowed from the housing industry, stud walls are one of the most versatile of scenic units. They are different from the Hollywood flat only in the type of material used and their load-bearing capabilities. Commonly constructed of structural lumber (typically 2 × 4), when covered, they can serve both as the wall surface produced by a regular flat and as the structural support for an upper platform or stage level. When left uncovered, but reinforced with bracing and plywood gussets (corner blocks), stud walls provide a rapid legging system for platforms. Standard stud walls utilize a single horizontal top cap and base plate with studs located on 2'-0" centers.

The following parameters need to be addressed before any Hollywood flat or stud-wall shop drawing can be considered adequate for construction

Component Part	Standard Material Choices
1. Stud	1 × 3, 1 × 4 for flats
	2 × 4, 2 × 6 (infrequent) for legging systems
2. Top cap / bottom plate	Match the choice of studs
3. Gusset	¼", ½" ply
4. Brace	1 × 3, 1 × 4, commercial metal bracing
5. Cover	Any hard-covering material
6. Fasteners	Nails, staples, screws

One of the most common assignments given a shop drafter is the layout of elevated staging units, commonly known as platforms. Two types of shop drawings are used to describe such staging. Both techniques use a top view orientation to match the orientation of the carpenter.

A **construction detail** specifies the framing and legging details of a single unit and notes all material and fastener choices. A **platform layout** is more of a schematic drawing, used to subdivide a large raised area into smaller, more manageable units for reasons of either fiscal or handling constraints. The platform layout identifies modular units, some possibly from an existing inventory ("stock"), others (known as "bastards") built for a specific use. Generally, little detail is provided other than arrangement, identification, and notes regarding assembly procedures. At times both layout and detail drawings are combined into a single drawing showing both stock and bastard units.

Construction Details

Shop drawings of stock platforms are rarely required, since most scenic studios have their own standard. Stock platforms are usually of whole-foot increments and are modular, using a 4 × 8 sheet as the base module. Platforms having dimensions such as 4 × 8, 4 × 6, 4 × 4, 3 × 8, and 4 × 4 triangles are considered stock units.

Framing details must be provided, however, for irregular or bastard platforms. As a convention when details of any platform are drawn, a top view of the unit is drawn, with the deck removed. Removing the deck allows the drafter to expose the frame and posts permitting these components to be drawn using visible rather than hidden lines. The shop drawing should clearly indicate all framing, the location of legs (posts), the location of braces and faced surfaces (frequently noted rather than drawn), and include notes specifying the types and locations of fasteners and the deck material. The drawing should contain a note stating that the deck is not shown.

20.4. A platform shop drawing

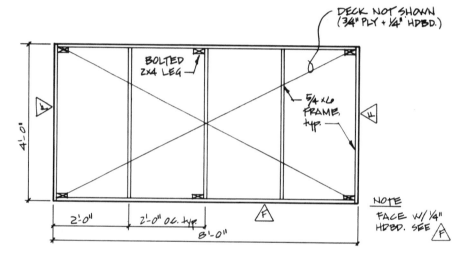

Regardless of the specification technique applied, the following parameters need to be addressed before any platform drawing can be considered adequate for construction.

Component Part		Standard Material Choices
1. Deck:	Material	¾" plywood, OSB or particle board
	Span	Framing members 24" o.c.
2. Frame:	Material	2 × 4 fir; 1 × 6 or 5/4 × 6 pine
	Span	Posts 48" o.c. max; 2-sided stress skin construction will allow up to 96" span
3. Post:	Material	1 × 3, 1 × 4, 2 × 4 (thinnest dimension must be greater than $\frac{1}{50}$ of height)
4. Brace:	Ribbon	1 × 3, etc.; use when leg is greater than 12" but less than 30" long
	Diagonal	1 × 3 etc.; use if leg is longer than 30", combine with ribbon brace
5. Facing:	Material	¼" or stiffer hardboard, ply, or equal
	Span	Fasten entire perimeter using deck standard

20.5. Cross brace and ribbon

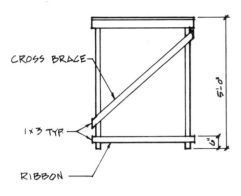

CROSS BRACE

1 × 3 TYP

RIBBON

5'-0"

6"

20.6. A platform section view

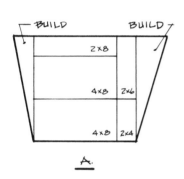

BUILD   BUILD

2×8	
4×8	2×6
4×8	2×4

A.

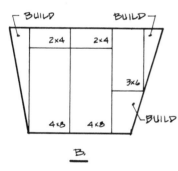

BUILD   BUILD

2×4	2×4
	3×6
4×8	4×8

BUILD

B.

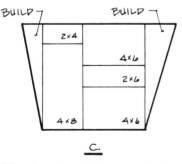

BUILD   BUILD

2×4	
	4×6
	2×6
4×8	4×6

C.

20.7. Alternative platform layout solutions

6. Fasteners: Deck   Nails, screws: 6″ o.c. along perimeter; 9″ to 10″ o.c. along interior frame

Frame   2 to 3 nails, screws: use a nail 2½ times the thickness of the material being nailed into place

Brace   Same as above

Side views or section views are used to detail posts, braces, deck, and facing. The section view is preferred, since it most clearly differentiates components, giving the "inside story" of the desired fabrication. To clearly communicate what is needed, the section drawing must reference the pieces shown in the top view, assuring the carpenter of the proper relationship of the pieces.

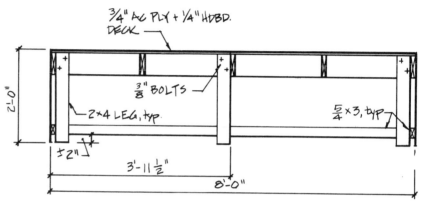

¾″ AC PLY + ¼″ HDBD. DECK

⅜″ BOLTS

2×4 LEG, typ.

5/4 × 3, typ.

2'-0"

±2″

3'-11½″

8'-0"

Platform Layout Drawings

Rarely is a single staging unit placed onstage; usually several are joined to create a platforming system. The exact configuration is most easily determined at the drafting table, where the number, style, and arrangement of stock units are determined and drawn into a platform layout. Using only platform outlines with an accompanying legend, all the necessary information is clearly transmitted. The legend looks and functions similar to a shopping list and should require no more work of the technician than the gathering of the specified units. Because of the simplicity of the drawing, it is possible, although not necessarily recommended, to work in ¼″ scale, a feature that will save both time and paper (fig. 20.7).

The first step in preparing a platform layout is to draw the outline of the entire area to be elevated. This is simply a tracing of the appropriate portion of the designer's ground plan. As a rule, begin by dividing the area into the largest possible "stock" sections, usually 4 × 8 modules, and work down to the smallest. Test alternative layouts using different combinations until the most efficient scheme is determined. The undefined areas will require the construction of specific, or bastard platforms.

The actual shop drawing given to the carpenter should be simplified as much as possible. The following procedure is recommended: After the large area is subdivided into component units, draw thin diagonal lines connecting the corners of the individual platforms. Next assign each platform size a letter of the alphabet; use that letter as a label. Locate the appropriate designation in the lower right-hand corner of the individual platform. (An alternative location is fine, but use a consistent location for each label.) Avoid using the center of the space, since this is often used for a locating a height or similar information. Then prepare the platform layout summary, itemizing the designation, number, and types of units required; letter and label it "platform legend."

20.8. Platform layout with platform legend

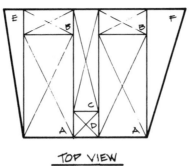

TOP VIEW

QTY	NAME	SIZE	HEIGHT	NOTES
		PLATFORM LEGEND		
2	A	4'-0" x 8'-0"	2'-0"	STOCK
2	B	2'-0" x 4'-0"		
1	C	2'-0" x 8'-0"		
1	D	2'-0" x 2'-0"	↓	
1	E	BASTARD		SEE DETAIL DWG
1	F	BASTARD	↓	↓

20.4 Wagons

Elevating a platform onto a set of wheels transforms the unit into a wagon. The use of wagons mobilizes scenery, making possible multiple stage pictures. Wagon construction techniques range from simple to complex; the focus here is again on the type of information needed to specify construction needs. Beyond that, the drafter will need to employ both experience and intuition.

A simple 6" high wagon may be created with the addition of casters bolted to the underside of the platform's plywood deck. Casters are placed in the same approximate locations as legs used to support a platform unit. A spacer block is often placed between the deck and caster mounting plate to adjust the wagon to the required height. This deck attachment technique is not advised for use with wood deck products having little or no grain, such as particle board and flakeboard (OSB). For wagons higher than 8", often a standard platform is mounted on a castered frame known as a **caster plate.** Typically made of 2 × 6s "on face," joined by half-lap joints or ½" to ¾" oversized gussets (12"–15" leg), caster plates are a structural form of the standard theatre flat. Casters are bolted to the underside of the plate (the side where the gussets are located), while the legs of the platform are secured to the top surface by using angle brackets. Wherever possible, position a caster directly under each platform leg. The caster plate serves to maintain caster alignment and to transfer the load of the platform to the stage floor. Often the caster plate doubles as a means to secure a facing material to the side seen by the audience.

Construction drawings of wagons that require caster plates need separate top-view drawings of both the platforming system and the caster plate. Begin by drawing register marks, such as a center line and datum line, to assure accurate alignment of component parts. Draw the platform frame

20.9. A wagon

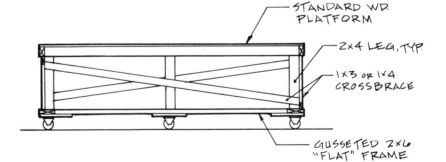

STANDARD WD. PLATFORM

2x4 LEG, TYP.

1X3 OR 1X4 CROSSBRACE

GUSSETED 2X6 "FLAT" FRAME

20.10. Caster plate detail

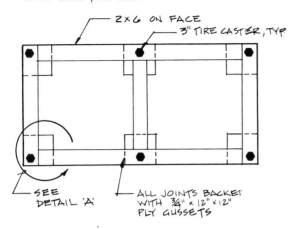

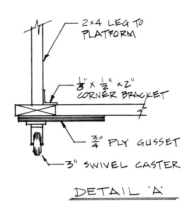

DETAIL 'A'

20.11. Caster layout for a jackknife
wagon

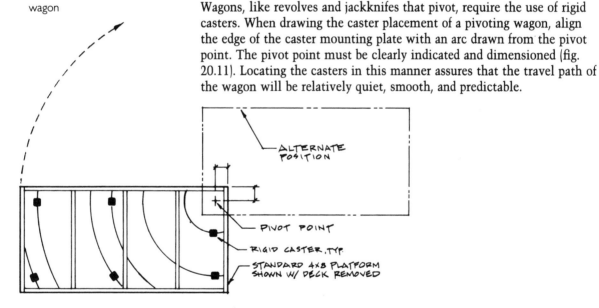

with the deck removed, but use thin diagonal lines to indicate the decking layout. The caster plate drawing shows the framing, the gussets (optional), recommended fasteners, and the caster locations. Caster locations are usually identified by use of a symbol. A filled-in hexagon, as shown in figure 20.10, is very useful for this purpose, since it is bold and not a symbol likely to appear in some other context on the drawing. A detailed section view showing the relationship of caster, leg, and facing to the frame help to clarify the construction to the carpenter.

Wagons, like revolves and jackknifes that pivot, require the use of rigid casters. When drawing the caster placement of a pivoting wagon, align the edge of the caster mounting plate with an arc drawn from the pivot point. The pivot point must be clearly indicated and dimensioned (fig. 20.11). Locating the casters in this manner assures that the travel path of the wagon will be relatively quiet, smooth, and predictable.

20.5 Stairs

The stair unit is one of the most complex units of standard scenery to draft. The complexity of stair units comes through their need to be comfortable for the human body, to elevate the actor to a given height, and to fit within a given space. This requires some understanding of the structural problems associated with them. Stairs are made up of three components (fig. 20.12).

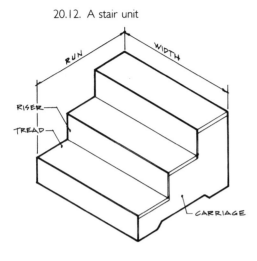

20.12. A stair unit

Components	Definition	Standard Materials
Treads	Walking surface	2 × 12, ¾" ply (single or doubled)
Risers	Height of the step	1 × lumber, plywood
Carriages or stringers	Structural members that support treads and risers	2 × 12, ⁵⁄₄ × 12, or ¾" ply with nailing cleats

Because the human body instantly reacts to the height and width of a given step, a constant riser/tread relationship must be maintained. If the riser/tread relationship is not constant, the actor is forced to move awkwardly to compensate for the inconsistency. At best this creates a strange stage picture, at worst this situation can cause an accident.

A variety of rules of thumb have been developed in the construction trade to aid the determination of tread depth and riser height. These are not absolute rules but guidelines to use in determining the most desirable answer.

Stair Construction Rules of Thumb

Rule	Example
Tread width + riser height = 17.5"	T + R = 17.5" 10" + 7.5" = 17.5"
Tread width + (2 × riser height) = 25"	T + 2R = 24" to 25" 10" + 2(7.5") = 25"
Tread width × riser height = 75"	T × R = 75" 10" × 7.5" = 75"

Treads should be no less than 10" and no more than 12" in width.

Additional Rules

1. More formulas:
   a. Length of a carriage^2 = total rise^2 × total run.^{2}
   b. Number of risers = total rise/riser height.
   c. Riser height = total rise/number of risers.
2. Subtract the thickness of the tread from the first rise when laying out a carriage.
3. Add a center carriage for stairs wider than 2'-6" to assure tread stiffness.
4. Provide railings for all stairs but especially offstage stairs. The top edge of the handrail should be located 2'-8" above the tread at the nosing line.
5. Allow a minimum of 6'-8" (80") headroom for stairs located under a platform or through a trap.

The run of a stair unit is determined by multiplying the tread width × the number of treads. The rise of a stair equals the riser height × the number of risers. To maintain comfort, in an unrestricted area, the total run should = 1⅓ × the total rise. Frequently onstage space for stairs is very restricted, limited perhaps by other scenery or the theatre walls. Shortening the run dimension will, of course, increase the steepness of the stairs. Acceptable practice requires that the steepness not be more than 50° nor less than 20°.

Design drawings of stair units are often nothing more than the information given on the ground plan unless the stair is highly ornamental or unusual. Shop drawings should show two views, usually a front and side view or a front and section. Because of the large amount of information needed to detail tread, riser, and carriage arrangements, 1″ scale is often used.

20.13. Front elevation and section of an open rise stair

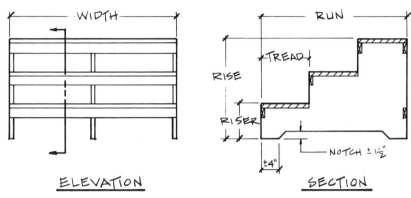

ELEVATION   SECTION

20.14. A ship's ladder

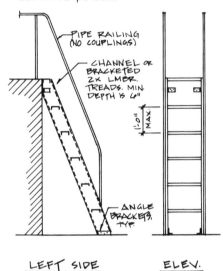

LEFT SIDE   ELEV.

If space considerations require the angle of a stairway to be greater than 50°, then the stair may be replaced with a **ship's ladder** or a **straight ladder**. A ship's ladder has the same components as a stair unit, only the riser height is increased to compensate for the rapid height change. Treads are a minimum of 6″ and the riser height is no greater than 12″.

If a vertical ladder is required, the ladder should be a minimum of 1′-6″ in width and be at least 6″ away from the vertical surface to which the ladder is attached. Rungs should be no more than 12″ apart and no less than 1″ in diameter. Many construction techniques are possible, but those that place loads on fasteners rather than materials should be avoided.

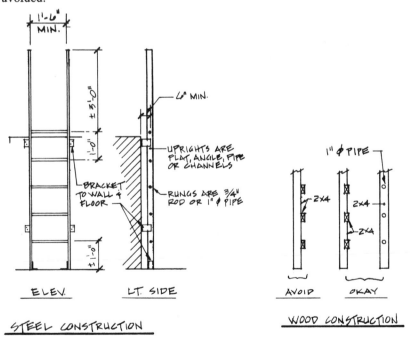

ELEV.   LT. SIDE   AVOID   OKAY

STEEL CONSTRUCTION   WOOD CONSTRUCTION

20.15. Straight ladder construction

20.6 Problems

Worksheet 20.1
Given the outline of a flat that is also to serve as a support for a second-story platform, develop a shop drawing showing the stud wall layout, material choices, and full dimensions. Note: The wall is to be covered in ¼" flake board. Be sure to provide framing to support seams.

Worksheet 20.2
Given the outline of a 4 × 8 platform that has been legged to a height of 2'-0", using standard 2 × 4 bolted legs, provide the framing, legging, and facing details of the stock platform. Provide dimensions and material and assembly notes.

Worksheet 20.3
Given the ¼" scale outline of a stage platform, divide the area into stock units and complete a platform legend, using the format provided in the text.

Worksheet 20.4
Provide frame and legging details for the cantilevered platform unit given. Indicate the materials to be used for deck, frame, and stud wall. Dimension and notate all work. Avoid hidden lines by using a section view when detailing the platform components. Note: When a design demands the use of platforms other than stock units, further details need to be provided. Worksheet 20.4 deals with a cantilevered platform with a stud wall legging system. Due to the need to provide support for the cantilevered portion of the platform, the use of stock platforming is not an option. Framing of 2 × 6 members on 2'-0" centers is selected to run the full length of the cantilever. To tie the framing members together and provide a deck, 4 × 8 sheets of ¾" ply are oriented with the 8'-0" dimension along the width. This means that additional framing will be required to support the seams in the three sheets of plywood required.

Worksheet 20.5
Develop a shop drawing of the step unit required to access a platform 3'-6" high, as shown in the isometric drawing. Provide complete dimensions and notation.

20.7 Checkpoints

√ Hollywood-style flats and stud walls use framing materials in their "on edge" direction for additional stiffness and strength.

√ Platforms are drawn in two views: top and side. In the top view, the deck is removed to avoid hidden lines.

√ Platform layouts are keyed and the information about the layout is summarized in a table called the "platform legend."

√ Caster locations on wagons and caster plates are drawn using symbols and are accompanied with a detail drawing for clarity.

√ Stairs are drawn in 1" scale for clarity of detail and should follow the rules of thumb given for safety and comfort.

OPEN

FRONT ELEVATION

SCALE. $\frac{1}{2}" = 1'-0"$

TOP VIEW

A   A

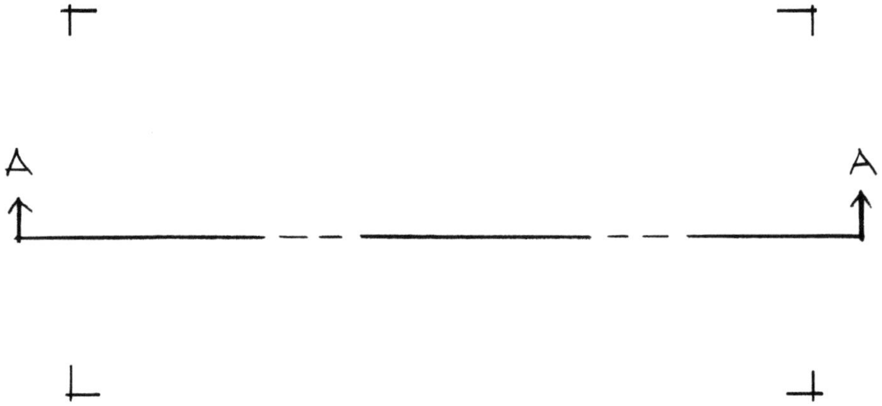

SECTION A·A

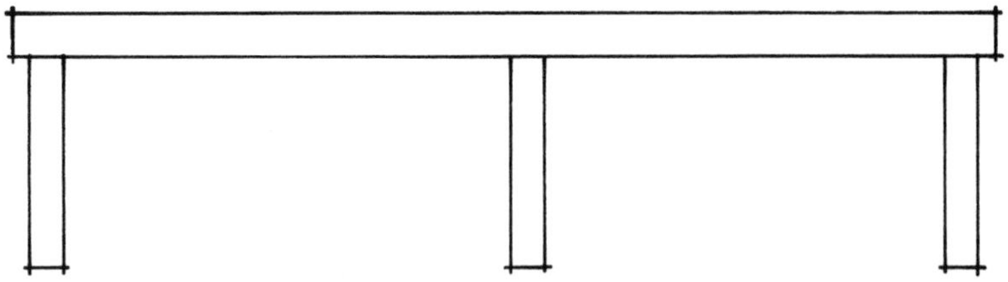

Name:	SHOP DRAWINGS: WEIGHT-BEARING	
Date:		

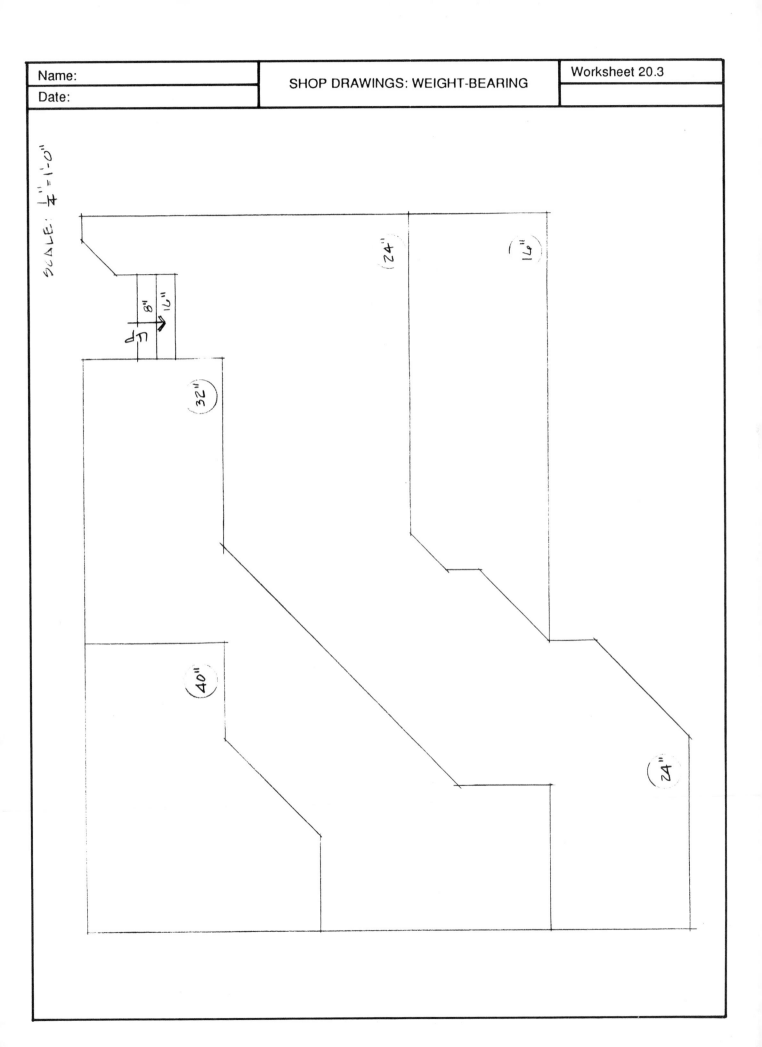

SCALE: $\frac{1''}{2} = 1'\text{-}0''$

EDGE OF
CANTILEVER

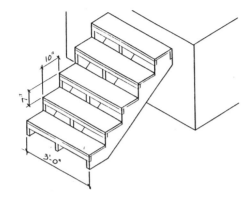

10"

7"

3'-0"

DRAW RT. SIDE OR SEC.
SCALE: 1"=1'-0"

21 Shop Drawings: Irregular Flats, Shapes, and Soft Goods

21.1 Two-dimensional Irregular Shapes

Most of the scenic units discussed in these chapters on shop drawings have had rectilinear shapes. Most scenery, however, does not fit into this convenient world of right angles. For the sake of this discussion these nonrectangular scenic units have been given the label of "irregular shapes." Usually these pieces have irregular profile lines. (A profile is an outline shape, drawn either with a straight edge or freehand, i.e., the skyline view of a group of buildings or the leaves on a tree.)

The development of useful shop drawings for irregular shaped units requires a knowledge of actual construction practices. It is important to recognize that in the scenic studio it is difficult to accurately project angles other than right angles. The carpenter can make use of a tape measure, framing square, and the axiom of the "3–4–5 triangle" for 90° angles, but there is no such ready combination of tools to develop other angles. Given the long distances that need to be projected in the construction of scenery, it is necessary to examine other methods of dimensioning oblique and acute angles.

21.2 Dimensioning Two-dimensional Irregular Shapes

One way to provide the information necessary for the construction of irregular units is to surround the object with a grid of right-angle dimensions, i.e., a system of coordinate points (fig. 21.1). These points are developed by placing the unit within a rectangle, equal in size to the object's extreme outside dimensions. One corner of the rectangle is selected as the "0, 0" point of intersection on an "X,Y" grid. Once this is done, all significant points are located within the rectangle and measurements evolve from the base lines. This technique is useful when dimensioning an object with oblique straight lines.

21.1. Perpendicular dimensions of an irregular shape

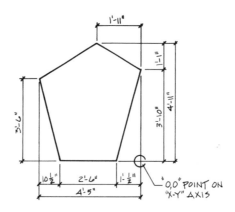

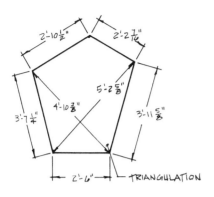

21.2. Triangular dimensioning of an irregular shape

A second method of describing the layout of a unit with oblique angles is through the use of triangulation. In this procedure, shown in figure 21.2, an irregular flat is subdivided into triangles, using temporary diagonals. The object can easily be reconstructed by using the compass and the process of triangulation. This operation is easily repeated in the scenic studio. Once a base line and perpendicular have been established on the studio floor, the outline of the flat is determined using trammel points and triangulation (see chap. 14). Triangulation is usually faster than developing a rectangular grid, but when working with extreme oblique angles it is not as accurate.

In neither system should the actual angle measurements be used unless they have been checked mathematically using trigonometry to determine that the angles and given lengths of the sides are precise. No drafter, regardless of experience or skill, can work in small scale with enough precision that this information can be determined solely by graphic means.

21.3 Profile Flats

Profile flats are among the most fascinating of scenic units to build. With good painting techniques, a flat piece of wood and canvas can be made to seem perfectly three-dimensional. The fabrication of profile flats, however, requires a different approach to framing and handling than does conventional flattage.

First, layout the shape (profile) by using the designer's front elevation. This is done on either a hard material, such as plywood, or on craft paper with a grid-to-grid or projection-transfer system. With the full-scale profile developed, framing is then applied to support the irregular shape. A working drawing of the framing should be developed in advance to reduce the decisions required of the carpenter and to increase efficient use of time and materials. Realize that the working drawing of the framing will be somewhat "conceptual" in nature. This is due to the inexact nature of the initial layout process. What is now reality may not precisely match the original drawing supplied by the designer.

Profile edges are usually formed by ¼" plywood joined to standard 1× framing, using a rabbet joint, or ¾" plywood gusseted to the 1× frame. No more than 6" of ¼" ply should be left unsupported by framing members. The 1× frame is developed by the drafter, such that the largest possible rectangles are drawn, utilizing the strength and easy construction of the right angle. Framing members that are in the longest dimension carry through all other internal members. The bottom rail always carries through the frame.

21.3. Profile flats

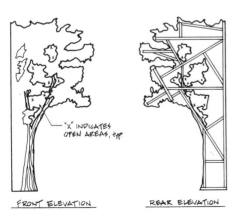

FRONT ELEVATION   REAR ELEVATION

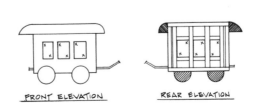

FRONT ELEVATION   REAR ELEVATION

Ground rows and similar large profile units may need to fold for storage and ease of handling. Since the extent of a person's reach is approximately equal to his or her height, one dimension of the unit, either open or folded, is generally kept under 6'-0". Standard bi-fold and three-fold construction techniques are used, with framing members extending through to the edge of the profile in any location where the joints are hinged. Removable stiffening is required across folded joints if the unit is meant to rest in a single plane.

Working drawings for profile flattage must include the following information:

1. Overall height and width of the unit
2. Width of component units (if a folding unit)
3. Other measurements that must be held (significant dimensions only)
4. Location of fold lines (if necessary)

Other conventions that are helpful to the carpenter and therefore should be included are:

1. Crosshatching the plywood profile edge
2. High-contrast outline with thin lines used for frame, dimensions, etc.
3. Local notes specifying materials, hardware, assembly instructions, etc.
4. A labeling system to indicate clearly all components
5. A superimposed grid of one- or two-foot squares, labeled for easy reference

21.4 Three-dimensional Irregular Shapes

Scenic designers often call for the construction of three-dimensional irregular or curvilinear shapes such as rocks, trees, and columns. Like the drawings for profile flats, shop drawings for three-dimensional structures are also of a conceptual nature, owing to the need to develop full-scale patterns in the scenic studio. Typical construction for such irregular shapes includes small flat frames that interconnect ¾" plywood profiles. An appropriate support covering is then added, followed by a finished skin. The shop drawing should provide:

1. Overall dimensions (length, width, and height)
2. Section views of those profiles critical to the overall shape
3. Type and location of framing materials needed to ensure structural integrity
4. Notes detailing the anticipated use of the object onstage

The specifications of the shop drawing serve to guide the scenic carpenter toward an appropriate approach to the given problem. However, it is nearly impossible to adequately depict the construction of a three-dimensional object, a piece of sculpture, in a two-dimensional shop drawing. Often a fully notated design drawing serves the experienced carpenter equally well. Actually from the perspective of both designer and carpenter, the very best kind of shop drawing for the fabrication of three-dimensional pieces is a painted model.

21.4. Three-dimensional irregular shapes

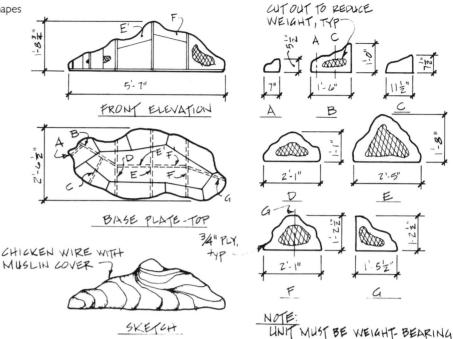

21.5 Soft Goods

Soft goods is an area of scenery that often encounters inadequate description of fabrication details. This specialized area includes drops, curtains, ground cloths, and any number of fabric-based scenic pieces, both woven and synthetic. Design elevations of soft goods are frequently painted elevations from which the line information is transferred from the original drawing to the full-sized piece of fabric by using some type of projection technique. Frequently the piece is sewn, hemmed, grommeted, and battened without the preparation of a shop drawing. This practice is not to be recommended, since it bypasses the overall system of checks built into the system of design and shop drawings.

21.5. Fabrication details for a muslin drop

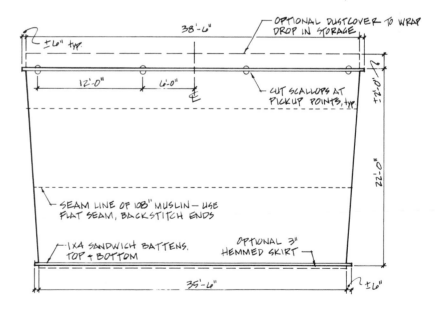

The information necessary in the construction of soft goods includes:
1. The type of curtain (traverse, tableau, austrian, etc.) or drop (regular, cut, scrim, border, leg, roller, etc.)
2. Overall dimensions (height and width)
3. Kind of fabric
4. Placement of seams and stitching instructions (drops should be seamless or have horizontal seams; curtains have vertical seams with nap direction specified)
5. Hanging instructions
6. Edge finishing instructions (webbing, sandwich batten, pipe/chain pocket, keystone, hem, skirting)
7. Surface preparation and painting technique, if any, to be used

While detailed information is required, most soft good specifications involve extensive notation in addition to simple drawings. There are a few details, however, that can and should be drawn to clarify written language. Some of the more standard of these details are shown in figure 21.5.

Given the lack of detail appearing on a drawing that shows the overall size of the goods, it is common to see soft goods drawn in a scale less than the standard ½" = 1'-0". While such practice does not usually affect clarity, a change of scales may be responsible for some confusion regarding actual size. When using a scale other than ½" = 1'-0" scale, be doubly certain to provide all needed dimensions.

21.6. Fabrication details for a swag curtain

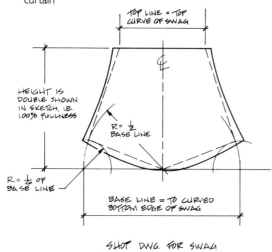

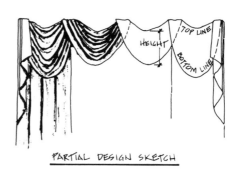

21.6 Problems

Worksheets 21.1, 21.2
Given the rear elevations of two irregular flats, develop working drawings of each in ½" = 1'-0" scale. Provide complete notation and dimensioning for each.

Worksheet 21.3
Given the **front elevation** of a ground row, develop a ½" = 1'-0" scale working drawing. Dimension and notate as needed. Show the locations of all hardware, using USITT Graphic Standards. Note: The unit must fold into a package approximately 6'-0" by 10'-0".

Worksheet 21.4
Given the front elevation of a drop to be constructed out of 72″ wide #140 muslin and rigged with a sandwich batten for hanging, develop a ½″ = 1′-0″ scale working drawing. Include details for hanging, pipe pocket, skirt, and seams. Dimension and notate as needed.

21.7 Checkpoints

√ Two-dimensional irregular flats are dimensioned by using a coordinate reference or through triangulation.

√ Profile flats and irregular three-dimensional scenic units require working drawings that are "conceptual" in nature owing to the potential inaccuracy of the initial layout process.

√ Shop drawings for soft goods contain a variety of specifications that are best noted or shown as details.

OPEN

OPEN

SCALE: $\frac{1}{2}'' = 1'-0''$

SCALE: $\frac{1}{2}'' = 1'-0''$

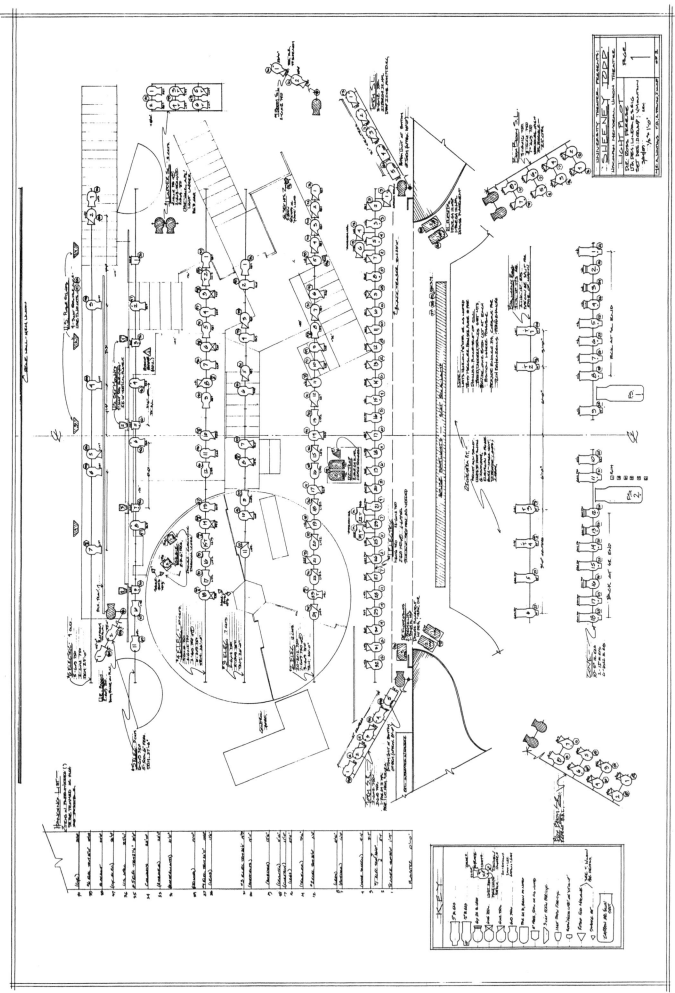

22.1. Lighting plot, Sweeney Todd. Courtesy Linda Essig, lighting designer

22 Lighting Design Drawings

22.1 And Then There Was Light

As with scenic designers, the lighting designer uses graphic communication to translate design work from idea to onstage reality. A major distinction, however, is that the lighting designer is not actually picturing the intended look of the design, rather, the lighting designer uses drafting to convey a plan to accomplish the design. In this sense, lighting design drafting is more similar to a shop drawing than a design drawing.

To facilitate handling the great amount of information that needs to be transmitted from the designer to the electrics crew, a concise language of lighting symbols and notation has been developed and adopted as an industry standard by USITT. With the adoption of these standards, lighting designers are able to save considerable drafting time, since a specific key of symbols no longer needs to be created for each plot. (As is discussed later, a key must still be included, but it will contain selected units drawn from the USITT standard.) The use of standard symbols also provides designers a greater degree of mobility, since the standard is common to all lighting specialists regardless of which part of the country they are working. Most schools now teach this shorthand language to better prepare students for professional careers.

22.2 The Necessary Parts of Lighting Communication

The most basic element of lighting design communication is the **light plot.** The light plot is a horizontal section that indicates the stage setting, acting areas (optional), instrumentation, hanging locations, focus, color, and circuitry (this information is sometimes added by the master electrician). The light plot serves as the primary source of information throughout the lighting design process.

A center-line **section view** of the proposed lighting hang is also required. The section assists in checking appropriate beam angles, the value of proposed masking and its impact on the lighting design, as well as identifying scenic obstacles. Section views also show trim heights of onstage electrics and can clarify the location of actual hanging positions. In complex situations, two sections may be required to fully describe the design.

Lighting design graphics also include supplementary lists, usually referred to as "paperwork." Paperwork helps the designer organize the information provided on the plot in a variety of manners to meet specific needs. A **storyboard** (usually a series of storyboards) may be prepared that tracks through the script and attempts to capture individual cues or moments onstage. Storyboards are similar to scenic renderings, however, drawing light is a much more difficult task and these boards should be taken as only suggestive of the final look onstage. An **equipment list** is prepared that lists all equipment by position, including instruments and accessories such as booms, boom bases, cable, and two-fers. This list can be sent to a rental company to develop a cost estimate, or it can be useful in checking the theatre inventory against what the designer has requested.

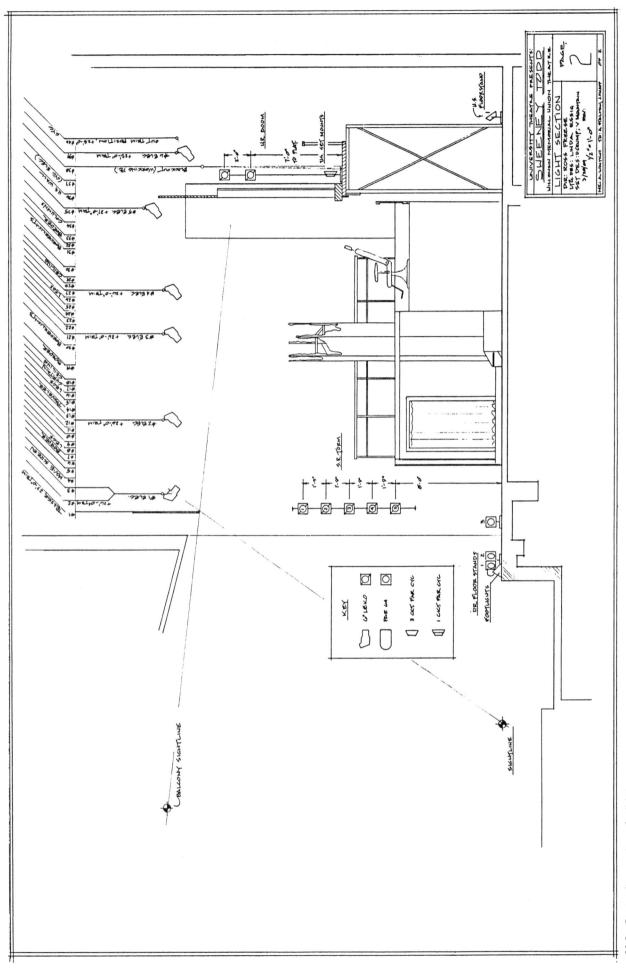

22.2. Center-line section of a lighting plot, *Sweeney Todd*. Courtesy Linda Essig, lighting designer

22.3. Production photo, *Sweeney Todd.* Courtesy University Theatre, University of Wisconsin-Madison

LIGHTING EQUIPMENT SHOP ORDER

SHOW: Sweeney Todd   **LIGHTING DESIGNER:** L.Essig

PRODUCER: The University Theatre   March 28, 1989
University of Wisconsin-Madison

THEATER: Memorial Union Theater

LOAD-IN DATE: April 16, 1989

COVE:
    10 - 5 1kW ERS, clamps, frames
     2 - 12 1kW ERS, clamps, frames
     6 - 6x22 1kW ERS, clamps, frames
    Jumpers & twofers

BALCONY RAIL:
    4 - 12 1kW T&S ERS, clamps,
       temp. holders, frames
    2 - 12 1kW ERS, clamps, frames
    Jumpers & twofers
    Pans & irons as needed

BOX BOOM LEFT:
    4 - 6x16 750W ERS, frames
    2 - 6x12 750W ERS, frames
    1 - 6x9 750W ERS, frame
    Jumpers & twofers
    4 - DT sidearms

BOX BOOM RIGHT:
    4 - 6x16 750W ERS, frames
    2 - 6x12 750W ERS, frames
    1 - 6x9 750W ERS, frame
    Jumpers & twofers
    4 - DT sidearms

BOX BOOM RIGHT:
    4 - 6x16 750W ERS, frames
    2 - 6x12 750W ERS, frames
    1 - 6x9 750W ERS, frame
    Jumpers & twofers
    4 - DT sidearms

S.L. TORM:
    3 - 6x12 750W ERS, frames
    2 - PAR 64 1kW MFL, frames
    Jumpers & twofers
    5 - ST sidearms
    Supply one cable

S.R. TORM:
    2 - 6x12 750W ERS, frames
    3 - 6x9 750W ERS, frames
    1 - PAR 64 1kW MFL, frame
    Jumpers & twofers
    5 - ST sidearms
    Supply one cable

FIRST ELECTRIC:
    1 - 6x16 750W ERS, clamps
   23 - 6x12 750W

22.4. Shop order (equipment list), *Sweeney Todd.* Courtesy Linda Essig, lighting designer

The **hook-up** is organized by channel or dimmer number and lists the instruments that are controlled by each. The **focus chart** lists each instrument by position on which specific focus notes can be made. The **color cut list** schedules the color(s) chosen for each instrument and the appropriate sizes needed of each so that all frames can be prepared in advance of the hang. The **cheat sheet** identifies systems of focus along with color and serves as a rapid source of information in the development of cues.

HOOK-UP

SHOW: 'SWEENEY TODD'
DESIGNER: LINDA ESSIG
FOR: 1>9 @ 4KW
#1 ELEC.   ETC. 'IMPRESSION'

PAGE 1 OF 8
DATE: 3/89
THEATRE: MEMORIAL UNION

CHAN	D.	POSITION-NO	TYPE	FOCUS	COLOR	NOTES
1A		#1 ELEC -22·24	2-6x9 750	JOHANNA'S BALCONY	R88 T=R77·806	'GREEN FINCH' TEMPLATES
		T+S				
1B		#1 ELEC - 9	1-6x16 750	JUDGE'S COURT DL	N/C	DALT
2		#1 ELEC 7·13·20·26	4-6x12 750	CTR STEPS FILL ↗↖	7·13-N/C 20·26-GAM 79	(2 CKT3.)
3		#1 ELEC 3·16	2-6x9 750	BALCONY FILL	3-N/C 16-GAM 79	
4		#1 ELEC 5·15·21	3-6x9 750	PARLOR FILL	5·15-N/C 21-GAM79	↑↑↖
5		#1 ELEC - 8	1-6x12 750	DL DOWN	R65	
				↗ DOWN	R65	

22.5. Hook up, *Sweeney Todd*. Courtesy Linda Essig, lighting designer

FOCUS CHART FOR: 'SWEENEY TODD'
POSITION: #1 ELEC

13 APR. '89

CHAN/SW	PLUGGED W		FOCUS			F	TYPE	COLOR
1	1E·2	10L, +4		• DL ←			6x12 750w	R87
9	SL TORM 2·3	SL		US	S.E.			
		SR		DS	S.E.		LEKO	
2	1E·1	4L, +4		• DL ←			6x12 750w	R87
9	SL TORM 2·3	SL		US O.O. RAIL				
		SR		DS	S.E.			
3	1E·16	ON J.'s BALCONY		• BALCONY FILL			6x9 750w	N/C
3		SL @WALL		US HEAD HIGH				
		SR TO PLAT.		DS OFF STAIRS				
4	1E·6	4L, +12		• H.S. LEFT ↖			6x12 750w	L142
13	SL TORM	SL OFF PLAT		US OFF WALL				
		SR		DS				
5	1E·15·21	10R, +10		• PARLOR FILL			6x9 750w	N/C
4		SL		US OFF BRICK				
		SR		DS TO PLAT				
6	1E·4	4, +12		•US LT. ↖			6x12 750w	L142
13		SL		US				
		SR		DS				
7	1E·13·20 ·26	2ND FROM TOP		•CTR. STEPS. FILL			6x12 750w	N/C
2		SL		US AT MOLDING				
		SR		DS AT STRINGER				
8	—	10L, +4		• DL. DOWN			6x12 750w	R65
		SL		US OFF STAIRS				
		SR		DS				
	-4			• JUDGE'S COURT			6x16 750w	N/C
				US O.O. PLAT				
				~ S.E.				
		—					6x12 750w	R87

22.6. Focus chart, *Sweeney Todd*. Courtesy Linda Essig, lighting designer

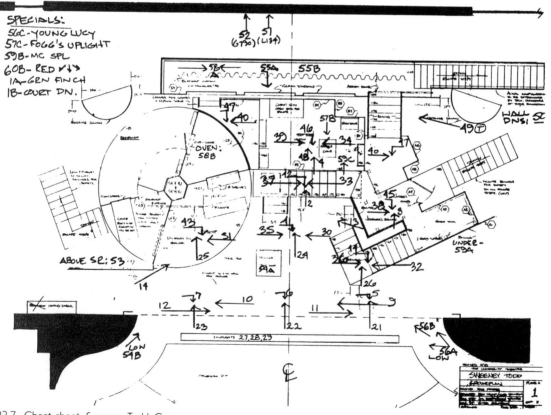

SPECIALS:
56C - YOUNG LUCY
57C - FOGG'S UPLIGHT
59B - MC SPL
60B - RED ↖↗
1A - GRN FINCH
1B - COURT DN.

22.7. Cheat sheet, *Sweeney Todd*. Courtesy Linda Essig, lighting designer

22.3 The Light Plot

The light plot is the central source for information in lighting design and therefore is the first step in developing the graphic communication of a lighting design. But before a lighting designer can even begin the light plot, some basic information must first be gathered. The lighting designer needs:

1. The scenic design ground plan
2. The scenic design center-line section or sections
3. The plan view of the theatre
4. The section view of the theatre
5. Indications of circuit layout, hanging positions, and control board type
6. Inventories of equipment and accessories

Once all of this information has been assembled, the lighting designer is ready to begin to design and draft the plot. For some designers, design and drafting is a one-step process. For other designers, ideas are sketched first on scratch paper, then assembled into the final plot by a drafter, frequently the assistant lighting designer (ALD).

Most drafters or designers use an overlay technique in drawing the plot, since both set and lighting drawings are drawn in ½″=1′–0″ scale. A large clean sheet of drawing media, typically 30″ × 42″ (E-size), is placed over either the plan of the theatre or the scenic design ground plan, and the plot is developed from there. The light plot is oriented from the auditorium side of the theatre. Typically all instruments, hanging locations, and notes are drawn before the scenery and the architectural features of the theatre building are added. (Other options are to draw in the set and building features first, then use an erasing shield to assist in removing lines that interfere with instruments and notes, or employ pin-bar techniques with a 40%–50% screen used to reduce the set and building features. The latter reduces drawing time and eliminates the danger of erasing necessary information.)

An early step in the plot development process is the division of the stage space into **acting areas.** These areas serve to assist the lighting designer in determining system focus and cueing control. Acting areas average about 6′-0″ to 10′-0″ in diameter, are indicated with broken circles that approximate the beam spread of the instruments being used to light the show, and are identified using ½″ or larger capital letters. This same letter designation will later be used in the notation on each instrument indicating its focus.

22.8. The stage divided into acting areas

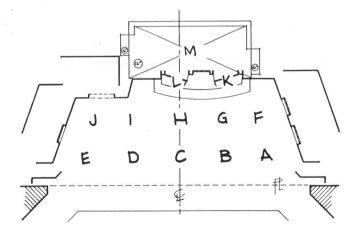

A lighting template is used to draw the appropriate symbols for the instruments selected in their chosen **hanging positions**. Instruments are drawn perpendicular or parallel to the horizontal pipe upon which they are being hung, with the pipe located at approximately the center of the instrument. They may be pointed upstage, downstage, stage right, or stage left, but no other hanging orientation is recommended. All onstage pipes are drawn in their actual location. Front-of-house (FOH) locations are foreshortened to eliminate the large unused areas of paper that would occur if these locations were actually drawn in scale from the stage.

22.9. Lighting templates

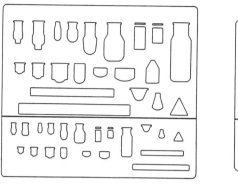

PLAN   SECTION

22.10. USITT standard lighting symbols. Reprinted by permission of USITT

FRESNELS   PARHEADS   ELLIPSOIDALS

3"   PAR 38   3½"x6"
6"   PAR 56   x8"
8"   PAR 64   x10"
12"   4½"x6½"
                  SCOOPS   6"x9"
2-PANEL   x12"
BARNDOOR   10"
4-PANEL   x16"
BARNDOOR   14"

PROJECTORS   BEAM PROJECTORS   8"x7¾"

EFFECTS   10"   x9"

SLIDE   16"   x10"
(35 MM)
                                   x11"

STRIPLIGHTS

FLOOR   10"x12"
MOUNT

PIPE   FOLLOWSPOT
MOUNT

OTHER

PRACTICAL   ERS BY   30° VAR. FOCAL   Z   IRIS   O   GOBO   •
             DEGREE   LENGTH

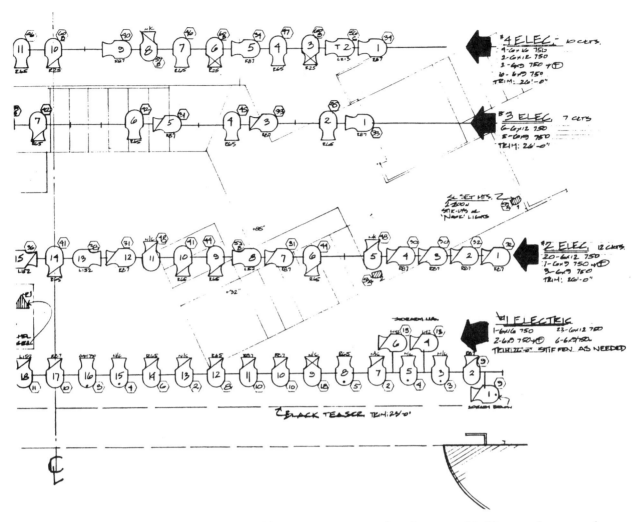

22.11. Horizontal lighting pipes, *Sweeney Todd.* Courtesy Linda Essig, lighting designer

Vertical hanging positions such as booms and ladders are drawn on the plot in their actual location in plan view with a dotted line, or more commonly, a solid outline shaded in. A leader is then extended from the actual location to a nearby space on the drawing, which affords the room to draw the vertical position in a modified front view.

The plot indicates not only where instruments are to be hung but what type of instrument is to be hung in each location. The USITT standard symbols identify various sizes and types of lighting instruments; nevertheless, despite the general acceptance of the standards and the availability of templates that use them, **all plots must include a key of symbols** usually located in the lower left-hand corner of the sheet. This key ensures that even someone who is unfamiliar with the USITT standards will be able decipher the information on the plot.

Although the standard symbols provide specific descriptions of the equipment needed, even more information is necessary for the successful translation of the design into reality. A standard notation arrangement has been accepted as well. This system provides the following information for each instrument: focus, color, instrument number, wattage, circuit, and channel/dimmer. A general symbol template may be handy for adding in all of this additional information. Frequently wattage and instrument manufacturer are included in the key and do not appear at the unit location.

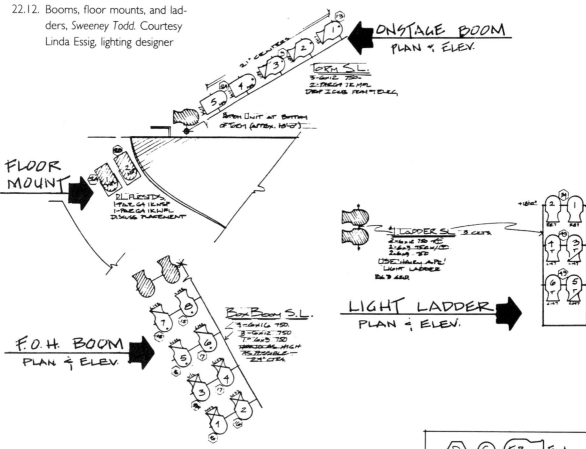

22.12. Booms, floor mounts, and ladders, *Sweeney Todd.* Courtesy Linda Essig, lighting designer

FLOOR MOUNT

ONSTAGE BOOM
PLAN & ELEV.

LIGHT LADDER
PLAN & ELEV.

F.O.H. BOOM
PLAN & ELEV.

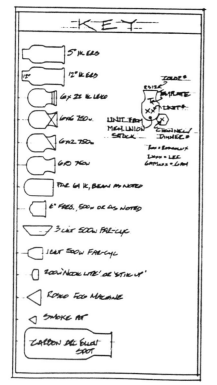

—KEY—

22.13. Typical light plot key, *Sweeney Todd.* Courtesy Linda Essig, lighting designer

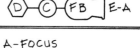

A—FOCUS
B—INSTRUMENT NUMBER
C—CIRCUIT NUMBER
D—DIMMER NUMBER
E—COLOR
F—WATTAGE

22.14. USITT standard layout for instrument notation. Reprinted by permission of USITT

Once all of the instruments are located, each instrument should be numbered. Each hanging location begins with its own number 1. Units are numbered from stage left to stage right on horizontal pipes and from top to bottom on vertical pipes. A **summary inventory** of each hanging position is added at the right end of each pipe or where graphically clearest. This summary provides the trim height of the batten and a list of the instruments and accessories that are to be hung on the pipe.

22.5 Finishing Up the Plot

With the instruments located, numbered, listed, and notated, the process of providing the related information begins. Instruments along individual pipes and hung above the stage floor on booms need to be dimensioned to specify their exact locations. When instruments are hung on standard 1'-6" centers, dimensions are not necessary, but a note to that effect is appropriate. To further aid in locating instruments, **a horizontal scale** is drawn just downstage and parallel with the plaster line, in addition a **vertical scale perpendicular** to the plaster line is drawn offstage right. The scale in front uses the intersection of the center line and the scale line as 0 and is marked in 6" increments from that point in each direction. Only the whole feet marks, over even-numbered feet marks, are labeled. The vertical scale uses the set line or plaster line as 0 and follows the same markings as the horizontal scale. (An alternative is to tick off 18" markings on each pipe, omitting those marks that fall within the area of an instrument.)

22.15. Placing scales on a light plot

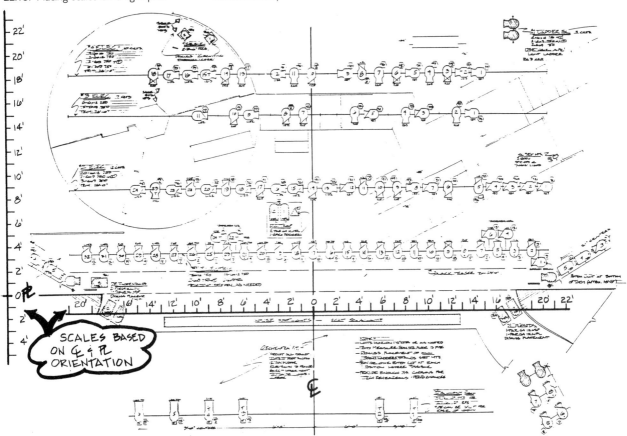

The set may now be indicated with thin lines. This information is provided solely for reference purposes, and only the necessary detail should be drawn, so as not to interfere with the rest of the information on the plot. With the numerous layers of information contained on the plot, proper line weight once again becomes critical. In order from the heaviest to the lightest, lines should be darkened in this order:

1. Instrument symbols
2. Pipes (broken at each instrument, not drawn through)
3. Ground plan and section lines of the theatre space
4. Dimensions and lists
5. Scenic information

6. Sightlines
7. Lettering guidelines

As with all other drawings, an appropriate **title block** should be located in the lower right-hand corner. In this block the director, scenic designer, lighting designer, and master electrician should be identified.

22.6 Lighting Design Sections

The **lighting section** follows the same techniques as the scenic section. By using a cutting plane that passes through the center line of the theatre, either a stage-left or stage-right viewing orientation may be drawn. Usually the lighting designer again opts to use overlay drafting techniques with the section view provided by the scene designer as the base sheet. Small circles are used to indicate horizontal pipes, and section symbols of the instruments are positioned in their approximate hanging positions and angles. Trim heights of battens and ladders are given, and sightlines and masking are detailed.

22.7 Color Keys

22.16. A color key for *Sweeney Todd*. Courtesy Linda Essig, lighting designer

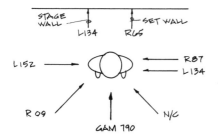

Although it is conventional practice to list the color of each instrument directly at the unit, some designers include on their plot an optional feature known as a **color key.** This graphic technique schematically shows the color systems employed on a typical acting area. An actor standing within an area is indicated by a schematic figure, and arrows are drawn that indicate the directions various color systems are lighting the actor. Each arrow is noted with the color coming from the direction. Any lighting that is not focused on the actor but has impact on the overall composition of the design (set lighting) is indicated pointing to a straight line upstage of the actor.

22.8 The Importance of Graphic Quality

Even though good paperwork and an excellently drafted plot do not a good lighting design make, the quality with which design ideas are presented does impact on the perception of a lighting designer's abilities. Clarity and completeness take on considerable significance in this profession, given that the light plot serves as the shop drawing that directs the work of the master electrician and electrics crew. The quality of the crew's work will be no better than the work of the lighting designer. A lighting designer's graphic abilities and organizational skills are clearly evident in the paperwork produced. This paperwork serves as the foundation upon which a lighting designer is able to demonstrate a mastery of the art of lighting design.

22.9 Checkpoints

√ Lighting plots are the primary source of information in lighting design.

√ Lighting plots are part of a large package of paper work that is necessary for the successful translation of design idea to stage reality.

√ USITT standards for symbols and instrument notation aid in conveying necessary information in a concise manner

23   The Final Project

23.1 Putting It All Together

The purpose of this chapter is to incorporate the book's cumulative information into a project designed to challenge the drafter's ability to comprehend and implement the concepts explored. "The Final Project" could also be called "The Portfolio Piece," since a well-done project would be a strong component of any professional portfolio intended to exhibit theatre design and technical skills.

Two alternative designs are provided in this chapter as models for the purpose of establishing parameters for this type of project. *Candida*, a realistic three-act play by George Bernard Shaw, requires a traditional box set. So familiar is this type of setting that even beginning drafters will find this project easily approachable. As a challenge, this version of *Candida* offers "forced perspective" wall units, moldings, set dressing, a "full" ceiling, and various approaches to masking. In addition there is the opportunity to enhance research abilities while addressing the numerous furniture props that must grace most Shavian productions.

The set for Bertolt Brecht's episodic *Arturo Ui* is less complex in visual detail than *Candida* but far more challenging technically. The many interacting working pieces of this design demand attention to storage, tracking, tolerances, and many of the problems associated with large-scale movable scenic units.

Students and instructors should feel free, and in fact are encouraged, to substitute "like" projects when looking for a satisfactory portfolio piece. The two models shown here serve simply as examples, offered as a means to articulate likely parameters for an assigned portfolio project. Regardless of the project chosen, however, the completed project should fit the following guidelines:

1. Every unit of scenery and masking (props are not included) must be described in terms of shape, dimension, and surface finish.
2. All units must be clearly and individually labeled and cross-referenced.
3. All USITT Graphic Standards must be observed.

23.2 Elements of the Final Project

In any project assignment, primary emphasis should be given to developing graphic communication skills. All aspects of technical drawing such as accuracy, labels, dimensions, notation, line weight, reproduction quality, cross-references, and standardized conventions must be given needed attention. It cannot be overstressed that all drawings need to be consistent with USITT Graphic Standards.

A second important aspect of any major drafting assignment is that little, if any, design work should be required of the student drafter. The devel-

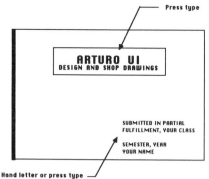
23.1. Project title sheet

Press type

ARTURO UI
DESIGN AND SHOP DRAWINGS

SUBMITTED IN PARTIAL
FULFILLMENT, YOUR CLASS

SEMESTER, YEAR
YOUR NAME

Hand letter or press type

opment of design skills is unarguably important, but the split focus of design and drafting demands can only serve to muddy the focus of the project. Make the exercise a drafting assignment exclusively.

Third, since the scope of these projects is professional, the final product should look professional. Use only standard-sized cut sheets, sequentially ordered and bound with a binding strip and perhaps a title sheet as shown in figure 23.1. The actual submission should be requested as blue- or black-line prints only. Originals such as vellum or tracing paper drawings should not be submitted.

23.3 A Project Overview

A project of this size can be overwhelming to many students unless the concepts and standards to be observed are carefully discussed. Consider an approach in which basic units such as ground plans, center-line sections, shape descriptions, detail drawings, and the various types of shop drawings are discussed preliminarily in class. Be prepared to give away any and all trade secrets. Keep in mind this is a drafting assignment, not a design or problem-solving exercise. Similarly if time constraints do not permit the time to complete the project as described, reduce the number of plates required. Given the demands of shop drawings for specific detailed information, it might be wise in any case to be selective rather than all encompassing.

Because of time constraints, light plots are not included as part of these projects, nor is CADD. Should students wish to incorporate either subject in their project, it would be wise to reduce the number of plates otherwise required. Except as noted above, both sets of project parameters however do incorporate full sets of both working and shop drawings. Although the day of specialization eventually comes, beginning students of theatre drafting need exposure to the variety and depth of information required by the professionals who use these drawings to create or fabricate scenery and props.

23.4 Guidelines for Dimensioning Ground Plan and Center-Line Section Drawings

The dimensions on ground plans are used to establish:
1. Heights of levels
2. Location of significant points of walls or units with respect to the plaster (datum) and center lines
3. Tolerances between units and/or masking

Note that the dimensions shown on a ground plan are never used to describe the size of a scenic unit. That information should be located on working drawings that provide the shape description of all units.

The dimensions used on sections are sparse and used only to clarify:
1. Depth
2. Trims (masking and/or flying units)
3. Selected heights (even these can be reduced in number, if a scaled human figure is placed on the drawing to give a sense of scale)

23.5 *Candida:* Parameters

This production of *Candida* is an unproduced project designed by Dennis Dorn. It is a conventional box set, complete with ceiling and offstage masking units. All molding is three-dimensional, all wall surfaces are painted and stenciled. Wall construction should use standard flat construction. For easy handling and possible tour capability, units should be designed to be no larger than 6'-0" wide when folded.

Problem

Given the following information:

a. 3/16" scale plan view (fig. 23.2)

b. 3/16" scale center-line section, looking SR (fig. 23.3)

c. 1/4" scale front elevations of units A–G (fig. 23.4)

prepare worksheets according to the instructions below; all drawings are to be submitted as blue-line prints.

a. Draw worksheets D1–D4 (designer working drawings) on D-size vellum sheets.

b. Draw S1–S5 (shop drawings) on either D-size or C-size vellum sheets. If you use 18 × 24 sheets, more sheets are necessary; number them accordingly.

c. Bind both sets of drawings into a single set with a cover sheet formatted as shown in figure 23.1.

D1. Provide a 1/2" scale ground plan showing all scenic elements, sightlines, masking , dimensions, and required notation. Label all units clearly.

D2. Provide a 1/2" scale section taken along the center line looking SR. Show all scenic units, masking , audience sightlines, location of dedicated lighting battens, overall set dimensions, and notation as needed.

D3–D4. Provide 1/2" scale, shape descriptions of all set components, including set returns (A, G); built masking, including ceiling, false portal, and large-scale details of moldings, doors, windows. Three-dimensional units such as the fireplace should be described in three views including plan and section. All views must be labeled, dimensioned, and notated as necessary. Cross-reference sheets as needed.

S1. Provide a technical director's version of the design ground plan (D1), showing all bracing and joinery. Indicate and label all braces, jacks, stud walls, or other devices that might be utilized to provide the necessary structural rigidity.

S2. Provide rear elevations of all wall units, including masking and set pieces. Include plan view and/or section views where useful. Provide complete notation, dimensioning, and labeling. Show all stiffening and joining hardware, picture toggles, and bracing required.

S3–S4. Provide rear elevations of the portal units and ceiling, including section views where useful, plus large-scale details of molding constructions (showing components parts), fireplace, doors, windows, braces, jacks, stud walls, and other devises utilized for structural rigidity.

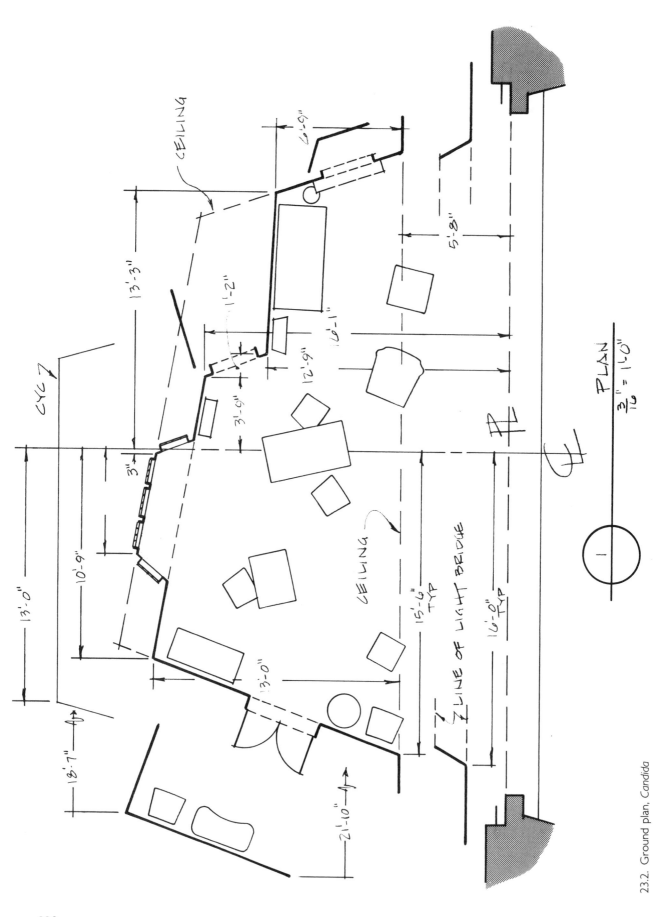

23.2. Ground plan, Candida

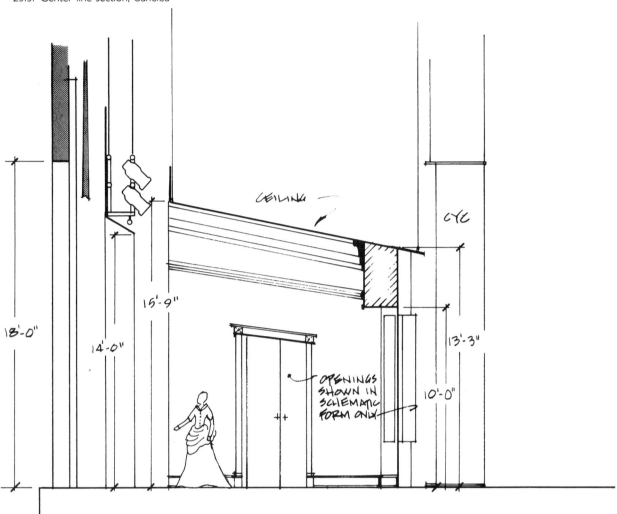

18'-0"

14'-0"

15'-9"

CEILING

CYC

13'-3"

10'-0"

OPENINGS
SHOWN IN
SCHEMATIC
FORM ONLY

2 ℄ SECTION, LOOKING SR
$\frac{3}{16}$" = 1'-0"

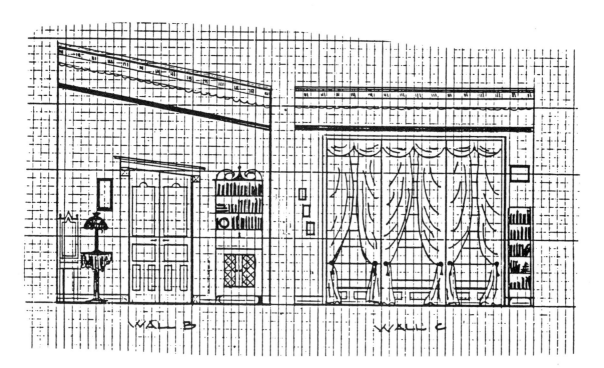

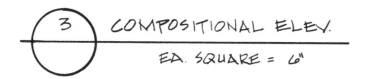

③ COMPOSITIONAL ELEV.

EA. SQUARE = 6"

23.6 *Arturo Ui*: Parameters

This project is similar to a production of *Arturo Ui* designed by Eugene Warner for the Amherst College Masquers. The finish was that of a galactic blue box, spattered with a range of metallic colors. All surfaces were treated the same, regardless of the actual material used, which included masonite, muslin, shark's-tooth scrim, and white pine.

Problem

Given the following information:

a. ³⁄₁₆″ scale plan view (fig. 23.5)

b. ³⁄₁₆″ scale center-line section, looking SR (fig. 23.6)

c. ³⁄₁₆″ scale front elevation of the entire set (fig. 23.7)

d. ½″ scale views of a swastika unit, not in the original design (fig. 23.8) prepare worksheets according to the instruction below; all drawings are to be submitted as blue-line prints:

a. Draw worksheets D1–D4 (designer working drawings) on D-size vellum sheets.

b. Draw S1–S5 (shop drawings) on either D-size or C-size vellum sheets. If you use 18 × 24 sheets, more sheets are necessary; number them accordingly.

c. Bind both sets of drawings into a single set with a cover sheet formatted as shown in figure 23.5.

D1. Provide a ½″ scale ground plan showing all scenic elements, sightlines, masking , dimensions, and required notation. Label all units, using reverse and repeat (R&R) conventions where appropriate.

D2. Provide a ½″ scale section taken along the center line, looking SR. Show scenic units, masking , sightlines, overall dimensions, and needed notation.

D3–D4 Provide shape descriptions of all set components, including built masking. Label, dimension, and notate all views as necessary. Cross-reference sheets as needed.

S1. Provide rear elevations of all wall units, including masking and set pieces. Include plan view and/or section views as required. Complete notation, dimensioning, and labeling as necessary. Show all hardware, stiffening, joining required. Show units assembled or provide assembly schematic or isometric. Note: All drawings are to be ½″ = 1′-0″ scale or larger. If uncertain as to the most appropriate scale, ask in class.

S2. Provide framing plans of all wagons, caster plates, stationary platforming, including details and section views of above. Detail interlock mechanisms, caster locations, locomotion devices(s), track guides, and platform-to-caster plate fastening. Specify all hardware including dimensions and manufacturer (where appropriate.)

S3. Provide plan view and enlarged section of false deck; rear elevation, section, and plan of swastika; upstage escape stairs, railings, decks, etc.

S4. Provide a rigging plan showing all spot lines, rope runs, loft blocks, headblocks, etc. The oblique walls require nearly all pick points to be spot lines. The theatre's permanent line sets are useful only for tailed-down lighting battens. Label, dimension, and notate as necessary to locate all components. Provide a legend of necessary components, i.e., bill of materials.

S5. Provide elevations of all soft goods, including masking legs. Specify dimensions, construction notes, rigging pick points, associated hardware, etc.

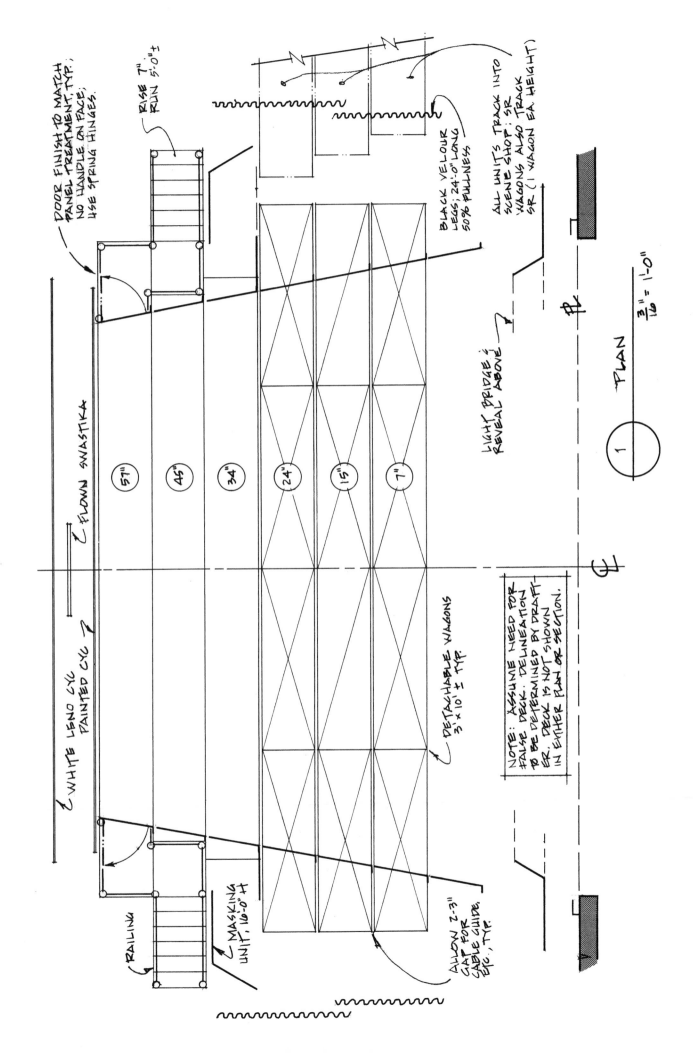

DOOR FINISH TO MATCH PANEL TREATMENT, TYP.; NO HANDLE ON FACE; USE SPRING HINGES.

RISE 7"
RUN 5'-0"±

BLACK VELOUR LEGS; 24'-0" LONG 50% FULLNESS

ALL UNITS TRACK INTO SCENE SHOP; SR WAGONS ALSO TRACK SR (1 WAGON EA HEIGHT)

℄ FLOWN SWASTIKA

57"

45"

34"

24"

15"

7"

℄ WHITE LENO CYC PAINTED CYC

LIGHT BRIDGE ℄ REVEAL ABOVE

DETACHABLE WAGONS 3' × 10'± TYP.

NOTE: ASSUME NEED FOR FALSE DECK. DELINEATION TO BE DETERMINED BY DRAFTER. DECK IS NOT SHOWN IN EITHER PLAN OR SECTION.

RAILING

℄ MASKING UNIT, 10'-0"±

ALLOW 2-3" GAP FOR CABLE GUIDE, ETC., TYP.

℄

℄

1 PLAN
   $\frac{3}{16}" = 1'-0"$

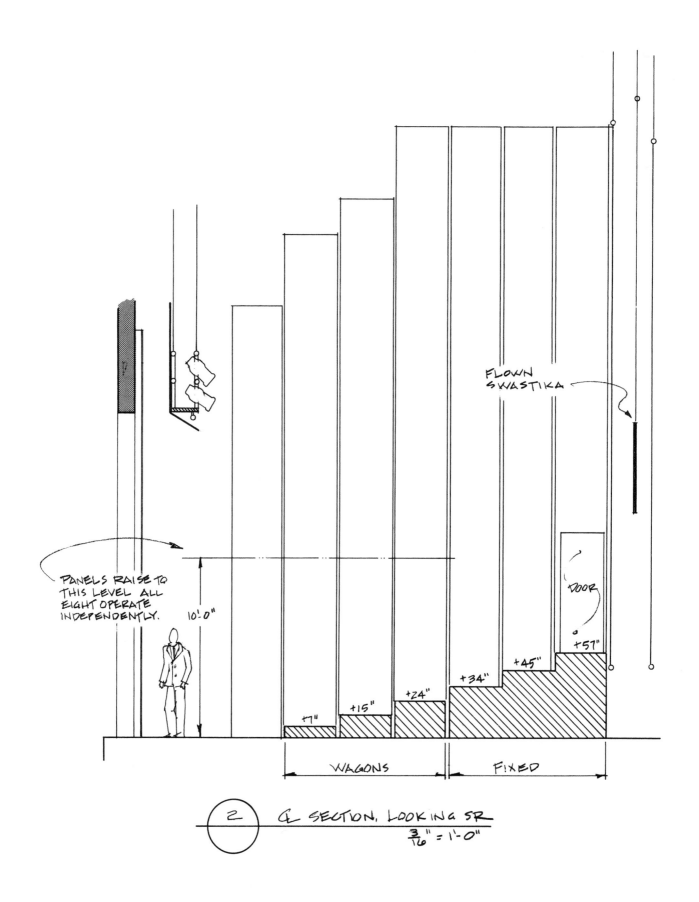

PANELS RAISE TO
THIS LEVEL ALL
EIGHT OPERATE
INDEPENDENTLY.

10'-0"

FLOWN
SWASTIKA

DOOR

+7"

+15"

+24"

+34"

+45"

+57"

WAGONS

FIXED

2 ℄ SECTION, LOOKING SR

$\frac{3}{16}$" = 1'-0"

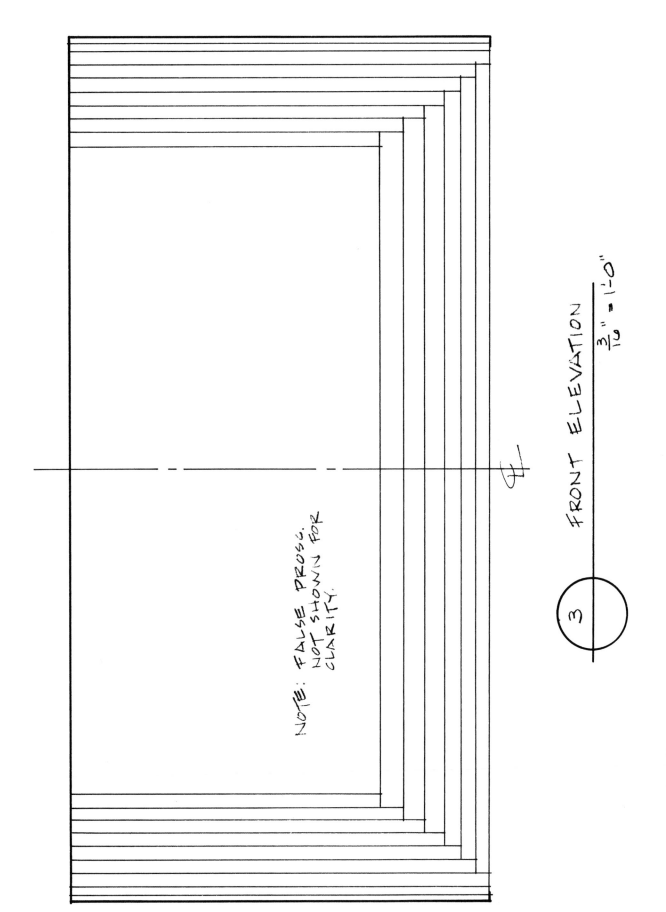

NOTE: FALSE PROSC.
NOT SHOWN FOR
CLARITY.

₵

3 FRONT ELEVATION
$\frac{3}{16}" = 1'-0"$

23.7. Front elevation. Arturo Ui

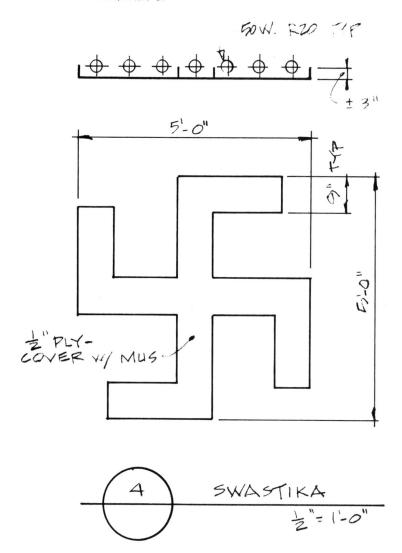

50W. R20 TYP

± 3"

5'-0"

TYP

9"

6'-0"

½" PLY-
COVER W/ MUS.

4 SWASTIKA

½" = 1'-0"

APPENDIXES
INDEX

Appendix A

A Standard Graphic Language for Scenic Design and Technical Production By the USITT Graphic Standards Board

Background

There are two primary needs for standardized graphic language in the technical theatre industry. Theatre work is performed in a condensed time span that prohibits inefficient communication. The need for a standardized language to achieve effective communication is intensified by the mobility of the members of the trade. Professional (and some educational) designers and technicians frequently work by mail or telephone and travel from theatre to theatre or shop to shop. Their drawings must be meaningful to the members of each staff with whom they work. The most effective manner to attain that meaning is with a common graphic language. The second need for a consistent graphic language is of importance to educators preparing students for entry into the profession of scenic design or technical theatre. Lacking published standards, the educator can only assume a graphic language that is acceptable to the industry. If his or her assumptions are incorrect, he or she may provide improper training to students and hamper their professional growth.

A standard is an example for comparison and an authority that serves as a model. The word **graphic** implies the presentation of a picture described in sufficient detail to meet the intended needs. In combination these two words depict the purpose of this project: to present a series of models that may be used to aid the scenic drafter. Typically, graphic standards are begun when individuals or groups start to codify the existing practice. Usually it is felt that any new standard should have a basis in established drafting methods if it is to have value. Obviously, the theatre has arrived at this point without a uniform method, and some see no need for establishing a consistent mode. However, an agreed-upon set of standards, like those of other industries, would tend to improve the efficient use of graphic material in the theatre.

The Graphic Standards Board of USITT's Education Commission has been empowered by the commission to devise a set of graphic standards for recommendation to the USITT membership as the standard graphic language for theatrical production. Standards will be recommended in the area of 1) scenic design and technical production, 2) lighting design, 3) audio design.

The initial effort of the Graphic Standards Board has been in the area of scenic design and technical production. The board members have examined studies in this area conducted by Don Calvert, Harvey Sweet, Stephan M. Zapytowski, Sr., and others, and have used these studies as the basis for the recommendations that follow.

General Description

The concept of a standard must evolve from a logical basis. In this case, that basis is rooted in the only inflexible rule of technical drawing: that any graphic communication must be clear, consistent, and efficient. While these recommendations will not include specific guidelines for the spacing of objects on each plate, any graphic presentation should adhere to the general recommendation of clarity—do not crowd or unevenly space individual items on a plate. Equally important, all line weights, line types, symbols, conventions, and lettering should be consistent from plate to plate and in a given set of drawings. This does not mean that everyone will be expected to letter in the same manner or draw their arrowheads in precisely the same way. It means that each drafter should be able to establish his or her "style" within the guidelines of the recommended standards and conform to that style throughout the drawings for a particular project or production. Finally, the standards and symbols used in any recommended guide should be efficient—both in ease of drawing and in ease of comprehension for the reader.

Ground Plan

A great deal of drawing technical theatre, both in presentation and symbology, is directly related to the drawing of the floor plan or ground plan. The specific definition of the ground plan is as follows: A floor or ground plan is a horizontal offset section with the cutting phase passing at whatever level, normally a height of 4'-0" above the stage floor, and is required to produce the most descriptive view of the set.

Line Weights

The USITT recommends a modified ANSI standard two-thickness line system. The approved line weights are as follows:

Pen: Thin: .010" to .0125" width (ANSI standard = .016)
        Thick: .020" to .025" width (ANSI standard = .032)
Pencil: Thin: .3 mm
        Thick: .5 mm

In either pen or pencil, an extra-thick line, .035" to .040" (.9 mm) may be infrequently used, as necessary, for emphasis (plate border, suitable section cutting plane line, etc.)

Conventions

There are a number of standard theatrical units such as chandeliers, shelves, and fireplaces that because of their varying styles and sizes should not be represented by standard symbols but need to be easily and repetitively drawn.

The drawing of these items should subscribe to the general guideline offered under the definition of the ground plan. In general, shelves, fireplaces, and similar items should be drawn by using a section cutting plane 4'-0" above the stage floor unless another view would be more descriptive. An item such as a chandelier should be indicated by a circle utilizing a hidden line, as it is not at the previously indicated 4'-0" cutting plane height. The circle should be drawn, in scale, the diameter of the chandelier at its widest point. The graphic should be placed in its proper position on the floor plan. Other suspended objects such as beams, drops not in contact with the stage floor (e.g., an act 2 drop on the act 1 floor plan), would be drawn in their appropriate outline, using the hidden line type. Another recommended convention involves the drafting of flats on the ground plan. They should be drawn in scale thickness and should have the space darkened between the two visible lines that are outlining the thickness of the flat.

Lettering

Lettering should be legible, and the style should allow for easy and rapid execution. Characters that generally conform to the single-stroke Gothic style meet these requirements. Only uppercase letters should be used on drawings unless lowercase letters are needed to conform with other established standards or nomenclature.

Title Block

The title block should be in the same location on all drawings of a single project. The title block should be located in either the lower right-hand corner of the drawing or in a strip along the bottom of the drawing. In either case, the block should include the following information:

1. Name of producing organization and/or theatre
2. Name of production; act and scene, if appropriate
3. Drawing title
4. Drawing number
5. Predominant scale of the drawing
6. Date the drawing was drafted
7. Designer of the production
8. Drafter, if different from the designer
9. Approval of drawing, if applicable

A.1. USITT-approved line types

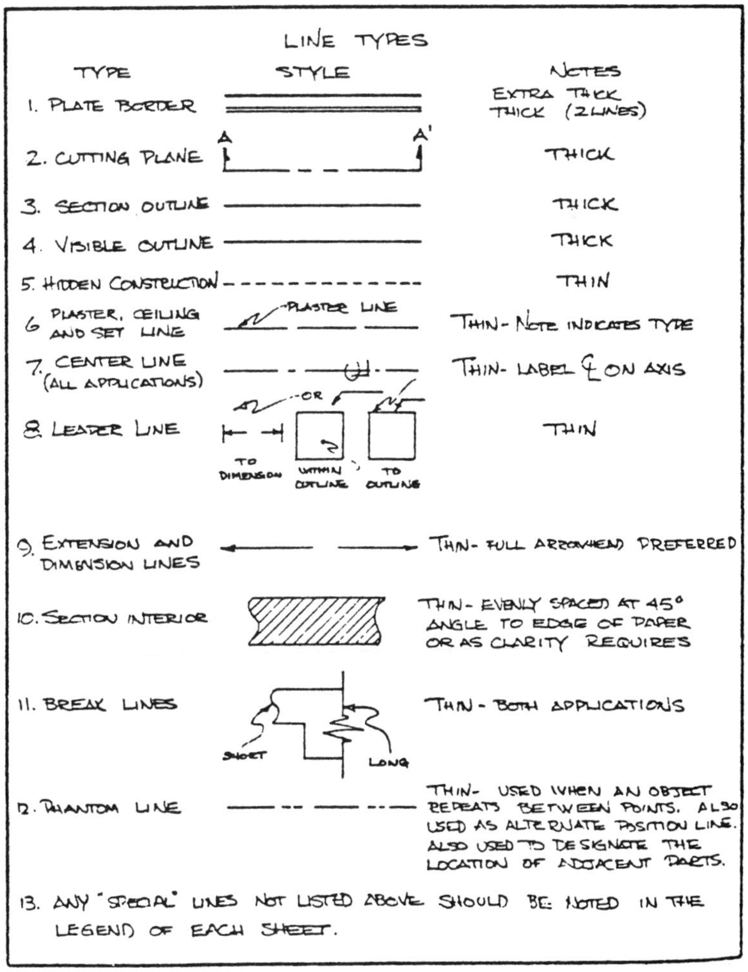

243

A.2. USITT-approved symbols for
ground plans and stage hardware

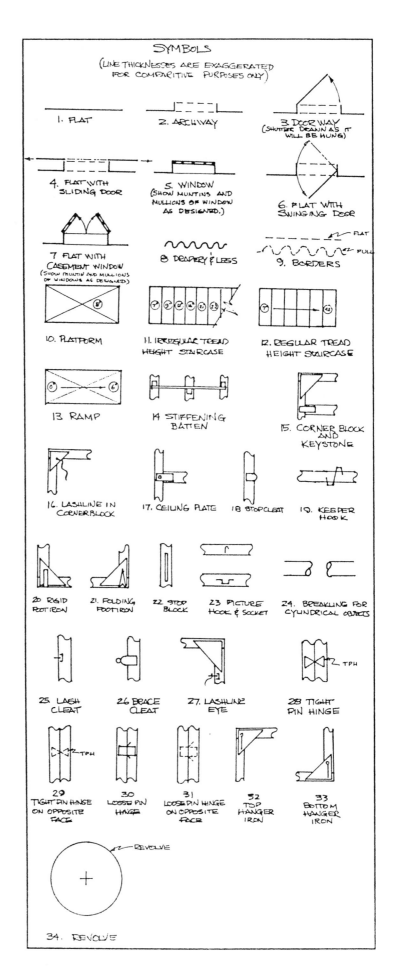

A.3. USITT-approved standard dimensioning practices

Dimensions

1. Dimensions must be clear, consistent, and easily understood.
2. Dimensions should be oriented to read from the bottom and/or the right hand side of the plate.
3. Metric dimensions less than one meter are to be noted as a zero, decimal point, and portion of meter in numerals. All measurements one meter and greater shall be given as a whole meter number, decimal point, and portion of meter: 0.1m, 0.52m, 1.5m, 2.35m.
4. Dimensions less than 1'-0" are given in inches without a foot notation, such as: 6", $9\frac{1}{2}$", etc.
5. Dimensions 1'-0" and greater include the whole feet with a single apostrophe followed by a dash and then inches followed by a double apostrophe: $7'-0\frac{1}{2}$", $18'-5\frac{1}{4}$", 1'-3".
6. Dimensions that require more space than available between extension lines are placed in proximity to the area measured, parallel with the bottom edge of the sheet, and directed to the point of reference by means of a leader line.

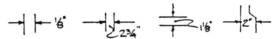

7. Platform and tread heights are given in inches above the stage floor. Such heights are placed in circles at or near the centers of the platform or tread; ⑥", ㊷".
8. Direction of arrows (when used to indicate elevation change on stairs, ramps, etc.) points away from the primary level of the drawing.

9. Radii

10. Diameter

11. Centers

12. Angles

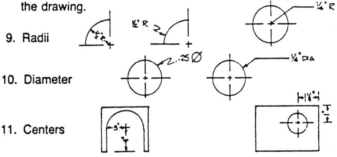

245

Appendix B   A Standard Graphic Language for Lighting Design By the USITT Graphic Standards Board

Background

The Graphic Standards Board of USITT's Education Commission was established in 1980 and was empowered by the commission to devise a set of graphic standards for recommendation to the USITT membership as the standard graphic language for theatrical production. A scenic graphic standard was presented in the spring 1982 issue of of *Theatre Design and Technology*. This article is concerned with the presentation of the lighting graphic standard.

For the current phase of its work the Graphic Standards Board has examined studies of current lighting graphic practice conducted by J. Michael Gillette, Stephen M. Zapytowski, Sr., and others. The board has surveyed many texts and other publications containing information on lighting graphics and has participated in two very stimulating sessions with members of USITT at the Corpus Christi and Orlando conferences. It is on the basis of this several years' work that the Board makes the recommendations that follow.

General Description

The concept of a standard must evolve from a logical basis and in this case, that basis is rooted in the only inflexible rule of technical drawing: that any graphic communication must be clear, consistent, and efficient. While these recommendations will not include specific guidelines for the orientation of information on individual plates, any graphic presentation should adhere to the general recommendation of clarity. Equally important, all line weights, line types, symbols, conventions, and lettering should be consistent from plate to plate and in a given set of drawings. This does not mean that everyone will be expected to letter in the same manner or draw their arrowheads in precisely the same way. It means that each drafter should be able to establish a "style" within the guidelines of the recommended standards and conform to that style throughout the drawings for a particular project or production, and that all departure from the guidelines should be indicated on that drawing by suitable notes or legends. Finally, the standards and symbols used in any recommended guide should be efficient—both in ease of drawing, and in ease of comprehension for the reader.

Light Plot

A light plot is a tool used by the lighting designer to convey in a precise manner to the electrician, information needed to rig a lighting design.

The specific definition of the light plot is as follows: A light plot is a ho-

246

rizontal offset section with the cutting plane passing at whatever levels are required to produce the most descriptive view of the instrumentation, in relation to a set (or sets), needed to light a production.

Line Weights

The USITT recommends a modified ANSI standard two-thickness line system. The proposed line weights are as follows:

Pen: Thin: .010″ to .0125″ width (ANSI standard = .016)
      Thick: .020″ to .025″ width (ANSI standard = .032)
Pencil: Thin: .3 mm
         Thick: .5 mm

In either pen or pencil, an extra-thick line, .035′ to .040″ (.9 mm) may be infrequently used, as necessary, for emphasis (plate border, suitable section cutting plane line, etc.).

Conventions

The setting is usually drawn on a light plot and is needed to help the electrician understand physical and spatial relationships between instrument and scenery. This is information that may be critical to the crew member who must rig the lights but may not be familiar with the totality of information the lighting designer used to construct the plot. While both lighting instruments and scenery may be drawn on a light plot, the dominant portion of the drawing should be the lighting graphic. Thus it is recommended that the solid "thick" line be used to draw lighting symbols and a solid "thin" line be used to draw scenery outlines and that the lighting portion of the plot take precedence over the scenic portion. Thus a portion of the set could be omitted if it interferes with lighting symbols or notes.

Generic Instrument Types

There is a great diversity in types, styles, and manufacturers of lighting instruments used in the theatre today. Consequently, any graphic language that attempted to create a specific symbol for each of these instruments would be too unwieldy to be of any value. The material studied by the Graphic Standards Board did strongly suggest that a body of very common instrument types is in general use, and that the most good could be done by addressing these groups. Instead of devising symbols for each specific manufacture or type of 6 × 9 ellipsoidal reflector spotlight, it is suggested that a single "generic" symbol be used to represent the entire 6 × 9 ERS family. If required by local practice, the specific brand of 6 × 9 ERS should be listed in the **legend.**

There are a number of instruments families represented in the lighting graphic standard, including fresnels, beam projectors, PAR cans, etc. There, however, will be instances in local practice where instruments outside the scope of this graphic standard will be used. In this case the board has recommended s set of miscellaneous shapes that may be used to construct symbols for any nonstandard or unusual instruments. Any such invention must be properly identified in the **legend.**

Legend

Each light plot must have a legend that indicates the meaning of each symbol used on the light plot.

Lettering

Lettering should be legible, and the style should allow for easy and rapid execution. Characters that generally conform to the single-stroke Gothic style meet these requirements. Only uppercase letters should be used on drawings unless lowercase letters are needed to conform with other established standards or nomenclature.

Title Block

The title block should be in the same location on all drawings of a single project. The title block should be located in either the lower right-hand corner of the drawing or in a strip along the bottom of the drawing. In either case, the block should include the following information:

1. Name of producing organization and/or theatre
2. Name of production
3. Drawing title
4. Drawing number
5. Predominant scale of the drawing
6. Date the light plot was drafted
7. Designer of the production
8. Drafter, if different from the designer
9. Approval of drawing, if applicable
10. Dates of revisions

Graphic Standards Board:

    Stephen M. Zapytowski, Sr., Chair
    Don Calvert
    J. Michael Gillette
    Charles Richmond
    Frank B. Silberstein
    Harvey Sweet
    William B. Warfel

B.1. USITT-approved symbols for fresnels and lensless instruments

B.2. USITT-approved symbols for ellipsodial reflector spotlights

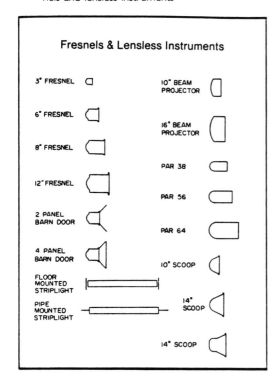

B.3. Miscellaneous USITT-approved symbols

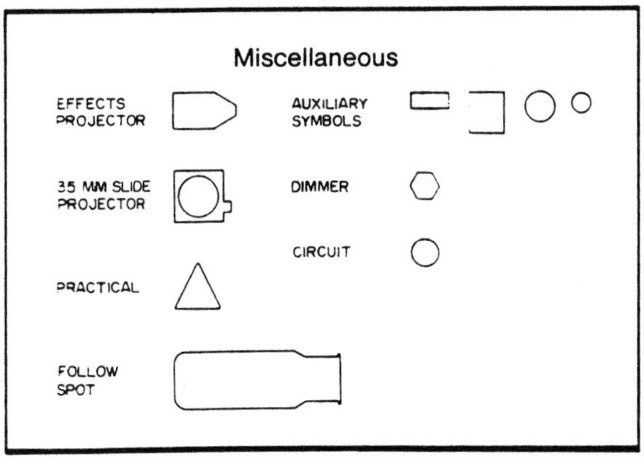

B.4. USITT-approved standard practice for instrument notation

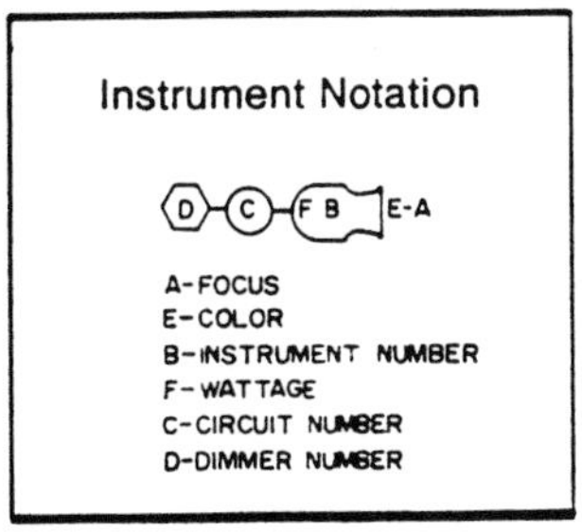

Miscellaneous

EFFECTS PROJECTOR		AUXILIARY SYMBOLS	
35 MM SLIDE PROJECTOR		DIMMER	
		CIRCUIT	
PRACTICAL			
FOLLOW SPOT			

Instrument Notation

A-FOCUS
E-COLOR
B-INSTRUMENT NUMBER
F-WATTAGE
C-CIRCUIT NUMBER
D-DIMMER NUMBER

Appendix C   Triangles, Arcs, and Chords

RIGHT TRIANGLES:

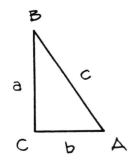

FIND	GIVEN	SOLUTION	FIND	GIVEN	SOLUTION
A	a,b	$\tan A = a \div b$	a	A,b	$b \tan A$
	a,c	$\sin A = a \div c$		A,c	$c \sin A$
	b,c	$\cos A = b \div c$			
			b	A,a	$a \div \tan A$
	a,b	$\tan B = b \div a$		A,c	$c \cos A$
B	a,c	$\cos B = a \div c$			
	b,c	$\sin B = b \div c$	c	A,c	$a \div \sin A$
				A,b	$b \div \cos A$
Area	a,b	$ab \div 2$			

OBLIQUE TRIANGLES: Solve by using one of the following groups of formulas

THE LAW OF SINES:

$$\frac{a}{\sin A} = \frac{b}{\sin B} = \frac{c}{\sin C}$$

MOLLWEIDE'S FORMULAS:

$$\frac{a + b}{c} = \frac{\cos \frac{1}{2}(A - B)}{\sin \frac{1}{2} C} \qquad\qquad \frac{a - b}{c} = \frac{\sin \frac{1}{2}(A - B)}{\cos \frac{1}{2} C}$$

$$\frac{b + c}{a} = \frac{\cos \frac{1}{2}(B - C)}{\sin \frac{1}{2} A} \qquad\qquad \frac{b - c}{c} = \frac{\sin \frac{1}{2}(B - C)}{\cos \frac{1}{2} A}$$

$$\frac{c + a}{b} = \frac{\cos \frac{1}{2}(C - A)}{\sin \frac{1}{2} B} \qquad\qquad \frac{c - a}{b} = \frac{\sin \frac{1}{2}(C - A)}{\cos \frac{1}{2} B}$$

PROJECTION FORMULAS:

$a = b \cos C + c \cos B$

$b = c \cos A + a \cos C$

$c = a \cos B + b \cos A$

THE LAWS OF COSINES:

$a^2 = b^2 + c^2 - 2bc \cos A$

$b^2 = c^2 + a^2 - 2ca \cos B$

$c^2 = a^2 + b^2 - 2ab \cos C$

ARCS: $a = \dfrac{\pi r A}{180}$

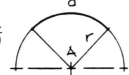

CHORDS: $c = 2r \dfrac{\sin A}{2}$

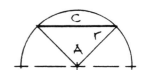

Appendix D   Conversion Factors for Metric Units

Measurement of Length

(Use meters on all drawings with a scale ratio larger than 1:200. Use millimeters on drawing with a scale ratio less than 1:200.)

1 meter = 3.2808 feet or 1.0936 yards
1 millimeter = 0.03937 inch
1 kilometer = 0.6213 mile

1 mile = 1.6093 km
1 yard = 0.9144 m
1 foot = 0.3048 m
1 inch = 25.44 mm

Measurement of Area

(Area is expressed by linear dimensions, normally written with the width first and depth or height second.)

$1 \text{ km}^2 = 0.3861 \text{ mile}^2$
$1 \text{ m}^2 = 10.7639 \text{ ft}^2$ or 1.196 yd^2
$1 \text{ mm}^2 = 0.0016 \text{ in}^2$

$1 \text{ mile}^2 = 2.590 \text{ km}^2$
$1 \text{ yd}^2 = 0.8361 \text{ m}^2$
$1 \text{ ft}^2 = 0.0929 \text{ m}^2$
$1 \text{ in}^2 = 645.16 \text{ mm}^2$

Measurement of Volume

$1 \text{ m}^3 = 1.30795 \text{ yd}^3$ or 35.3147 ft^3
$1 \text{ mm}^3 = 61.0237 \times 10^{-6} \text{ in}^3$

$1 \text{ yd}^3 = 0.7646 \text{ m}^3$
$1 \text{ ft}^3 = 16.387 \text{ mm}^3$
$1 \text{ in}^3 = 16.387 \text{ mL } (\text{cm}^3)$

Measurement of Liquids

$1\text{L} = 0.03531 \text{ ft}^3$
   $= 0.2642 \text{ gal}$
   $= 1.0567 \text{ qt}$
$1 \text{ mL} = 0.0610 \text{ in}^3$

1 gal = 3.7854 L
1 qt = 946.35 mL
1 pt = 473.18 mL
1 fl oz = 29.57 mL

Measurement of Weight

1 g = 0.035 oz
1 kg = 2.205 lb
1 metric ton = 2204.62 lb

1 oz = 28.35 g
1 lb = 0.4536 g
1 ton = 907.19 kg

Appendix E   Standard Dimensions Useful to Theatre Drafters[1]

Architectural

(Note that all dimensions are given in inches.)

Group	Subgroup	Category	Height	Width	Depth
Doors	Door types	Interior	80	30–36	1⅜
		Exterior	80–84	30–36	1¾
		Screen/ storm	80–84	30–36	1⅛
		Knob	36		
	Hinges	Top	7 (from top)		
		Center	Space equally		
		Bottom	10 (from bottom)		
Trim		Chair rail	30–32	—	—
	Early century	Base	—	8–10	1
		Casing	—	3½	¾
	Modern	Base	—	3½	½
		Casing	—	2¼	½
Work surfaces		Kitchen/ shop	36	—	26–30
		Service counter	42	—	24–36
Devices	(dimensions on center)	Switch/bell	42		
		Receptacle	12		
		Outlet	12		
		Handicap outlet	30		
		Phone	48		
		Intercom	60		

Equipment

Group	Subgroup	Category	Height	Width	Depth
Appliances	Kitchen	Refrigerator	66	30	30
		Stove/ range	45/36	30	27
		Dishwasher	34	24	24
		Sink	36	33	22
		Microwave	16	24	18
	Laundry	Clothes washer	36	28	28
		Clothes dryer	36	30	28
		Single washtub	36	24	27

Fixtures	Bathroom	Toilet/seat	30/15	22	28–30
		Pedestal lavatory	32	24	19
		Bathtub	13	30–33	60–66
		Shower	80	36/36	36/42
		Shower head	74		

Furnishings

(Note that all dimensions are given in inches and have been rounded upward to the nearest whole number.)

Group	Subgroup	Category	Height[2]	Width[3]	Depth
Table	Dining	Rectangular	29–30	66/80	36/42
		Square	"	36/42 sq	—
		Round	"	42/48 dia	—
		Trestle	"	60/72	34/36
	Occasional	Rectangular	17–28	21–48	19–28
		Square	"	15–32 sq	—
		Round	18–23	16–30 dia	—
		Television	16	24–36	16
	Desk	Secretary	83	40	25
		Double-pedastal classic	29	58	29
		modern	29	60/70	30/36
		Credenza	29	75	24
	Folding	Service table	29	72/96	30/36
		Card	28	30 sq	—
Storage	Dining	Buffet	30	54–66	18–20
		with hutch	78	—	—
		Breakfront	95	76	14
	Office	2 dr letter file	26	15	29
		5 dr letter file	60	15	29
		Legal file	—	18	—
		5 dr. flat file	15	29–41	29/38
		flat file base	6	—	—
		Bookcase	36–72	36	10
Pianos	Grand	Concert	39	64	116
		Music room	39	60	84
		Parlor	40	58	75
		Baby	36	55	53
	Upright	Spinet	40	58	25
		Studio	46	57	25
	Bench	Standard	19	30	14

Furnishings

(Note that all dimensions are given in inches and have been rounded upward to the nearest whole number.)

Group	Subgroup	Category	Height[2]	Width[3]	Depth
	Stool	Standard	19–25	15 dia	—
Bedroom	Mattress	Bunk	Varies	30/33	75
		Twin	21	39	75
		Double	"	54	75
		¾	"	48	75
		Above beds extra-long	—	—	80
		Queen	"	60	80
		King	"	78	80
Bedroom	Furniture	Dresser	29	42–72	20
		Chest	54	37	20
		Night table	16	18 sq	—
		Dressing table	29	42–48	18–22
Seats	Chairs non-upholstered	Kitchen Ladder-back	40/18	16	20
		Bentwood	35/18	16	20
		Stacking	30/17	21	22
		Folding	30/17	19	20
	Chairs upholstered	Arm	39/19	26	24
		Wing	45/19	32	30
		Lounge	35/17	34	32
		Dining room	32/18	20	20
	Sofas	Love seat	35/18	60	30
		Small sofa	34/18	66	32
		Traditional	34/18	86	42
	Bench	Park	29/17	72	23
		Straight-back	44/16	60	24
		Sun lounge	39/12	28	82
		Public areas	17	72	20
		Trestle	17	60–72	14
	Stool	Bar	24/30	16–18 dia	—
		Hearth	17	14 dia	—
		Ottoman	16	24	18
		Round hassock	15	20 dia	—

[1]Most standards are taken from American Institute of Architects, *Architectural Graphic Standards,* 8th ed. (New York: John Wiley & Sons, 1988).
[2]First number is overall height; second number is seat height.
[3]Combine first numbers (width and depth) to create one standard combination; combine the second numbers to create a second standard size.

Appendix F   Welding Symbols

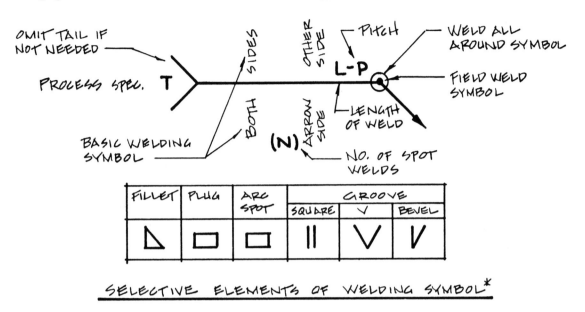

OMIT TAIL IF NOT NEEDED

PROCESS SPEC.   **T**

BASIC WELDING SYMBOL

BOTH SIDES

SIDES

OTHER SIDE

ARROW SIDE

(N)

PITCH

L-P

LENGTH OF WELD

WELD ALL AROUND SYMBOL

FIELD WELD SYMBOL

NO. OF SPOT WELDS

FILLET	PLUG	ARC SPOT	GROOVE		
			SQUARE	V	BEVEL
◺	▭	▭	‖	V	V

SELECTIVE ELEMENTS OF WELDING SYMBOL*

FILLET WELD SYMBOLS

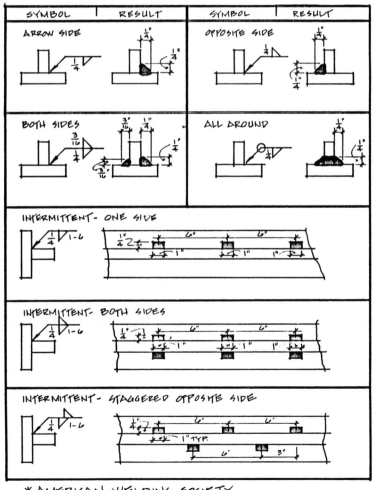

SYMBOL	RESULT	SYMBOL	RESULT
ARROW SIDE		OPPOSITE SIDE	
BOTH SIDES		ALL AROUND	

INTERMITTENT- ONE SIDE

INTERMITTENT- BOTH SIDES

INTERMITTENT- STAGGERED OPPOSITE SIDE

*AMERICAN WELDING SOCIETY

Appendix G   Abbreviations

A

Alternate	ALT
Ampere	AMP
Auxiliary	AUX
Average	AVG

B

Back to Back	B to B
Bevel	BEV
Black	BLK
Break	BRK
Building	BLDG

C

Center Line	CL
Center to Center	C to C
Check	CHK
Circle	CIR
Countersink	CSK
Cubic	CU
Cubic Foot	CUFT

D

Diagonal	DIG
Diameter	DIA
Do Not Cover	DNC
Dowel	DWL
Down	DN
Down Stage	DS
Drawing	DWG
Drawn	DRN

E

Each	EA
Electric	ELEC
Elevation	EL
Estimate	EST
Extra Heavy	XHVY
Extra Strong	XSTR

F

Fabricate	FAB
Face to Face	F to F
Figure	FIG
Foot	(') FT
Front	FRT

G

Gallon	GAL
Gauge	GA
Grade	GR
Grind	GRD
Ground	GRD

H

Hardware	HDW
Hydraulic	HYD

I, J, K

Inch	(") IN
Inches per Second	IPS
Inside Diameter	ID

L

Left	L
Length	LG
Lumber	LBR
Loose Pin Hinge	LPH

M

Manual	MAN
Manufacture	MFR
Maximum	MAX
Metal	MET
Minimum	MIN
Motor	MOT
Mounted	MTD
Mounting	MTG
Muslin	MUS

N

Nominal	NOM
Not Applicable	NA
Not to Scale	NTS
Number	NO

O

On Center	OC
Original	ORIG
Outside Diameter	OD

P

Page	P
Pattern	PATT
Perpendicular	PERP
Plaster Line	PL
Please Note	PN
Plywood	PLY
Pound	LB
Power	PWER

Q, R

Radius	R
Remove	REM
Return	RET
Reverse	REV
Reverse and Repeat	R&R
Rev. Per Min.	RPM
Right	R
Round	RD

S

Sheet	SHT
Stage Left	SL
Stage Right	SR
Steel	STL
Stock	STK
Straight	STR
Structural	STR

Support	SUP	Tight Pin Hinge	TPH	Vertical	VERT
Surface	SUR	Tolerance	TOL	Volume	VOL
Symbol	SYM	Tongue and Groove	T&G		
		Total	TOT	**W, X, Y, Z**	
T		Typical	TYP	Weight	WT
Taper	TPR			White Pine	WP
Template	TEMP	**U, V**		Width	W
Thick	THK	Unit	U	Wood	WD
Thousand	M	Vacuum	VAC	Yard	YD

Appendix H   A Recommended List of Basic Drafting Tools

Drawing board with cover, minimum 31″ wide (or equivalent) for home use

T-square (30″ long) or parallel rule with transparent edge blade

8″ 45° triangle

12″ 30°–60° triangle

6″ protractor

12″ architect's ruler

Set of drafting instruments: 6″ dividers and 6″ bow compass

Irregular (French) curves, need two or three different shapes

Erasing shield

Plastic eraser

Kneaded eraser

Ames Lettering Guide

Lead holder, need two or three

Lead pointer

Sandpaper pad or small piece of sandpaper

H, 2H, 4H leads, two each

Drafting tape

Dusting brush

Cleaning pad or powder

Circle template (3″ diameter and smaller)

Index

Dennis Dorn is professor of theatre and technical director at the University of Wisconsin-Madison, where he has taught since 1976. A graduate of the University of Wisconsin and the Yale School of Drama, Dorn has previously been associated with SUNY-Brockport, Amherst College, the Yale Rep, and the Guthrie Theatre. In addition to his teaching, Dorn is an active member of USITT, involved in both Midwest and national programming, and is a continuing contributor to *Theatre Design and Technology*.

Mark Shanda is the technical director and director of undergraduate studies in the Department of Theatre at the Ohio State University in Columbus, Ohio. Prior to joining the faculty at Ohio State he was a visiting lecturer and the acting technical director at the University of Wisconsin-Madison. He holds an M.F.A. degree in theatre technology from the University of Wisconsin and received his undergraduate education at Iowa State University. Shanda was the technical director at the Fireside Dinner Theatre in Fort Atkinson, Wisconsin, and for three years was the technical director for the Madison Opera Company. In addition, he has been a consultant on a variety of theatre renovations as well as several new theatre construction projects and has taught theatre technology workshops at the International Thespian Society Festival.